THE COMPLETE IDIOT'S GUIDE TO

The Civil War

Third Edition

by Alan Axelrod, Ph.D.

ALPHA

A member of Penguin Group (USA) Inc.

For Anita—again and yet again.

ALPHA BOOKS

Published by the Penguin Group

Penguin Group (USA) Inc., 375 Hudson Street, New York, New York 10014, USA

Penguin Group (Canada), 90 Eglinton Avenue East, Suite 700, Toronto, Ontario M4P 2Y3, Canada (a division of Pearson Penguin Canada Inc.)

Penguin Books Ltd., 80 Strand, London WC2R 0RL, England

Penguin Ireland, 25 St. Stephen's Green, Dublin 2, Ireland (a division of Penguin Books Ltd.)

Penguin Group (Australia), 250 Camberwell Road, Camberwell, Victoria 3124, Australia (a division of Pearson Australia Group Pty. Ltd.)

Penguin Books India Pvt. Ltd., 11 Community Centre, Panchsheel Park, New Delhi—110 017, India

Penguin Group (NZ), 67 Apollo Drive, Rosedale, North Shore, Auckland 1311, New Zealand (a division of Pearson New Zealand Ltd.)

Penguin Books (South Africa) (Pty.) Ltd., 24 Sturdee Avenue, Rosebank, Johannesburg 2196, South Africa

Penguin Books Ltd., Registered Offices: 80 Strand, London WC2R 0RL, England

Copyright © 2011 by Alan Axelrod

International Standard Book Number: 978-1-61564-078-2
Library of Congress Catalog Card Number: 2010912367

13 12 11   8 7 6 5 4 3 2 1

Interpretation of the printing code: The rightmost number of the first series of numbers is the year of the book's printing; the rightmost number of the second series of numbers is the number of the book's printing. For example, a printing code of 11-1 shows that the first printing occurred in 2011.

Printed in the United States of America

Note: This publication contains the opinions and ideas of its author. It is intended to provide helpful and informative material on the subject matter covered. It is sold with the understanding that the author and publisher are not engaged in rendering professional services in the book. If the reader requires personal assistance or advice, a competent professional should be consulted.

The author and publisher specifically disclaim any responsibility for any liability, loss, or risk, personal or otherwise, which is incurred as a consequence, directly or indirectly, of the use and application of any of the contents of this book.

Most Alpha books are available at special quantity discounts for bulk purchases for sales promotions, premiums, fund-raising, or educational use. Special books, or book excerpts, can also be created to fit specific needs.

For details, write: Special Markets, Alpha Books, 375 Hudson Street, New York, NY 10014.

Publisher: *Marie Butler-Knight*

Associate Publisher: *Mike Sanders*

Senior Managing Editor: *Billy Fields*

Acquisitions Editor: *Tom Stevens*

Development Editor: *Lynn Northrup*

Senior Production Editor: *Janette Lynn*

Copy Editor: *Monica Stone*

Cover Designer: *Rebecca Batchelor*

Book Designers: *William Thomas, Rebecca Batchelor*

Indexer: *Johnna Vanhoose Dinse*

Layout: *Ayanna Lacey*

Proofreader: *Laura Caddell*

Contents

Introduction

Of the 1,556,000 soldiers who served in the Union army during the Civil War, 359,528 were killed and 275,175 were wounded. Of the approximately 850,000 men of the Confederate forces, at least 258,000 died, and some 225,000 were wounded. This means that 41 percent of the Union soldiers and 56 percent of the Confederate soldiers who fought were either killed or wounded.

The population of the Northern states in 1860, the year before war began, was 22 million, including 4 million men of combat age. That of the Confederate states was 9 million (of whom almost 4 million were slaves), including 1,140,000 men of combat age. The 1,117,703 casualties on both sides represented 3.6 percent of the total U.S. population; however, 21 percent—more than one fifth—of the nation's young men were killed or wounded between 1861 and 1865.

The United States spent $15 billion on the war in an era when an unskilled laborer earned about a dollar a day. The South, of course, emerged from the war having lost its chief agricultural labor system—slavery—and with most of its factories and railroads destroyed, along with some of its richest croplands.

None of us lived through the war, yet the war seems, somehow, a part of us. It is a kind of hunger, judging from the rate at which we consume books on the subject. No fewer than 65,000 volumes have been devoted to the Civil War since it ended in 1865, and in any recent year, 1,500 to 2,000 Civil War titles are actively in print. The first great American movie, D. W. Griffiths's 1915 *The Birth of a Nation*, was a Civil War epic, and *Gone with the Wind* was a box-office phenomenon when it was released in 1939 and remains at the top of many filmgoers' list of favorites.

We continue to argue about the war, too. Was it *really* about slavery? Should Lincoln have just let the Southern states go their own way? Was the cause of the South evil, just misunderstood, or, at least in some ways, right? Were Lee and Stonewall Jackson overrated? Was Grant a "butcher" and Sherman a "war criminal"? Was Lincoln a great man or a single-minded tyrant? And is a civil war possible today, with angry political activists and voluble politicians throwing about such terms as *states' rights* and *nullification*, and the governor of Texas even speculating on the subject of *secession*?

No events in nineteenth-century American history—and only a handful of *current* events—seem more important to us, more relevant to us, or more familiar to us than those of 1861 to 1865. Yet no matter how important, relevant, or familiar, those events, a century and a half in the past, are not only distant in time, but often complex and confusing to interpret. The Civil War is one of those subjects we both care about and feel we *should* care about. We know *something* about it, but we feel we should know *more*. The names of battles and generals are familiar to us, but only vaguely. We are attracted to the subject of the Civil War, but we're not quite sure why. And schoolbook history, with all its dates, midterm exams, and pop quizzes—well, none of that was much help.

The Complete Idiot's Guide to the Civil War, Third Edition, will not tell you *everything* you need to know about the Civil War. But it *will* tell you all you need to know to get started in an exploration of a true-life drama by which we can measure the remarkable heights and unspeakable depths humanity touches, and through which we can learn something about who we were, are, and might yet be.

Part 1, Fire-Bell in the Night, takes us to the very hour at which the Civil War began, then looks back before this time, to the roots of slavery in the New World. For it was in slavery that the war began, despite all the effort to avoid it through argument, excuse, and compromise.

Part 2, Rally Round, shows how the Americans, a most unmilitary people, suddenly transformed themselves into soldiers, and how the North, many times greater in wealth and population than the South, saw its army beaten in opening battles more terrible than either side had imagined possible.

Part 3, Die to Make Men Free, takes us to the moral turning point of the war. The Battle of Antietam was the first in which the Union could claim a victory, however narrow and however bloody, and this gave President Lincoln the platform from which to issue an emancipation proclamation. From now on, whatever else the war meant, it would be a war to end slavery, a struggle "to make men free."

Part 4, That the Nation Might Live, begins with a military turning point of the war: Gettysburg, not only the most momentous single battle of the Civil War, but also the largest battle ever fought on this continent, and one of the great military contests in all history. Despite Union victory here, the North, we will see, was plagued by riot, racism, subversion, and other forms of dissension.

Part 5, The Last Full Measure, begins with the installation of Ulysses S. Grant as the Union's general-in-chief. Now, increasingly, the war became a contest in deadly earnest between Grant and Lee, while Grant's principal subordinate, William Tecumseh Sherman, fought Joseph E. Johnston, John Bell Hood, and, ultimately, the people of the South. This part of the book concludes where, for all practical purposes, the Civil War ended, at Appomattox Court House, with Lee's surrender of the Army of Northern Virginia.

Part 6, Taps and Reveille, begins with the assassination of Abraham Lincoln, whose death doomed the nation, and the South in particular, to more than a decade of punitive and destructive Reconstruction policy, which created, in turn, a climate of regional resentment, social intolerance, and racial hate. This part concludes with an acknowledgment of the war's unfinished business, the twenty-first-century revival in some quarters of Civil War cultural and political rhetoric, and a look at how the Civil War continues to live in our collective memory.

Extras

In addition to the main narrative, photographs, portraits, and maps in *The Complete Idiot's Guide to the Civil War, Third Edition*, you'll find other types of useful information, including definitions of key terms; an array of historical sites open to the public; battle statistics and other war-related numbers; and a collection of Civil War facts, anecdotes, and trivia. Look for these sidebars:

DEFINITION

The Civil War was fought with words as well as bullets. Here are definitions of the era's key words.

COUNT OFF!

Here you will find battle statistics and other informative numbers related to the war.

WAR NEWS

This sidebar offers Civil War anecdotes, trivia, and informative facts.

SITES AND SIGHTS

Many Civil War battlefields and other sites are maintained today as public parks, historical monuments, and museums. This sidebar presents some of the most interesting and important.

Special Thanks to the Technical Reviewer

The Complete Idiot's Guide to the Civil War, Third Edition, was reviewed by an expert who double-checked the accuracy of what you'll learn here, to help us ensure that this book gives you everything you need to know about the Civil War. Special thanks are extended to Keith Poulter, whose many insights and contributions have greatly enriched this edition.

Keith Poulter was born in 1940 during a Luftwaffe air raid on London, and quickly developed a keen interest in military history. A former intelligence officer and university teacher, he is currently the publisher-editor of the leading Civil War magazine, *North & South* (northandsouthmagazine.com), and of *Military Chronicles* magazine. He resides in California's San Joaquin Valley.

Trademarks

All terms mentioned in this book that are known to be or are suspected of being trademarks or service marks have been appropriately capitalized. Alpha Books and Penguin Group (USA) Inc. cannot attest to the accuracy of this information. Use of a term in this book should not be regarded as affecting the validity of any trademark or service mark.

Fire-Bell in the Night

When did the Civil War begin? Answer at Fort Sumter, on April 12, 1861, and you'd be partly right. The roots of the war, however, descend to August 1619, when Virginia tobacco farmers purchased their first consignment of 20 slaves from Dutch traders. From that moment, the slavery issue festered through the colonial and early national periods, inexorably tearing the emerging nation apart.

In this part, you'll read about the tortured attempts to compromise on slavery, about men who could tolerate no compromise, and about one man who tried to arm the slaves to win their freedom for themselves. This part ends with the inauguration of Abraham Lincoln, who came to Washington to preside over a "house divided against itself," and a people rushing headlong toward war.

Beginnings

In This Chapter

- The fall of Fort Sumter
- Slavery comes to America
- Opposition to slavery
- Attempts to compromise on the slavery issue
- The Missouri Compromise

What caused the Civil War? Most schoolbooks say it was the issue of slavery—the South wanted it, the North wanted to abolish it—but these days especially, you may hear an impassioned, even angry, argument that slavery was secondary to "states' rights," a concept I'll explain shortly. It is true that slavery wasn't the only issue of the Civil War. Nevertheless slavery always looms behind, or towers above, all other motives for the war. If there had been no slavery, no other issue, including states' rights, would have triggered secession and war.

So this chapter begins with the first day of the war—April 12, 1861—then reaches back to slavery, the seeds of war planted some 242 years earlier.

Fort Sumter, South Carolina: April 12, 1861

Life moved at a leisurely pace in the peacetime army of what had been the United States of America. The construction of Fort Sumter, on an artificial island of New England granite transported to Charleston Harbor, had begun in 1829. It was still unfinished on the day after Christmas 1860, when Major Robert Anderson assumed command of a garrison of two U.S. Army artillery batteries—68 soldiers, 9 officers, and 8 bandsmen, along with a handful of civilian workers. Less than a week earlier, on December 20, 1860, South Carolina had *seceded*—proclaiming itself no longer a state of the Union. Backed by militiamen and volunteers loyal to their state, South Carolinians quickly seized federal property, including military installations and arms.

 DEFINITION

To **secede** is to withdraw from membership in an organization, association, alliance, or, in the case of what became the 11 Confederate states, to withdraw from the union of the United States.

In the predawn hours of April 12, 1861, the Confederates (that's what the citizens of seven Southern states now called themselves) aimed against Sumter the bristling guns of batteries at Morris, James, and Sullivan islands, and Forts Moultrie and Johnson, as well as the town of Mount Pleasant.

Pierre Gustave Toutant Beauregard, a dashing Louisianian, was an excellent engineer and a fine artillerist, having been educated in that art by his West Point instructor, none other than Major Anderson. Now in command of the Confederate forces that had laid siege against Sumter since January, Beauregard sent, under a flag of truce, two men rowing out to the fort in Charleston Harbor. They presented Anderson with a chivalrous note demanding surrender and promising safe conduct, adding that the "flag which you have upheld so long and with so much fortitude, under the most trying circumstances, may be saluted by you on taking it down."

For his part, Anderson, a Kentuckian married to a Georgian, was torn between loyalty to the Union and sympathy with the South. To Beauregard's messengers he handed a reply, resigned rather than defiant, explaining that his "sense of honor, and of my obligations to my government" prevented his surrender. "Gentlemen," he told the envoys, "if you do not batter us to pieces, we shall be starved out in a few days."

Four more rowboatmen called on Anderson after midnight on April 12, warning that bombardment was about to commence. Anderson replied that, barring further orders or supply from "my government," he would evacuate by April 15. Not soon enough, Beauregard's emissaries declared; the bombardment would begin in one hour.

*Dashing, ostentatiously chivalrous, not brilliant but competent, Confederate
General Pierre Gustave Toutant Beauregard (1818–1893) commanded the bom-
bardment of Fort Sumter, firing on his former West Point artillery instructor,
Major Robert Anderson.*
(Library of Congress)

The honor of letting fly the first shot was offered to Virginian Roger Pryor. Pryor
had resigned his seat in the U.S. Congress to join the Confederate army on March 3,
1861, and was what the divided nation called a *"fire-eater,"* he had exhorted the people
of South Carolina to "Strike a blow!" But now he shook his head, protesting weakly
that he "could not fire the first gun of the war." It was long believed that 67-year-old
Edmund Ruffin, a rural Virginia newspaper editor and a crusty, wild-eyed defender
of slavery, pulled the lanyard for the first shot at 4:30 A.M., but it is now known that
Lieutenant Henry S. Farley, the first Southern cadet to resign from West Point on
the approach of war, was actually responsible. In any event, through Friday the 12th
and into Saturday the 13th, some 4,000 rounds followed the first shot.

DEFINITION

On the eve of the Civil War, a **fire-eater** was a Southerner who enthusiastically and unconditionally advocated secession.

Edmund Ruffin, a 67-year-old rural Virginia newspaper editor and rabid defender of slavery, was long credited with firing the first shot of the Civil War. It is now known that Lieutenant Henry S. Farley was the first to let fly.
(National Archives and Records Administration)

Four thousand rounds! All of it was solid shot 12- or 20-pound iron projectiles pro-pelled by black powder at great velocity. They penetrated or battered down most of whatever they hit. Astoundingly, however, when Major Anderson finally surrendered after two days and nights of continuous bombardment, no one had been killed or even seriously wounded. The casualties, it turned out, were yet to come.

The first was Roger Pryor. Reluctant to fire the first shot of the war, he now rushed into the shattered fort as one of Beauregard's negotiators of surrender. Taking a seat at a table in Sumter's empty hospital while the terms he dictated were put into writing, he was overcome with thirst, seized a bottle close to hand, quaffed it, and, finding it peculiar tasting, thought to glance at the label, "Iodine of Potassium."

The fire-eater had poisoned himself. The fort's surgeon hauled him outside, pumped his stomach, and saved his life.

SITES AND SIGHTS

The Fort Sumter National Monument, administered by the National Park Service and encompassing Forts Sumter and Moultrie, can be reached by ferries operated by Fort Sumter Tours, Inc. Call 1-800-789-3678 for hours of operation and fees. Boats depart from the City Marina in downtown Charleston and from Patriots Point, in nearby Mount Pleasant. Admission requires a fee. For information, contact Park Superintendent, 1214 Middle Street, Sullivan's Island, SC 29482.

The Confederate flag flies over the ruins of Fort Sumter. Most of the damage seen here was inflicted by Union guns late in the war.
(Massachusetts Commander, Military Order of the Loyal Legion, and the U.S. Army Military History Institute)

The next day, Beauregard permitted Anderson to order a 50-gun salute to his fallen colors. When the Federal artillery thundered, a stray ember touched off some powder in a keg. The blast injured five people and killed one—Union Private Daniel Hough, the first soldier to die in the American Civil War. In the next four years, at least 618,000 others would join him.

Jamestown, Virginia: August 1619

The Civil War began long before Fort Sumter's fall.

In May 1607, a band of English settlers sailed into Chesapeake Bay, proceeded 30 miles up what they called the James River, and planted Jamestown, the first permanent English colony in America. A dozen years later, in August 1619, Virginia tobacco farmers purchased their first consignment of 20 slaves from Dutch traders.

These 20 souls, bought and sold, were hardly the first slaves transported to the New World. By 1619, Spanish and Portuguese slavers had brought more than a million Africans, in bondage, to their Caribbean and South American colonies. Unlike the wealthy planters in the colonies of Spain and Portugal, however, few of the hard-scrabble English farmers could afford African slaves.

At first, *indentured servitude*, whereby British men and women bound themselves to a limited period of service in return for passage to the New World, was a far more common source of cheap labor. But, by the close of the seventeenth century, the price of slaves fell and American colonists' wealth increased. More and more planters made the investment in a slave who, though he or she cost twice as much as an indentured servant, yielded a full lifetime of labor. More, in fact. The children of slaves were born slaves, and their children likewise—and so on, generation after generation, in perpetuity. Slavery was an eternal bargain.

DEFINITION

Indentured servitude was a form of voluntary servitude, in which a person bound himself to work for another for a fixed period (usually seven years) in return for passage to the New World.

A "Peculiar Institution"

At least it was a bargain in places where much land was controlled by a few wealthy planters. It was a bargain where the work was so backbreakingly miserable that free white laborers shunned it. As the seventeenth century gave way to the eighteenth, slavery had taken little hold in the Northern colonies, where farms were small and typically worked by the families who owned them. Here, slaves were an unnecessary expense. In the North, too, certain religious groups opposed slavery on moral grounds. The Quakers took the lead in this opposition as early as 1724.

But in the South, where some plantations were vast, slavery became integral with the region's economy. Nowhere was this more true than in South Carolina, whose planters were always the most ardent defenders of what came to be called (in polite circles) the "peculiar institution." Many Southerners were small farmers who owned few or no slaves, but slavery became a part of Southern life, for slave owners and nonslave owners alike.

By the 1720s, rice plantations covered the tidal and inland swamps of the Low Country, and indigo thrived in the higher, drier elevations. At this time, African slaves accounted for 64 percent of South Carolina's population. They lived, many of them, in malarial swamps, worked by their masters until disease or exhaustion brought them the death that finally set them free.

Three Fifths of a Man

1776: Thomas Jefferson, a Virginian who owned slaves, selected fellow members of the Continental Congress to draft a "Declaration of Independence" from Great Britain and proposed that the document denounce slavery. His fellow Southerners wouldn't hear of it and, 11 years later, when the Constitution was drawn up, it alluded to the future possibility of abolishing the importation of slaves (Article I, Section 9), but it also recognized and protected the institution of slavery (Article IV, Section 2.3).

The Constitution did even more.

Boston lawyer James Otis had helped stir the Revolution by declaring that "Taxation without representation is tyranny." With independence hard won, the framers of the Constitution sought to hammer out an equitable representative government. But they were bedeviled by the stubborn fact that the more representatives a state could claim, the more influence it would have in the federal government. For most purposes, Southerners were pleased to count their slaves as property. But when it came to apportioning representation in Congress, they suddenly preferred to count them as human beings. Seeking to minimize Southern influence, Northerners argued that slaves should be altogether excluded from the calculation.

At length, a compromise was reached. For purposes of levying taxes and apportioning representation, slaves were to be counted in the official census, but only as three fifths of a person. The so-called *Three-Fifths Compromise*, embodied in Article I, Section 2.3 of the Constitution, was the first of many tortured compromises American slavery would spawn. Like those later acts, the Three-Fifths Compromise was expedient in that it put off immediate conflict, but it settled nothing. The issue of slavery continued to smolder, and, with each subsequent compromise, it burned hotter and hotter—until it exploded.

DEFINITION

The **Three-Fifths Compromise** is represented in Article I, Section 2.3 of the U.S. Constitution. It stipulates that slaves (though that word is not used) may be counted as three fifths of a person for purposes of levying taxes and apportioning representation in Congress.

Against the American Grain

If the Constitution condoned slavery, growing numbers of Americans were finding the South's "peculiar institution" intolerable. Almost all of these people—the most radical of whom were called *abolitionists* because they wanted to abolish slavery entirely—lived in the North, where there had never been a huge demand for cheap agrarian labor on a vast scale. (However, at least in 1861, most Northerners were not abolitionists, and certainly racism was pervasive in the North.)

Freedom-Loving Quakers and Enlightened Colonists

As already mentioned, the Quakers mounted organized opposition to slavery by 1724. Rhode Island, a haven of toleration since its founding by dissident minister Roger Williams in 1636, abolished slavery in 1774. Elsewhere in the North, individual protests grew in number and volume.

The Feds Take a Stand

And even the federal government took action. A year before the Constitution was ratified, Congress enacted the Northwest Ordinance of 1787. It spelled out the basis for the government of what was then called the Northwest Territory—the vast region west of Pennsylvania, north of the Ohio River, east of the Mississippi River, and south of the Great Lakes—and for the eventual admission into the Union of its constituent parts. Most important, the ordinance outlawed slavery in the lands of the Northwest Territory. Not only was it the first federal pronouncement against slavery, but inasmuch as the ordinance regulated the expansion of the country—the nation's future—it loudly hinted that this future should be one without slavery. The ordinance also ensured that, at some time, three to five more "free" states would counterbalance the slave states, thereby checking and diminishing slaveholding interests and influence in Congress.

A Simple Machine

The thought behind the antislavery aspects of the Northwest Ordinance was to end slavery gradually, as the nation grew. And it might have happened just that way because, as immigration from Europe increased after the Revolution, cheap labor became more plentiful, and there were growing indications that the economic utility of slavery was diminishing. Moreover, the markets for the chief slave-produced crops of the South—tobacco, rice, and indigo—though large, were finite, what today would be called "mature markets," with little potential for growth.

But there was another Southern crop of some importance. Along the Southern coast, black-seed, long-staple cotton was cultivated. Before it could be exported for weaving into cloth, it had to be cleaned of its seeds. This was easy to do with black-seed cotton; the seeds could be expelled simply by passing the cotton bolls through a pair of rollers. The trouble was that black-seed cotton could be grown only in a limited coastal area. The vast interior lower South grew only green-seed, short-staple cotton, the seeds of which stubbornly resisted cleaning. Even with slave labor, the work was time-consuming and expensive, and the potential of cotton as a source of profit for the lower South was proportionately limited.

Eli Whitney, Inventor

Then, in 1794, a young Northerner named Eli Whitney cobbled together a simple machine that neatly and quickly cleaned short-staple cotton. Whitney secured a patent, and partnered with Phineas Miller to make and service the new "cotton gins." The machines were so successful—and so elegantly simple—that the partners found themselves pirated out of business by 1797 as planters made their own gins or bought cheaper knockoffs. "An invention can be so valuable as to be worthless to the inventor," Whitney later moaned.

A New Economy

During the first half of the nineteenth century, thanks to the cotton gin, cotton exports exceeded the value of all other American exports *combined.*

The cotton gin created a new economy for the South and had, in the process, renewed, reaffirmed, and increased the demand for slave labor to pick the cotton, feed the gins, bind the bales, and load them for shipment.

COUNT OFF!

In 1790, the United States produced about 3,000 bales (500 lbs. each) of cotton. In 1801, after the widespread introduction of the cotton gin, production was 100,000 bales; in 1820, 400,000 bales; on the eve of the Civil War, cotton production reached 4,000,000 bales.

A Major Purchase

The vast Louisiana Territory, some 90,000 square miles of land west of the Mississippi River, was French until the defeat of France in what Europe called the Seven Years' War and America called the French and Indian War. In 1763, France ceded the territory to its ally Spain as compensation for the Caribbean territories Spain lost in the war. In 1800, however, Napoleon Bonaparte reacquired the territory by secret treaty in exchange for parts of Tuscany, which he pledged to conquer on behalf of Spain. Napoleon also promised to maintain Louisiana as a buffer between Spain's North American settlements and the United States. But no sooner was the secret treaty concluded than Napoleon abandoned his Tuscan campaign, and France and Spain fell to disputing. Beginning in 1802, Spain responded to its ally's broken promise by closing the Mississippi River to American trade—the first step in Spain's plan to retake the Louisiana Territory.

President Thomas Jefferson could not tolerate so complete a disruption of western trade. However, neither did he relish the prospect of Napoleon entering North America. True, the French armies were currently bogged down in the Caribbean, vainly fighting tropical diseases and the brilliant Haitian revolutionary, Toussaint-L'Ouverture. Just now, they posed little threat to the continent, but Jefferson also feared that the ongoing warfare between France and England would likely result in the English seizure of the Louisiana Territory. Any way he looked at it, it was a bad situation, and, short of going to war with France, Jefferson decided to resolve the crisis by sending James Monroe to Napoleon with an offer to purchase Florida and the port city of New Orleans—and thereby establish a sound American claim for the right to Mississippi River navigation.

Buying New Orleans was a very good idea. But Monroe, as it turned out, was offered something even better. Resolving to cut his Caribbean losses, Napoleon decided to withdraw from the Americas altogether. For him, all of Louisiana was now a liability. Even as Monroe was crossing the Atlantic, Napoleon's minister, Talleyrand, asked Robert R. Livingston, U.S. foreign minister to France, how much Jefferson would offer not just for New Orleans and Florida, but for the entire Louisiana Territory. A bargain was struck for 60 million francs.

Many Southerners saw the vast territory as a virtually unlimited cotton field.

"Title Page to a Great Tragic Volume"

But more cotton also meant more slaves. Abolitionists eagerly pointed to the Northwest Ordinance, which had (they said) established a nonslavery precedent for *all* new territories. Proslavery factions responded with legalistic brilliance: the Constitution, far more authoritative than the Northwest Ordinance, acknowledged and even protected slavery. Moreover, the Fifth Amendment, in the sacred Bill of Rights, guaranteed the security of property, which, after all, is what slaves were. Finally—and this was, for the South, the most compelling argument in support of their "peculiar institution"—the Constitution gave to the individual states all powers and authority not specifically reserved for the federal government.

The regulation of slavery was nowhere reserved to federal authority; therefore, it must be a right of the individual states. Those states that opposed slavery could abolish it within their own borders, but states that favored it within their borders had the right to maintain it.

The years following the Louisiana Purchase widened the gulf that slavery gouged between North and South. A major crisis came during 1818–1819, when the U.S. Senate consisted of 22 senators from Northern states and 22 from Southern states. Precariously, ever since the end of the Revolution, the balance between the nonslave-holding North and the slave-holding South had been preserved with the addition of each new state. Now the territory of Missouri petitioned Congress for admission to the Union as a slave-holding state. The balance suddenly threatened to shift.

Representative James Tallmadge of New York responded to Missouri's statehood petition by introducing an amendment to the statehood bill, calling for a ban on the further introduction of slavery into the state (but persons who were slaves in the present territory would remain slaves after the transition to statehood) and for the emancipation of all slaves born in the state when they reached 25 years of age. Thus, by attrition, slavery would be eliminated from Missouri. The House passed the Tallmadge amendment, but the Senate rejected it, adjourning afterward without reaching a decision on Missouri statehood.

When the Senate reconvened, a long, rancorous debate began. Northern senators held that Congress had the right to ban slavery in new states. Southerners asserted that new states had the same right as the original 13: to determine whether or not they would allow slavery.

At last, in March 1820, a compromise was knocked together: Missouri would enter the Union as a slave state, but, simultaneously, Maine (hitherto a part of Massachusetts) would be admitted as a slave-free state. So, for the moment, the slave state/free state balance was maintained. Looking toward the future, the so-called Missouri Compromise called for a line to be drawn across the Louisiana Territory at a latitude of 36°30', north of which slavery would be permanently banned, except in the case of Missouri.

As some saw it, the Missouri Compromise staved off civil war. To the aging Thomas Jefferson, however, the rickety compromise, "like a fire bell in the night, awakened and filled me with terror." With equal foresight, an even older John Adams regarded it as the "title page to a great tragic volume."

The Least You Need to Know

- The bloodless fall of Fort Sumter was the first battle of the Civil War, in which 620,000 Americans would eventually die.
- The large-scale cultivation of Southern crops such as rice, indigo, tobacco, and, most of all, cotton, created and perpetuated the demand for slave labor.
- Men would fight the Civil War for many reasons, but the root cause of the war was slavery. The North ultimately wanted to end it, and the South refused to part with it.
- The Missouri Compromise of 1820 staved off civil war, but also pointed to the likelihood of future violent conflict over the issue of slavery.

Liberty and Union, Now and Forever?

In This Chapter

- The Nullification Crisis
- The abolitionist movement and its leaders
- The Underground Railroad
- Texas independence and the Mexican War
- California gold rush

Those who deny that slavery was at the root of the Civil War usually mention, in addition to states' rights, economics, and claim that the North was always trying to economically dominate the South. They do have a point. Set aside the moral obscenity and emotional pain of involuntary servitude, and you will find that slavery was very much an economic issue. It sustained, even as it was sustained by, the Southern way of life.

This chapter explores the brutal, brute forces of an economy bound to slavery—a way of life that tore apart a people who had, less than a century earlier, declared themselves one.

The South Says No

Slavery was essential to the South's agrarian economic system, dedicated to producing raw materials for manufacture by others. Some of these raw materials, chiefly cotton, were shipped to textile mills in the North, but most of what the South produced was exported. Raw cotton was spun into cloth in the great mills of England and France, which in turn exported the manufactured product back to the United States.

Through the first quarter of the nineteenth century, the South enjoyed relatively free trade with its European customers, little hampered by tariffs and duties. This was a great boon to the agricultural economy of the South, but a burden to the fledgling industrial economy of the North. When Americans imported their manufactured goods, homegrown industry suffered.

To foster American industry, Congress passed a stiff *protective tariff* law in 1828, levying a hefty duty on imported manufactured goods. The Northeast embraced the legislation, whereas the South voiced its outrage. If tariffs made it too costly for Americans to buy European goods, Europe would buy less of the South's raw materials, and the region's export business would dry up. No wonder Southerners decried the 1828 measure as a "Tariff of Abominations."

DEFINITION

A **protective tariff** is a tax imposed on imported goods with the purpose of discouraging importation and, therefore, promoting the manufacture and sale of domestic goods.

Calhoun's Theory

John C. Calhoun, son of South Carolina's Piedmont region at the foot of the Appalachians, was a congressman whose fiery nationalism moved him to introduce the declaration of war against Britain in June 1812. So ardent was he during the War of 1812 that a colleague dubbed him the "young Hercules who carried the war on his shoulders." After the war, he promoted federal funding of a permanent road system and the creation of a standing army and modern navy. He even voted in favor of a protective tariff in 1816. The following year, President James Monroe appointed him secretary of war, and John Quincy Adams, Monroe's secretary of state, declared Calhoun to be "above all sectional and factious prejudices, more than any other statesman of this Union with whom I have ever acted."

But Calhoun wanted desperately to be president himself, and became increasingly cantankerous when he failed to win a nomination. He began to execute a 180-degree turn away from passionate nationalism and toward fanatical regionalism. In 1828, while serving as Adams's vice president, he responded to the "Tariff of Abominations" with an anonymous pamphlet, the *South Carolina Exposition and Protest*, arguing that the tariff could be declared "null and void" by any state that deemed it unconstitutional.

The idea of *nullification* was not original. James Madison and Thomas Jefferson introduced the concept when they wrote the Virginia and Kentucky resolutions of 1798 and 1799. The resolutions declared that the Alien and Sedition Acts (repressive, reactionary legislation enacted by a skittish Congress during the Federalist administration of J. Q. Adams's father, John Adams) violated the Bill of Rights. Because the Acts were therefore, unconstitutional, they could and should be nullified by any state that chose to do so, Jefferson and Madison argued.

Despite this impressive precedent, Calhoun had difficulty garnering support for nullification in 1828. Even most Southern states repudiated the concept, and Jefferson Davis himself, the Mississippian destined to become the president of the Confederate States of America, argued that the states had no such right. In any case, a major battle over the Tariff of Abominations was averted by the 1828 election of Andrew Jackson, a Southerner, who pledged tariff reform.

Yet the promised reform proved weak and the Tariff Act of 1832, passed during Jackson's administration, offended the South again. Calhoun abruptly resigned as vice president, gained election to the Senate, and the state of South Carolina called a convention that, on November 24, 1832, passed an Ordinance of Nullification forbidding collection of tariff duties in the state. Another South Carolina senator, Robert Y. Hayne, first presented Calhoun's nullification theory in the Senate, arguing that a state could not only nullify an unconstitutional law, but also that it could, as a last resort, even secede from the Union.

In reply to Hayne, Daniel Webster, senator from Massachusetts, made an eloquent defense of the powers of the federal government versus the alleged rights of the states, concluding with the stirring appeal, "Liberty and Union, now and forever, one and inseparable!"

Nullification brought the nation to a showdown between the will of a state and the law of the nation. And the scope of the crisis went well beyond the issue of the tariff. Calhoun and the other advocates of nullification were really fighting for protection of slavery, which would, in all likelihood, be abolished by a Northern majority in Congress someday—unless the doctrine of *states' rights* could be made to override the national majority.

DEFINITION

Nullification is the concept that a state may nullify and refuse to obey or enforce any federal law it considers unconstitutional. The concept rested on the related principle of **states' rights,** which is the doctrine that the individual states do command all powers and authority not *explicitly* assigned to the federal government by the Constitution.

Jackson Acts

Calhoun hoped and believed that Jackson (a Southerner, after all) would back down on the tariff. To the senator's chagrin, however, the president responded on December 10 with a declaration denying the power of any state to block enforcement of a federal law and threatening armed intervention to collect duties. He secured from Congress passage of a Force Act, empowering him to use the military to enforce the tariff.

With passage of the Force Act, outright civil war suddenly loomed; but, that same year, a compromise tariff was enacted, and, although South Carolina did "nullify" the Force Act, it also accepted the new tariff, which made the nullification moot because the Force Act would not be used. Bloodshed was averted for now, but the nullification and states' rights concepts refused to die and would provide a rationale for the break up of the Union less than three decades later.

The Liberators

The times were dangerous for the nation in general, and for the South in particular. With each passing year of the nineteenth century, Northern opposition to slavery grew stronger and increasingly militant.

Genius of Universal Emancipation

At first, William Lloyd Garrison (1805–1879) was typical of the liberal white Northerners who opposed slavery. A native of Newburyport, Massachusetts, he became coeditor of a genteel abolitionist periodical called *The Genius of Universal Emancipation*. But the more Garrison wrote about slavery the less genteel he became until, on January 1, 1831, he published the first issue of *The Liberator*, an abolitionist periodical that called for immediate emancipation.

The radical *Liberator* electrified the abolitionist movement. Three years after the debut of *The Liberator*, Garrison founded the American Anti-Slavery Society and declared that slavery would end when a majority of white Americans experienced a "revolution in conscience." Garrison sought just such a revolution. In 1842, he exhorted *Northerners* to break with the Union because the Constitution protected slavery. A pacifist who abhorred violence, Garrison nevertheless hailed John Brown's bloody 1859 raid on Harpers Ferry for the purpose of stealing guns to arm slaves for a general uprising (see Chapter 13).

A Life in Search of Liberation

A tonic too strong for many, even in the North, *The Liberator* was the most forceful white voice in support of abolition. In 1845, a gripping account of slavery and liberation by an escaped Maryland slave named Frederick Douglass was heard as the most compelling African American voice of liberation. His autobiographical *Narrative of the Life of Frederick Douglass* brought home both the collective inhumanity of slavery and the individual humanity of the slaves. Although both Garrison and Douglass sought to end slavery, Douglass disagreed with Garrison over breaking with the Union. Douglass wanted to work within the Constitution.

Frederick Douglass, an escaped Maryland slave, whose autobiography and stirring oratory brought home the collective inhumanity of slavery and the individual humanity of the slaves.
(UPI/Corbis-Bettmann)

Murder in Virginia

As the South saw it, violent words were dangerous enough, but seething under the chivalrous surface of Southern society was fear of violence beyond mere words.

The fear was well founded. Nat Turner was a slave on the plantation of Joseph Travis in Southampton County, Virginia. A fiery lay-preacher, Turner gathered a band of rebellious fellow slaves and, just before dawn on August 22, 1831, he and his followers killed every white member of the Travis household. Then they swept through the countryside killing every white they encountered during the next 24 hours—perhaps 60 people in all.

The white response was, in turn, swift and bloody. Turner and 50 of his band were captured and summarily tried. Twenty were hanged. Dissatisfied with this display of "justice," bands of white avengers ranged the countryside, torturing and killing whatever blacks they happened to run across. In Southern society, slavery was ultimately an issue of life and death.

> **COUNT OFF!**
>
> By 1861, one third of the total Southern population of 12,000,000 were slaves; 384,000 whites were slave owners, but only about 1,800 whites owned more than 100 slaves.

Notes from Underground

Legislative pressure, public eloquence, and physical violence were not the only weapons wielded against slavery. Beginning in the 1830s, a loose network of white abolitionists and free blacks created an *Underground Railroad* to smuggle slaves out of the South and into the free states of the North. The "conductors," as the secret operatives of the system were called, transferred the fugitives ("passengers" or "freight") gradually northward from one secret safe house ("station") to another. During the 1830s, '40s, and '50s, 50,000 to 100,000 slaves "followed the North Star" to freedom by way of the Underground Railroad (even though the railroad's "terminals" never reached into the Deep South—southern Georgia, Alabama, Mississippi, Florida, and Texas).

> **DEFINITION**
>
> The **Underground Railroad** was a secret network that helped fugitive slaves escape from the South to the free states of the North and, sometimes, into Canada.

Although the rewards of freedom were greatly prized, the risks were grave. "Conductors" were menaced, beaten, and even killed, and fugitive slaves, once retaken, were often severely punished as an example to others. When the Supreme Court ruled in 1842 (*Prigg* v. *Pennsylvania*) that states were not required to enforce the Fugitive Slave Law of 1793 (which provided for the return of slaves who escaped to free states), Southern opposition to the Underground Railroad became especially intense and bitter.

War and Gold

As the nation inexorably tore along the seam dividing North from South, increasing numbers of Americans turned their eyes westward. In the years before the Civil War, traffic on the Oregon Trail and the other overland trails multiplied. In the nation's time of trouble, the West held hope and, it seemed, the future.

Mexican Sunset

While the prairies of the Midwest and the plains of the West began to fill, the Southwest, still the territory of the Republic of Mexico, was also being settled by a growing number of American colonists.

Stephen Austin brought more than 1,200 American families to Texas in 1822. By 1836, the American population of Texas had swelled to 50,000, while Mexicans numbered a mere 3,500.

The large American colony chafed under Mexican rule. In particular, the Texas colonists objected to Mexican laws forbidding slavery. Austin tried to negotiate with the country's president, Antonio Lopez de Santa Anna, for a degree of autonomous Mexican statehood for Texas, but failed. In 1835, he urged Texans to support a Mexican revolt against Santa Anna, thereby triggering the Texas Revolution, which ended in the defeat of Santa Anna at the Battle of San Jacinto (April 21, 1836). The beaten dictator signed a treaty granting Texas its independence.

The new republic immediately agitated for annexation to the United States. Congress and the president met this with reluctance, however. Not only would it mean adding another slave state to the Union, upsetting the delicate balance of compromise, but it would also surely touch off a war with Mexico. When France and England made overtures of alliance to Texas, outgoing President John Tyler finally urged Congress to adopt an annexation resolution, and Tyler's successor, James K. Polk, admitted Texas to the Union on December 29, 1845.

 SITES AND SIGHTS

The Alamo, a Franciscan mission officially known as the Mission San Antonio de Valero, became an American icon as the site of the battle between a small band of Texans (led by Jim Bowie and William B. Travis, including Davy Crockett) and a large contingent of Mexican soldiers commanded by Antonio Lopez de Santa Anna, from February 23 to March 6, 1836. Recent scholarship suggests that the number of Alamo defenders, traditionally believed to be 189, might have been closer to 257.

Located on the Alamo Plaza in San Antonio, the Alamo is one of the nation's most-visited tourist attractions. Contact: 210-225-1391.

In the meantime, England and France also demonstrated undue interest in California, held so weakly by Mexico that it was ready to fall into any waiting hands. Polk offered Mexico $40 million for California. When the offer was spurned, Polk supported the Bear Flag Rebellion there, and the territory's independence from Mexico was proclaimed.

Mexico disputed the boundary of the new state of Texas during this time, too; Polk dispatched troops and, on May 13, 1846, the U.S.-Mexican War began. It ended on September 17, when Santa Anna, once again in power, surrendered after a series of stunning American victories.

Agreement to the Treaty of Guadalupe Hidalgo (ratified by the U.S. Senate on March 10, 1848) ended the war and included provisions for the Mexican cession to the United States of New Mexico (which included parts of the present states of Utah, Nevada, Arizona, and Colorado) and California. Mexico also renounced claims to Texas above the Rio Grande.

Optimists believed the vast new Western territories would relieve some of the North-South tension; pessimists pointed to the necessity of making any number of urgent and potentially explosive decisions as to whether a territory acquired as the spoils of war would join the Union as a free state or a slave state.

The Mexican War meant something else as well. It was the baptism in blood of such commanders as Ulysses S. Grant, Robert E. Lee, and many other Northern and Southern officers, who were destined in less than two decades to meet, as foes, on fields much closer to home.

Gold Rush

Johann Augustus Sutter was a hard-luck case. Born in Kandern, Germany, in 1803, he went bankrupt there and, one jump ahead of his creditors, fled to the American southwest. There he plunged into the Santa Fe trade, going bust two more times before he settled in Mexican California in 1838 and built a large ranch in the central valley. On January 24, 1848, one of his employees, James Wilson Marshall, went out to inspect the canal of a new mill Sutter had built. Something shiny in the sediment at the bottom of the millrace caught his eye. It was gold.

Sutter's luck had changed.

Or so it seemed. Within a month and a half, all of Sutter's employees had deserted him in search of gold. Unstaffed, the Sutter ranch began to fall apart. Worse, his claims to the land adjacent to the mill were judged invalid. As those around him (it seemed) grew rich, Sutter went broke again. He died, bitter and bankrupt, in 1880.

Tough luck for him, but for the rest of the country, the California gold rush of 1849 was on! All over the nation, men dropped their tools, left their jobs, kissed their families good-bye, and headed for the south fork of the American River to find their fortunes. This human tidal wave hastened the entry of California into the Union. It became the 31st state in 1850 and, once more, Congress was compelled to rush to bitter, divisive compromise to preserve the balance between free-state and slave-state legislators. Bathed in the warm glow of California gold, America drifted ever closer to civil war.

The Least You Need to Know

- The Nullification Crisis of 1832 to 1833, an early contest between the sovereignty of individual states and the authority of the federal government, nearly triggered civil war in the 1830s.
- John C. Calhoun turned the Nullification Crisis into a battle over states' rights, which ultimately meant a struggle to preserve and protect slavery.

- The Underground Railroad smuggled a small but significant number of slaves to freedom, and slave revolt was a constant Southern fear.
- The opening of the Southwest dramatically upset the balance between slave states and free states, propelling the nation to its final great crisis before the war.

Descent into War

In This Chapter

- The Compromise of 1850 and the Kansas-Nebraska Act
- John Brown and the raid on Harpers Ferry
- The birth of the Republican Party
- Enter President Lincoln
- The first states secede

The clumsy Missouri Compromise of 1820 (see Chapter 1) sagged, wheezed, and finally broke under the weight of the California gold rush. At the height of the gold rush in 1849, more than 80,000 fortune seekers poured into the region. Statehood for the newly acquired territory became so urgent an issue that South Carolina Congressman John C. Calhoun warned it could lead to civil war.

This chapter tells how the very steps that averted civil war for one more decade also made that war inevitable.

The Tortured Course of Compromise

During the first year of the Mexican War, 1846, Congress wanted to bring the conflict to a quick end and debated a bill to appropriate $2 million to compensate Mexico for what the lawmakers euphemistically termed "territorial adjustments." Seizing opportunity, Pennsylvania Congressman David Wilmot introduced an amendment, the "Wilmot Proviso," which would have barred the introduction of slavery into any land acquired as a result of the Mexican War.

South Carolina's Calhoun angrily countered with four proposed resolutions:

- First, that all territories, including those acquired as a result of the war, were to be regarded as the common and joint property of the states.

- Second, that Congress acts as agent for the states and can, therefore, make no law discriminating among the states and depriving any state of its rights with regard to any territory.

- Third, that the enactment of any national law regarding slavery violates the Constitution, including the doctrine of states' rights.

- Fourth, that the people have the right to form their state governments as they wish, provided only that such government is republican in principle.

Failure to accept these resolutions and to take action accordingly, Calhoun threatened, would surely mean civil war.

The Compromise of 1850

Action was not immediate. The year 1846 saw the commencement of a three-year debate on ways to brace and bolster the Missouri Compromise, but neither side was actually willing to compromise.

A standoff, Senator Lewis Cass of Michigan saw, would paralyze the government and probably lead to civil war. He therefore advanced the doctrine of *popular sovereignty,* which provided for the organization of new territories without mention of slavery one way or the other. Only when the territory wrote its own constitution and applied for admission as a state would the people of the territory itself vote whether it would be slave or free.

DEFINITION

Popular sovereignty was the doctrine and policy introduced in the Compromise of 1850. It provided for the people of a territory to vote on whether the territory would apply for admission to the Union as a free state or a slave state. The federal government would be bound by the people's decision.

To solve the immediate issue of California statehood, it was decided that California would be admitted to the Union directly instead of going through an interim territorial status. At this Southerners recoiled, correctly assuming that California would vote itself free. (It did, as would New Mexico, later.) So Senators Henry Clay of Kentucky and Daniel Webster of Massachusetts worked out a new compromise. California would be admitted as a free state, but the other territories acquired as a result of the Mexican War would be subject to popular sovereignty. Moreover, the slave trade in the District of Columbia (an embarrassment to foreign diplomats and other visitors from nations where slavery had long ceased to be tolerated) would be discontinued.

However, to further appease the South, a strong fugitive slave law was passed, explicitly forbidding Northerners from giving refuge to escaped slaves. Finally, the federal government agreed to assume debts Texas (admitted as a slave state in 1845) incurred before it was annexed to the United States.

As with previous compromises, that of 1850 offended as many interests as it placated. Abolitionists were appalled by the Fugitive Slave Law, whereas states' rights supporters saw the slave/free balance in Congress tilting ever northward.

Kansas Bleeds

The Compromise of 1850 augmented the Missouri Compromise, but four years later, when the territories of Nebraska and Kansas applied for statehood, Congress responded by repealing the Missouri Compromise altogether and passing the Kansas-Nebraska Act in its place. This extended the doctrine of popular sovereignty beyond territory acquired as a result of the Mexican War, entirely eliminating the 1820 slave/free line.

If the situation four years earlier had been explosive, the Kansas-Nebraska Act applied a match to the fuse. For although there was never any doubt that Nebraskans would vote themselves a free state, Kansas, to the south, was another matter. Proslavery Missourians and antislavery Iowans streamed across the territory's border—each side striving to achieve a majority. Many of the Missourians retreated to their home state after successfully electing a proslavery territorial legislature for Kansas, but the Iowans remained, and soon a guerrilla civil war developed between pro- and antislavery factions in what came to be called "Bleeding Kansas."

Typical of the violence was the 1856 raid against the antislavery stronghold of Lawrence. Proslavery Missourians, called border ruffians, raided the town in 1856, setting fire to a number of buildings, destroying a printing press, and killing several townspeople.

On the night of May 24, John Brown, a radical abolitionist who had taken command of the territory's so-called "Free Soil Militia," led four of his sons and two other followers in an assault on proslavery settlers along the Pottawatomie Creek. Brown and his militia put five unarmed settlers to the sword, pronouncing this retribution for the sack of Lawrence. Although Kansas was ultimately admitted as a free state in 1861, guerrilla violence was repeated there throughout the Civil War.

John Brown, avenger of the abolitionist cause in Lawrence, Kansas, and leader of a later raid on Harpers Ferry in an effort to arm the slaves.

Beyond Compromise

By the 1850s, the people of the United States were traveling inexorably beyond any compromise. The journey was made on roads emotional as well as legal.

The Little Woman Who Made This Great War

Harriet Beecher was born in 1811 in Litchfield, Connecticut, one of eleven children of a prominent Congregationalist preacher, Lyman Beecher. Harriet's brother, Henry Ward Beecher, would earn fame as a Brooklyn-based abolitionist. Harriet embarked on a career as a teacher at a school her sister, Catherine, founded in Cincinnati, Ohio. In 1836, she married a theology professor, Calvin Ellis Stowe, and began writing books.

During the 18 years she lived in Cincinnati, Stowe came to know slave owners from neighboring Kentucky, and she also met fugitive slaves. The experience made an impression. In 1850, her husband was appointed to a professorship at Bowdoin College, in Brunswick, Maine. There Harriet Beecher Stowe began to write a book about slavery.

Published in 1852, *Uncle Tom's Cabin, or Life Among the Lowly* tells the story of old Tom, a slave devoted to his kindly but debt-burdened Kentucky master, who sells him to the cruel Simon Legree. The novel was aggressively promoted by abolitionists even as it was denounced by Southerners, who passed local legislation to suppress distribution of the book throughout the region. Soon, the book was dramatized by a host of playwrights and thus reached an even wider audience than the 300,000 who bought the book in its first year of publication.

Uncle Tom's Cabin won the hearts and minds of many Northerners hitherto lukewarm on the issue of abolition. Reportedly, when President Lincoln received Stowe at the White House in 1862, he greeted her by saying, "So you're the little woman who wrote the book that made this great war."

Dred Verdict

The mayhem of Bleeding Kansas and the explosive popularity of *Uncle Tom's Cabin* were opening chords in the overture to the greater conflict to come. Another note was struck, to even more resounding effect, within the orderly confines of the Supreme Court. In 1857, the high court heard the appeal of one Dred Scott, fugitive slave.

Scott had belonged to John Emerson of St. Louis. An army surgeon, Emerson had been transferred first to Illinois and then to Wisconsin Territory, taking his slave with him. After Emerson's death in 1846, Scott returned to St. Louis, where he sued Emerson's widow for his freedom. He made his claim on the basis that he was now a citizen of Missouri, having been freed by virtue of his terms of residence in Illinois, where slavery was banned by the Northwest Ordinance, and in Wisconsin Territory, where the provisions of the Missouri Compromise made slavery illegal.

When the Missouri state court decided against Scott, his lawyers appealed to the Supreme Court. In a shocking breach of the constitutional separation of powers, incoming president James Buchanan (foolishly believing that a Supreme Court decision would settle the slavery issue once and for all) apparently talked Associate Justice Robert Cooper Grier, a fellow Pennsylvanian, into siding with the Southern justices in a decision against Scott. Writing for the majority, Chief Justice Roger B. Taney, native of the slave state of Maryland, upheld the Missouri court's decision. He wrote that neither free blacks nor enslaved blacks were citizens of the United States and, therefore, could not sue in federal court. Then he went further, ruling that the Illinois law banning slavery had no force on Scott once he returned to Missouri, a slave state. The law in Wisconsin was likewise without force, because, he said, the Missouri Compromise was unconstitutional, a violation of the Fifth Amendment, which bars the government from depriving an individual of "life, liberty, or *property*" without due process of law. If slaves were indeed nothing more than "property," no state could liberate them by simply taking them from their owners.

The Dred Scott Decision pleased the South, but also galvanized the abolitionist movement. By making slavery a Fifth Amendment issue, the Dred Scott Decision put the matter beyond compromise. If the constitutional rights of slave holders had to be universally upheld as long as slavery existed, slavery had to be universally accepted or universally abolished. There was no middle course, and, without a middle course, war was all but a certainty.

Some More Blood: The Raid on Harpers Ferry

At Pottawatomie Creek, Kansas, John Brown had demonstrated that he was a man of sharp, swift, bloody deeds. In 1857, he moved from Kansas to Boston, the national hotbed of abolitionism. There, with the support of six of the most prominent abolitionists—Samuel Gridley Rowe, Thomas Wentworth Higginson, Theodore Parker, Franklin Sanborn, George L. Stearns, and Gerrit Smith—he raised cash to finance a raid on the federal arsenal at Harpers Ferry, Virginia (present-day West Virginia). His intention was to use the guns and ammunition appropriated from the arsenal to arm the slaves of the South for a massive rebellion.

The Raid Begins

John Brown led 16 white men and 5 black men to the federal arsenal and armory at the confluence of the Shenandoah and Potomac rivers. He and his band quickly took the armory and Hall's rifle works nearby, and then hunkered down to defend the prize, holding hostage some 60 residents of Harpers Ferry and the surrounding area, including the great-grandnephew of George Washington. Brown dispatched two of his black "soldiers" to alert local slaves. He counted on this pair to rouse thousands to "swarm."

None came. And when the fighting started, the first civilian Brown's men killed was a free black man.

Citizens of Harpers Ferry laid siege to the arsenal. In an exchange of fire, two of Brown's sons were killed. Sporadic fighting continued through the morning and afternoon, when the survivors barricaded themselves and their hostages in a firehouse adjacent to the armory.

Enter Lieutenant Colonel Robert E. Lee

At this point, Lieutenant Colonel Robert E. Lee, U.S. Army, and his former West Point student, Lieutenant James Ewell Brown Stuart—known familiarly as Jeb—arrived with a company of U.S. Marines. Having been hurriedly called away from leave at his estate in Arlington, Virginia, where he was wrestling with the financial affairs of his late father-in-law, he was still wearing civilian clothing. Nevertheless, even out of uniform, Lee was a commanding presence. He arrived at Harpers Ferry amid wild rumors of a slave rebellion. Lee moved with calm deliberation. He let the night of the 17th pass; then, come morning, he sent Jeb Stuart under a flag of truce to demand Brown's surrender.

His fiery eyes flashing, Brown refused. Stuart emerged from the parley and waved his broad-brimmed cavalryman's hat in a prearranged signal for the marines to charge. They made short work of the firehouse door and rushed in; doing their best to protect the hostages, they put two of Brown's men to the bayonet.

WAR NEWS

The United States was so resolutely nonmartial, in attitude and spirit, before the Civil War that no army troops were available, even in the vicinity of a federal arsenal. A small marine detachment was handiest, so Lee became the only U.S. Army officer ever to command U.S. Marines.

The battle lasted all of three minutes. Marine Lieutenant Israel Green stabbed and pummeled Brown with his sword. Brown survived, but all except four of the other raiders were killed. Four citizens of Harpers Ferry, including the town's mayor, also perished, along with one marine.

John Brown's Body

The state of Virginia charged the wounded Brown and his surviving followers with treason, conspiracy to foment servile insurrection, and murder. Trial came swiftly and, 10 days after the raid, all were sentenced to hang.

But to the embarrassment of the Virginia government, John Brown did not die like the crazed fanatic Southerners thought him to be. At his sentencing, he spoke reasonably and eloquently, arguing that he had behaved in harmony with the New Testament injunction to "remember them that are in bonds, as bound with them." Brown concluded:

> Now, if it is deemed necessary that I should forfeit my life for the furtherance of the ends of justice, and mingle my blood further with the blood of my children and with the blood of millions in this slave country whose rights are disregarded by wicked, cruel, and unjust enactments—I submit; so let it be done.

On the day of Brown's execution, December 2, 1859, the nation's most respected philosopher and man of letters, Ralph Waldo Emerson, joined William Lloyd Garrison to memorialize Brown before a mass gathering of abolitionists in Boston. By hanging John Brown, the Southern state of Virginia had given the North a martyr to its most radical cause. For its part, after the Harpers Ferry raid, the South grew far less inclined to negotiate and talk peace.

The Shattered Party

Following passage of the Kansas-Nebraska Act in 1854, the Whig Party, traditional opponent of the pro-Southern Democratic Party, lost credibility with abolitionists. Antislavery voters resented the repeal of the Missouri Compromise and its replacement by popular sovereignty. In 1854, a host of small abolitionist parties, most importantly the Free-Soil Party, the Conscience Whig Party, the Liberty Party, and the Anti-Nebraska Democratic Party, joined forces as the Republican Party.

The new party failed to capture the White House with their first presidential candidate, the famous Western explorer John C. Frémont, but it did win more than 100 congressional seats. Two years later, the party's candidate for senator from Illinois, Abraham Lincoln, made a national name for himself by his eloquence in a series of debates against incumbent senator, Democrat Stephen A. Douglas. Douglas won reelection, but Lincoln emerged as the Republican presidential standard bearer. Lincoln opposed allowing the expansion of slavery into the territories, whereas Douglas wanted the matter left to a vote of the settlers themselves; neither candidate thought it constitutionally possible to abolish slavery outright in the United States.

As the Republicans swept the Whigs aside, their influence and relatively strong stand against slavery drove radical Democrats in the South to claim that if a Republican were elected president in 1860, the Southern states would secede from the Union.

Had they presented a united front and a single candidate, the Democrats might have defeated Lincoln in 1860. However, going into the elections, the Democratic Party was fatally splintered. Stephen A. Douglas sought the Democratic nomination, but by denouncing the proslavery constitution initially adopted by Kansas as fraudulent and contrary to the will of the territorial settlers, he had alienated the South. Douglas captured the nomination, but as the candidate of a shattered party. A breakaway group, called the Southern Democratic Party nominated Buchanan's vice president, John C. Breckinridge. Another splinter group, the Constitutional Union party, fielded its own candidate, further splitting the party.

COUNT OFF!

Although clearly victorious in electoral votes, Lincoln won only a plurality (more than any other *single* candidate) of the popular vote. He received only 1,866,452 popular ballots against 2,815,617 cast for *all* his opponents.

In the end, 123 electoral votes were divided among the various Democratic candidates, and 180 votes went to the Republican candidate, Abraham Lincoln.

The Union Dissolves

James Buchanan (1791–1868), 15th president of the United States, is remembered chiefly for two things: first, for his bachelorhood (he still stands as the only unmarried president the nation has ever elected); second, for an absence of leadership in the final crises leading to the Civil War.

Abraham Lincoln, 16th president of the United States.
(Harper's Pictorial History of the Civil War, 1866)

Personally opposed to slavery on moral grounds, he did nothing to oppose it officially and, indeed, usually caved in to proslavery interests. His only strategy for preserving the Union consisted of placating the South by suppressing Northern antislavery agitation and by enforcing the Fugitive Slave Act of 1850. He appealed to the suffering citizens of Bleeding Kansas to accept the unpopular proslavery "Lecompton Constitution" proposed for that state.

Once Lincoln was elected, the lame-duck Buchanan did not act when seven Southern states seceded. To be sure, he denounced their going, but he claimed he could find no constitutional means to stop them.

As for President-elect Abraham Lincoln, he believed it was best to remain silent on the crisis until inauguration day.

Buchanan waited, too, eager now for the arrival of March 4, 1861, when the gangly figure from Illinois (unfriendly newspapers compared him to an ape or a baboon, and it was a cruel slur that his enemies, both in the North and the South, eagerly repeated) would lift a terrible burden from his unwilling shoulders.

The Secession Commissioners

Others were not waiting. Between December 1860 and April 1861, five of the Deep South states that had seceded sent "secession commissioners" to one or more of the slave states that were considering (or might consider) seceding. There were 52 commissioners in all, who spoke to state legislatures and secession conventions, at public meetings and at private gatherings. Their objective was to spread the secessionist message across the South and to persuade additional states to secede. They were Southerners talking to fellow Southerners, speaking frankly and without the need to dissemble or take into account the sensibilities of outsiders. Their speeches and letters make clear what was driving secession impulse. For instance:

- "Louisiana looks to the formation of a Southern confederacy to preserve the blessings of African slavery." —George Williamson, Louisiana commissioner to Texas, official communication to the Texas convention

- "The Republican Party stands for 'one-dogma, the equality of the races, white and black.' [Secession is the only means by which] 'the heaven-ordained superiority of the white over the black race' could be maintained." —Stephen Hale, Alabama commissioner to Kentucky, letter to the governor

- "Mississippi ... will never submit to the principles and policy of this Black Republican Administration. She had rather see the last of her race, men, women and children, immolated in one common funeral pile [pyre], than see them subjected to the degradation of civil, political and social equality with the negro race." —William L. Harris, Mississippi commissioner to the Georgia General Assembly

In setting out to explain the reasons for secession to their fellow Southerners, these commissioners explain a great deal to us, too: that race and slavery were central to secession.

The Least You Need to Know

- The Compromise of 1850 and the Kansas-Nebraska Act staved off civil war, even as they further polarized the nation.
- Guerrilla warfare between proslavery and antislavery forces in Kansas was a violent prelude to the Civil War.
- The Supreme Court's decision in the *Dred Scott* case outraged even moderate Northerners and made it clear that the slavery issue had gone beyond compromise.
- John Brown's Harpers Ferry raid failed to incite a universal slave insurrection, but it galvanized the abolitionist cause, further polarized the nation, and brought civil war closer.

Bleak Inaugural

In This Chapter

- Secession follows Lincoln's election
- The South's economic and industrial handicaps
- A plot to assassinate President-elect Lincoln
- Lincoln's inaugural message

After Lincoln's election, seven Southern states immediately made good on their threat to secede:

1. First to leave the Union was South Carolina, on December 20, 1860
2. Mississippi followed on January 9, 1861
3. Florida on January 10
4. Alabama on January 11
5. Georgia on January 19
6. Louisiana on January 26
7. Texas on February 1

Four days later, delegates from these states met in Montgomery, Alabama, where they wrote a constitution for the Confederate States of America and named Mississippi's Jefferson Davis provisional president.

This chapter details the critical months and weeks leading up to the fall of Fort Sumter.

"Black" Lincoln

In Lincoln's day, presidents-elect had no transition teams, spin doctors, or big-money consultants to usher the new man into the White House. President-elect Lincoln did not even think to huddle with James Buchanan during the troubled interval before his inauguration. And even when the president-elect learned that Jefferson Davis had offered to negotiate peaceful relations with the Union, he kept silent.

Lincoln also knew that Senator John J. Crittenden of Kentucky was proposing, as a last-ditch alternative to war, the Crittenden Compromise—a set of six constitutional amendments to protect slavery while absolutely limiting its spread. Still, Lincoln stubbornly refused to commit himself to any position before taking office.

Abraham Lincoln was a lifelong opponent of slavery. He once said, "If slavery is not wrong, nothing is wrong." He shared the ultimate goal of the abolitionists but he was not one of them; they demanded the immediate abolition of slavery, whereas Lincoln believed the federal government had no right to interfere directly with slavery where it already existed. He also said that the Fugitive Slave Law, obnoxious as it was, should be obeyed, because it was the law of the land.

In an 1858 speech that echoed the gospel of Mark, Lincoln argued, "a house divided against itself cannot stand." That is, the United States could not remain half-slave and half-free, it must inevitably become all one or all the other. Lincoln was adamant that there must be no expansion of slavery into the territories, whether by congressional fiat or Douglas's "settler sovereignty." If slavery were hemmed in, Lincoln believed it would disappear sooner rather than later.

It is possible to criticize Lincoln for maintaining silence on these issues between his election in November and his inauguration in early March. He remained silent in the face of the secession, one by one, of the Deep South states. He remained silent as a doomed "peace conference" deliberated in Washington. He remained silent as Senator Crittenden proposed a package of compromises, and he remained silent as Jefferson Davis offered to negotiate a settlement.

Lincoln's view was that nothing he could say, prior to taking up the reins of office, would help, and might make matters worse. His position on slavery was on record for all to see. Why then should he repeat it? It had been misrepresented before by those hell-bent on secession, and it would simply be misrepresented again. In any case, he was not prepared to abandon the policies on which he and other Republicans had just been elected, most especially in the face of secession. In Lincoln's mind no compromise was possible over the question of union. Either the minority was prepared to accept the result of a democratic election, or they were not. If not, it was his duty as president to save the Union. And this was not merely a matter of preserving the American union, but also of demonstrating the viability of representative government for all time.

Davis's invitation was a trap. The secessionists would agree to no compromise, and empty negotiations would only dishearten the millions of Republican voters. The Crittenden proposals left the decision on slavery to the inhabitants of each territory—meaning that slavery might *not* be confined to the states where it currently existed. But Lincoln would not retreat from the policy on which he had been elected. Should he do so, he argued, the young Republican Party would be seen as "a mere sucked egg—all shell with no principle in it."

In fact, the die was already cast. "The time for compromise has now passed," said Davis in February, "and the South is now determined to maintain her position and make all who oppose her smell Southern powder and feel Southern steel if coercion is persisted in." Lincoln said, shortly after, "As to slavery, it must be content with what it has. The voice of the civilized world is against it; it is opposed to its growth or extension. Freedom is the natural condition of the human race, in which the Almighty intended men to live. Those who fight the purposes of the Almighty will not succeed. They always have been, and they always will be, beaten."

The Wayward Sisters

Because there were initially seven secession states, the press sometimes called them the "seven sisters," a reference from Greek mythology to the daughters of Atlas and Pleione, who were changed into the stars of the constellation Pleiades—even as the breakaway states transformed themselves into the stars of a new flag. In response to the first wave of secession, Winfield Scott, the distinguished but aged and infirm general-in-chief of the U.S. Army, advised President Lincoln simply to say to the seceded states, "wayward sisters depart in peace!" This advice came not from timidity, Scott was a hero of the War of 1812 and the architect of victory in the U.S.-Mexican War, but from a conviction that the Southern states could not survive long without the North. He felt if they were allowed to go, they would return, sooner or later, of their own free will. William H. Seward, Lincoln's secretary of state, seconded the advice, counseling the president to "let the erring sisters go."

Scott and Seward were not alone in their belief that the South—its industries poorly developed, its population one-third slave, and many of its free people dirt poor—was economically incapable of sustaining itself. Southern prospects did not, in fact, look promising. The 11 states that eventually made up the Confederacy had a population of 12 million, of which 4 million were slaves. By contrast, the 23 states of the Union (to which even more would be added during the course of the war) had a combined population of some 22 million, all free.

On the eve of war, some 20,000 Southern factories employed about 100,000 workers but Northern factories numbered well over 100,000, and employed in excess of a million workers. As to railroads, which would prove essential for transporting military supplies as well as troops, the South boasted a mere 9,000 miles of track—much of it limited by non-uniform and mutually incompatible gauges (track widths)—whereas the North was thoroughly networked with 20,000 miles of uniform-gauge track. How could the South hope to prevail?

COUNT OFF!

Union banks held 81 percent of the nation's deposits, as well as $56 million in gold bullion. The Union's international credit was virtually unlimited, whereas the South was cash poor, gold poor, and, to establish credit in the world, would have to gain international recognition as a sovereign nation.

Olive Branches

Representatives from the first secessionist states convened in Montgomery, Alabama, on February 8, 1861, and declared themselves the Confederate States of America. Jefferson Davis of Mississippi was elected president and Alexander Stephens of Georgia, vice president. Nevertheless, there were those in the North who thought that war could still be averted and the Union glued back together. One of these hopeful men was John J. Crittenden, senator from the *border state* of Kentucky.

DEFINITION

The **border states** were slave states that did not secede. They included Delaware, Maryland, Kentucky, and Missouri. West Virginia declared itself loyal to the Union and seceded from the rest of Virginia when that state left the Union. On June 20, 1863, West Virginia was admitted to the Union as a new state; ushered in as a slave state, it is usually counted among the border states. As for Kentucky, it declared itself neutral, but Kentuckians fought on both sides; Tennessee, which had many Union loyalists, was often considered a border state.

Crittenden Tries

Crittenden not only wanted to preserve Kentucky for the Union, he wanted to preserve the Union. In December 1860, he presented six constitutional amendments that would effectively revive the old Missouri Compromise of 1820 and extend the line dividing slave states from free states all the way to the Pacific. In addition, the federal government would see to the strict enforcement of the Fugitive Slave Law and would even indemnify owners of fugitive slaves whose return was prevented by antislavery elements in the North. Popular sovereignty would be extended to all the territories, and slavery in the District of Columbia was to be protected from congressional action.

Lame-duck President James Buchanan said nothing about the Crittenden Compromise, and President-elect Lincoln declined to address the proposal directly, but he instructed a Republican colleague to "entertain no proposition for a compromise in regard to the extension of slavery." And that was quite sufficient to deliver a mortal wound to the proposal. In January 1861, Crittenden tried to get a public hearing on the compromise, introducing a resolution calling for a national referendum on his proposals. The Senate never acted on the resolution.

Buchanan Acts—More or Less

On the night after Christmas 1860, six days after South Carolina seceded, Major Robert Anderson moved his small garrison from the highly vulnerable Fort Moultrie on Sullivan's Island, South Carolina, to the stronger Fort Sumter. As if it were a sovereign nation, South Carolina protested this action to President Buchanan. At last, the bachelor president was roused to action. Instead of surrendering the fort, he sent supplies and reinforcements, albeit via an unarmed civilian merchant steamer, the *Star of the West*.

As the vessel glided past Charleston, gunners drew a bead and opened up on her. The *Star* turned back. Fort Sumter would neither be reinforced nor resupplied, and James Buchanan once again hunkered down, nervously awaiting the transfer of authority to the new president.

Farewell

The morning of February 11, 1861, came to the town of Springfield, Illinois, chill and dreary, with a miserable cold drizzle. The victor in the presidential election of

1860, Abraham Lincoln, stood in the waiting room of the Great Western Railway depot and shook the hands of friends and local associates. There were no lighthearted congratulations, no bursts of laughter, nothing but kind, hopeful words and well-meaning, if wan, smiles.

At 8:00, the engineer in the idling locomotive blew the all-aboard, and the president-elect, together with his family and a handful of others, ascended the steps of the single passenger car. Lincoln stood on the observation platform and spoke to those who would remain behind:

> My friends, no one not in my situation can appreciate my feeling of sadness at this parting. To this place and the kindness of these people I owe everything. Here I have lived for a quarter of a century, and have passed from a young to an old man. Here my children have been born, and one is buried. I now leave, not knowing when, or whether ever, I may return, with a task before me greater than that which rested upon Washington ....

The next day would be Abraham Lincoln's fifty-second birthday. Although he called himself an old man, he was the youngest president the nation had yet elected.

Dangerous Inaugural Journey

The president-elect's train was scheduled to make stops at Indianapolis, Cincinnati, Columbus, Pittsburgh, Cleveland, Erie, Buffalo, Albany, New York City, Trenton, Newark, Philadelphia, and Harrisburg. At Baltimore, Lincoln was not only to stop, but also to change trains, going by carriage from the Calvert Street depot to Camden Station. But the day before Lincoln left Springfield, Allan J. Pinkerton, the eminent private detective hired by the president of the Philadelphia, Wilmington, and Baltimore Railroad, received a disturbing tip from the railroad's master mechanic. It seemed that "a son of a distinguished citizen of Maryland said that he had taken an oath with others to assassinate Mr. Lincoln before he gets to Washington, and they may attempt to do it while he is passing over our road."

Although most historians now believe that the Baltimore conspirators were a small group operating independently from any larger Confederate authority, Pinkerton concluded that Lincoln's assassination was being planned as the opening shot in a lightning campaign that would culminate in a rebel invasion of Washington, where-upon the demoralized North would abandon its design to enforce its will upon the South (the plotters hoped). Pinkerton learned that the assassination was to take place at the Calvert Street Station.

Pinkerton laid his observations and conclusions before the president-elect when he arrived in Philadelphia on February 21. According to recollections published in Pinkerton's memoirs, Abraham Lincoln received the news not with fear, but sadness.

The detective recommended cutting short Lincoln's itinerary and rushing him immediately to Washington. The president-elect protested that he had "promised to raise the flag over Independence Hall tomorrow morning, and to visit the legislature at Harrisburg in the afternoon." After these promises were fulfilled, however, he was willing to put himself entirely in Pinkerton's hands.

Pinkerton decided that, after the ceremonies at Harrisburg, a special train consisting of a baggage car and one passenger coach would carry Lincoln back to Philadelphia. There the detective would personally escort Lincoln from one depot to another, where he would board a Baltimore-bound train—not the one directly from Harrisburg, which the assassins were expecting, but the regular 11:00 train from Philadelphia. To ensure that no telegraph message could reach the conspirators to advise them of the change, George H. Burns, the American Telegraph Company's confidential agent, was assigned to see to it that telegraph traffic between Harrisburg and Baltimore was intercepted and delivered to Pinkerton.

At 5:45 P.M. John G. Nicolay, Lincoln's private secretary, handed the president-elect a note while he and his traveling party were in the dining room of a Harrisburg hotel. The men abruptly rose, and the president-elect changed out of his dinner clothes and into a traveling suit. According to Joseph Howard Jr., a reporter for *The New York Times*, Lincoln, acting on Pinkerton's instructions, carried a shawl upon one arm, as if he were an invalid, and had a soft felt hat tucked into his coat pocket. Lincoln was spirited into a coach, which took him to the depot. The train arrived in Philadelphia shortly after 10:00 P.M. He was then transferred by coach, with Pinkerton, to another depot.

Kate Warne, one of Pinkerton's female "operatives," had engaged the rear half of a Baltimore-bound sleeping car to accommodate "her invalid brother." At the depot, Warne approached the president-elect and greeted him loudly as her brother. Together, with Pinkerton and Lincoln's longtime friend Ward H. Lamon, she and Lincoln entered the sleeping car by its rear door.

Baltimore Transfer

It was 3:30 A.M. when the train pulled into Baltimore. Lincoln did not leave the sleeping car, which was drawn by horses over the horsecar tracks from the Philadelphia, Wilmington, and Baltimore depot to the Camden Street Station. The train that would take Lincoln's car to Washington was delayed almost two hours. Although those in the president-elect's party were nervous, Lincoln remained in his berth, joking easily with them. Even at so early an hour the depot was active, and Lincoln and the others caught snatches of rebel tunes, including "Dixie," a song introduced by the popular minstrel entertainer Dan Emmett in 1859 and had been taken up by the South as an unofficial anthem. "No doubt there will be a great time in Dixie by and by," Lincoln dryly observed to his companions.

The belated train arrived at last, set off, and reached Washington some time after 6:00 in the morning. As journalist Howard reported it, Lincoln wrapped his invalid's shawl around his shoulders and left the sleeping car with Lamon and Pinkerton. The crowd outside did not recognize him.

WAR NEWS

The "invalid shawl," which may well have been a fabrication of journalist Joseph Howard Jr., would haunt Lincoln's first days in Washington. Detractors, especially secessionist sympathizers in Maryland, spread the rumor that the president-elect had entered Washington disguised as an old woman, in a plaid shawl and "Scotch cap." Southern newspaper cartoonists (as well as some hostile Northern journalists) delighted in depicting the gangly westerner—the vaunted backwoods "rail splitter"—sneaking into the capital as a gawky, timid grandma.

Two Failures and a Tariff

The president-elect's party disembarked from the train, and Lincoln was bundled into a carriage, which set off for Willard's Hotel, on 14th and Pennsylvania Avenue, where the soon-to-be First Family would lodge prior to the inaugural ceremony.

The Peace Convention Fails

Elsewhere in Willard's, a "Peace Convention," called to order under sponsorship of the state of Virginia on February 4, was grinding on in vain. It was a gathering of old men, presided over by former President John Tyler, age 71, with 131 delegates from 21 states (including Southern states, but none of the seceded states). On March 1, the Peace Convention presented a handful of proposals to Congress, which simply refused to consider them.

Crittenden Fails

In Lincoln's time inauguration day was in March and, on March 2, 1861, two days before the ceremony, Senator Crittenden's proposal was narrowly defeated in the Senate. Unlike in 1820, 1850, and 1854, there would be no peace-patching compromise.

WAR NEWS

Senator John J. Crittenden's frustrated reconciliation efforts symbolized not only Kentucky's predicament, torn between the Union and the Confederacy, but the entire nation, plunging headlong into a war between brother and brother. The senator's son, George Bibb Crittenden, became a Confederate general; his other son, Thomas Leonidas Crittenden, served as a Union general.

The Morrill Tariff

Also on March 2, Congress passed the Morrill Tariff Act, sponsored by Vermont Representative Justin S. Morrill, a founder of the Republican Party. As a protective tariff intended to block importation of manufactured goods, the Morrill measure outdid even the "Tariff of Abominations," which brought on the Nullification Crisis and talk of secession some three decades earlier. The timing of the tariff could not have been more inflammatory to the South. It was the final, and entirely gratuitous, nail in the coffin for what had been the *United* States, and it is sometimes used to bolster the position of those who, even today, argue that the Civil War was more about the North's attempt to suppress the Southern economy than it was about saving the Union or abolishing slavery.

The "Essence of Anarchy"

By the time James Buchanan called upon the president-elect at Willard's to escort him, as tradition dictated, to the inauguration platform, the weather had changed from fair at dawn to overcast and cold and then to sunny again. The ceremony took place on the east portico of the Capitol; its dome under construction and unfinished appeared, eerily, decapitated, a highly disturbing image. Disturbing, too, was the bronze statue representing freedom, a classically robed woman with a sword in one hand and a wreath in the other, lying prostrate on the grass, awaiting the completion of the dome whose top she would grace.

The U.S. Capitol under construction, its dome yet to be completed.
(Harper's Pictorial History of the Civil War, 1866)

After witnessing the swearing-in of his vice president, Hannibal Hamlin of Maine, it was Abraham Lincoln's turn to speak. He addressed a crowd of some 10,000. "I have no purpose," Lincoln told the crowd, "directly or indirectly, to interfere with the institution of slavery in the states where it exists. I believe I have no lawful right to do so."

Thus "Black Lincoln" finally broke his silence with words intended to ring clearly through the South. But, he continued, "no government proper ever had a provision in its organic law for its own termination …. No state upon its own mere motion can lawfully get out of the Union." And he went on to pledge that the "power confided in me will be used to hold, occupy, and possess the property and places belonging to the government, and to collect the duties and imposts." With calm, clear, eloquently humane logic, Lincoln explained his view of the present crisis:

> Shall fugitives from labor be surrendered by national or State authority? The Constitution does not expressly say. Must Congress protect slavery in the Territories? The Constitution does not expressly say.
>
> From questions of this class spring all our constitutional controversies, and we divide upon them into majorities and minorities. If the minority will not

acquiesce, the majority must, or the government must cease. There is no other alternative; for continuing the government is acquiescence of one side or the other.

If a minority in such case will secede rather than acquiesce, they make a precedent which in turn will divide and ruin them; for a minority of their own will secede from them whenever a majority refuses to be controlled by such a minority ….

Plainly, the central idea of secession is the essence of anarchy. A majority held in restraint by constitutional checks and limitations, and always changing easily with deliberate changes of popular opinions and sentiments, is the only true sovereign of a free people. Whoever rejects it does, of necessity, fly to anarchy or to despotism. Unanimity is impossible; the rule of a minority, as a permanent arrangement, is wholly inadmissible; so that, rejecting the majority principle, anarchy or despotism in some form is all that is left ….

In your hands, my dissatisfied fellow countrymen, and not in mine, is the momentous issue of civil war. The government will not assail you. You can have no conflict without being yourselves the aggressors. You have no oath registered in Heaven to destroy the government, while I shall have the most solemn one to "preserve, protect and defend it."

Then Lincoln tempered logic with the impassioned poetry of an almost wistful patriotism. "I am," he said, "loath to close."

We are not enemies, but friends. We must not be enemies. Though passion may have strained, it must not break our bonds of affection. The mystic chords of memory, stretching from every battlefield and patriot grave to every living heart and hearthstone all over this broad land, will yet swell the chorus of the Union when again touched, as surely they will be, by the better angels of our nature.

The inaugural address concluded, Abraham Lincoln placed his broad palm on the Bible, shakily proffered by the aged hand of Chief Justice Roger Taney, and took the oath of office.

The Least You Need to Know

- Even after the first seven Southern states seceded, desperate efforts to avert war continued. The most important of these was the Crittenden Compromise.
- Economically and in numbers of population, the South's prospects for victory in a civil war were poor, though some felt the North could never subjugate so large an area.
- Allan J. Pinkerton and others successfully foiled an apparent plot to assassinate President-elect Lincoln.
- Lincoln's inaugural address made it clear that his purpose was to preserve the Union, not to abolish slavery in the states where it currently existed.

Rally Round

This part begins with views of the governments and armies of the North and South at the start of the war. You'll see how both sides sought European allies, how President Lincoln walked a tightrope across the "border states" (those slave states that had chosen—so far—not to leave the Union), and how the people of the North tasted the bitterness of defeat in the first major contest of the war—the battle at Bull Run.

You'll understand why the North looked to George B. McClellan, "the Young Napoleon," to save the nation, while an obscure commander named Ulysses Simpson Grant almost lost his army at a place called Shiloh. You'll witness a new kind of war on the sea, fought with ships of steel and iron. You'll understand how "Stonewall" Jackson was able to roll up one Confederate triumph after another, while the "Young Napoleon" was outgeneraled by Robert E. Lee, and how the Union lost a *second* battle at Bull Run—one that was far more devastating than the first.

"We'll Manage to Keep House"

In This Chapter

- The vulnerable U.S. capital
- Espionage and counterespionage
- Lincoln and his cabinet
- Davis and his cabinet
- The armies

Washington, D.C., the muggy, sleepy little seat of the government of the United States, had always been essentially a Southern city. Virginia's secession on April 17, 1861, suddenly put a hostile nation just across the Potomac. The newly declared enemies could see, hear, and even smell one another.

A mere three or four hundred marines at the U.S. Marine barracks on 8th and I Streets, and another 100 army troops at the Washington arsenal, were the only regular U.S. military forces stationed in Washington at the outbreak of the war. The citizens of the United States weren't militaristic, and they didn't like to maintain standing armies. But now it was reveille in Washington. The city would change. The people would change.

A Meeting with the President

William Tecumseh Sherman, having resigned from the Louisiana State Military Academy in February, came to Washington to pay a visit to the new president, report on the situation in the South, and offer his military services.

"Ah," Lincoln greeted him, "how are they getting along down there?"

"They think they are getting along swimmingly. They are preparing for war."

"Oh, well," the president replied, "I guess we'll manage to keep house."

To Sherman, it was as if Lincoln were in a trance. He immediately dropped the idea of reenlisting, bade the president farewell, and left Washington for St. Louis to head up a streetcar company.

Lincoln's response to the crisis was typical of most Northerners. If Southerners were exhilarated by the prospect of war, Northerners, but for a handful of the most ardent abolitionists, seemed enervated, as if the realities of the crisis had not yet penetrated.

City of Spies

Sherman returned to Washington and to military command soon enough, shortly after the fall of Fort Sumter. By then, the capital's torpor had turned to panic. The public parlors of Willard's Hotel buzzed with rumors of a rebel army massing in Virginia for an assault on Washington.

On Saturday, April 20, the city awoke to find itself entirely cut off from the North; pro-Confederate rioters in Baltimore had blockaded railroad traffic and seized the telegraph office. Many Washingtonians deserted the capital. Boards went up on the windows of many shops and homes. Volunteer groups, including the Potomac Light Infantry (one company), the National Rifles (one company), the Washington Light Infantry (a skeleton battalion of 160 men), and the National Guard Battalion, augmented the handful of regulars garrisoning the city. None of the volunteer outfits were worth much. The Potomac Light Infantry moved quickly into action by taking an emergency vote to disband until peace was restored. One shamefaced corpsman proposed a toast: "The P.L.I., invincible in peace, invisible in war!"

Other local militia companies hurriedly formed, including the Silver Grays' Home Guard, made up of veterans of the War of 1812. The only man older than those in the ranks of the Silver Grays was the U.S. Army's general-in-chief, hero of the War of 1812 and the Mexican War, and now a corpulent 75-year-old, Winfield Scott, known as "Old Fuss and Feathers." To Colonel Charles P. Stone, whom he had just appointed inspector-general for the District of Columbia, Army general-in-chief Winfield Scott wheezed in horror: "They are closing their coils around us, sir!"

    WAR NEWS

A panicky Prussian attaché in Washington sought to secure his official residence from attack by placing a large sign over the doorway to his building. He also wanted a Prussian flag, but couldn't get one delivered because of the disruption in rail service.

But Just Who Were "They"?

"They" weren't just the army supposedly massing in Virginia. As master detective Allan J. Pinkerton saw it, "they" were a

> … secret enemy, who [were] conveying beyond the lines the coveted information of every movement made or contemplated …. Men who formerly occupied places of dignity, power and trust …. Aristocratic ladies, who had previously opened the doors of their luxurious residences to those high in office and who had hospitably entertained the dignitaries of the land.

These and others "were now believed to be in sympathy with the attempt to overthrow the country, and engaged in clandestine correspondence with Southern leaders."

"They," in fact, were almost anyone in Washington. Although the city could breathe a sigh of relief when the seventh New York regiment marched in to garrison the capital, spies seemed to be everywhere. Army officers and federal officials defected to the South daily.

The commander of the Washington Navy Yard, Marylander Franklin Buchanan, was a rebel sympathizer. He resigned in April but honorably admonished his men to remain faithful to their government. (Soon after Buchanan's departure, it was discovered that many of the bombshells manufactured at the Navy Yard had been filled with inert sand and sawdust instead of explosive black powder.)

In the civil government, disloyalty was rife, from bureau clerks to Supreme Court Justice John A. Campbell, who carried on a correspondence with Confederate officials at Montgomery, even as he continued to sit on the high court.

In Lincoln's own White House, John Watt, employed as a gardener, confessed that he had sold official secrets. Watt had been trusted because he was a favorite of the president's wife, Mary Todd. But many questioned her loyalty as well, she being a Kentuckian with a brother and three half-brothers enlisted in the Confederate army.

A Question of Intelligence and Counterintelligence

Espionage and counterespionage were highly developed professions among the great powers of Europe, but they were virtually unknown to the U.S. civil and military establishments at the outbreak of the Civil War.

Allan J. Pinkerton, a Scottish immigrant who created the nation's first private detective agency in the 1850s, did private security work for the Illinois Central Railroad before the war. There he became acquainted with the railroad's president, former U.S. Army officer George McClellan, and was assigned to protect President-elect Lincoln during the rail journey to his inauguration (see Chapter 4). In November 1861, McClellan, who had returned to military service at the beginning of the war, was appointed general-in-chief of the Union army. He hired Pinkerton to conduct espionage work for him.

As we will see, the intelligence Pinkerton provided his employer was grossly inaccurate and helped to scare McClellan into excessive caution, and even inaction. Pinkerton proved far more successful as a director of counterespionage efforts (see "The Rebel Rose" in Chapter 6).

A Tale of Two Governments

The now-warring governments of the United States and the Confederate States of America were actually very much alike, at least on paper. The Confederate constitution adopted on February 8, 1861, at Montgomery, Alabama, largely copied the U.S. Constitution, except that it explicitly guaranteed the protection of slavery (but did not guarantee the right of secession).

Lincoln and His Cabinet

Abraham Lincoln was born on February 12, 1809, in a log cabin in Hardin (now LaRue) County, Kentucky. In 1816, the family moved to Indiana and, finally, to Illinois in 1830. Lincoln was mostly self-taught, driven by an insatiable thirst for knowledge. He tried any number of occupations and, like many others, volunteered as a militiaman in the war against the Indian leader, Black Hawk, during 1832. He discovered that military life held little appeal for him, but he did take "much satisfaction" in having been elected captain of his militia company and found in himself a talent for leadership. This moved the young backwoodsman to run for the Illinois state legislature. He lost, but ran again and was elected to four consecutive terms from 1832 to 1841.

Settling in the state capital of Springfield, Lincoln established a prosperous law practice, served a term (1847–1849) in the U.S. House of Representatives and then returned to the law, having, he admitted, lost "interest in politics."

Then came the Kansas-Nebraska Act of 1854. Lincoln was no abolitionist, but the doctrine of popular sovereignty, which potentially threw open to slavery vast new territories, reawakened the political animal in him. Lincoln believed that the Constitution protected slavery in states where it already existed, but he also thought that the Founding Fathers had put the "peculiar institution" on the way to extinction with the Northwest Ordinance, which banned its spread to new territories.

Lincoln ran unsuccessfully for the U.S. Senate in 1855; then, the following year, he left the Whig Party to join the newly formed Republicans. In 1858, he ran for the Senate against the Illinois incumbent, Stephen A. Douglas. He accepted his party's nomination on June 16, 1858, with a powerful speech against what he saw as the efforts of Douglas, Chief Justice Roger B. Taney, and Democratic presidents Franklin Pierce and James Buchanan to nationalize slavery. Rejecting their efforts, he also declared that compromise on slavery was doomed to fail.

As a result of his debates with Douglas, Lincoln gained national recognition for his eloquence, decency, and morally upright moderation, even though he lost the senatorial bid to his opponent. More than any other politician in 1860, Lincoln seemed to speak the Northern mind and, against a splintered Democratic field, was elected president of a disintegrating nation.

Once he was in office, some venerated him, others found him too timid with regard to abolishing slavery, and still others thought him too bold. A great many simply doubted his ability to lead.

Edwin M. Stanton derided the new president as the fabled missing link—the evolutionary step between ape and human—the "original gorilla." However, even though he knew what Stanton thought of him, Lincoln brought him into his cabinet to replace the corrupt Simon Cameron as secretary of war (January 11, 1862). That said a great deal about Lincoln. He understood that Stanton was ruthless and power hungry, but he also saw that he was a vigorous, tireless, and acute administrator: the man to get the job done.

The same was true of another key cabinet member, Secretary of State William H. Seward. He had lost the nomination to Lincoln in 1860 and entered the cabinet with great misgiving, believing that Lincoln was hardly equal to the job. At first, he highhandedly attempted to outmaneuver the president, thinking it best for the nation if he, Seward, pulled the strings and ran the government. But Lincoln, little by little, transformed Seward into a loyal subordinate and trusted advisor, and he made the best use of his critically important diplomatic talents.

Edwin M. Stanton, ruthless and power hungry, was also extremely capable. Lincoln took him into his cabinet to replace the corrupt Simon Cameron as secretary of war.
(Harper's Pictorial History of the Civil War, 1868)

Most troublesome of all was Salmon P. Chase, secretary of the treasury. Lincoln recognized that Chase served brilliantly in a post vital to the war effort, but Chase had also unsuccessfully contended for the 1860 presidential nomination and, unlike Seward, could never reconcile himself to the belief that the abler man had won. Persistently disloyal and insubordinate, he was finally dismissed by Lincoln in 1864. However, the president, never a petty man, wanted to keep Chase's judgment and intellect in service to the nation and nominated him to the post of chief justice of the Supreme Court after Taney's death, later in the year.

Davis of Mississippi

Like Lincoln, Jefferson Davis had been born in a log cabin, a son of the Kentucky backwoods. But the similarities ended there. Whereas Lincoln's father remained a poor backwoodsman, Davis's father comfortably settled the family on a plantation called Rosemont at Woodville, Mississippi, when the boy was only three, and prospered. In contrast to the self-taught Lincoln, Davis was sent away at the age of 7 to a Dominican boys' school in Kentucky, and at 13 was enrolled in Transylvania College at Lexington. Subsequently, he spent four years at West Point, graduating in 1828 with a second lieutenant's commission.

After serving in the Black Hawk War, he resigned his commission in 1835 and became a planter near Vicksburg, Mississippi. His bride, Sarah Knox Taylor, daughter of his commanding officer, Zachary Taylor, succumbed to malaria three months after the couple moved to the plantation. A devastated Davis secluded himself on his property, enlarging and developing it while devoting himself, with monastic zeal, to the study of philosophy, law, and constitutional law.

At the conclusion of seven years in virtual isolation, Davis was elected to the U.S. House of Representatives in 1845 and remarried. The following year, he resigned his seat in Congress to serve in the Mexican War as colonel of the First Mississippi volunteers. His brilliant victory at the Battle of Buena Vista in 1847 won him not only national but also international renown. Subsequently wounded, he entered the Senate, served as chairman of the Military Affairs Committee, and then was appointed secretary of war by President Franklin Pierce in 1853.

As civil war approached, Davis, strangely enough, came once again to resemble Lincoln. He was no secessionist, but instead made many public speeches urging reconciliation and compromise. Even after South Carolina became the first state to secede in December 1860, Davis voiced his opposition to secession. But he did believe that states had a constitutional right to secede, and he also believed that Abraham Lincoln, if elected, would coerce the South into renouncing slavery, thereby bringing its economic disaster.

On January 21, 1861, 12 days after his home state of Mississippi seceded, Davis bade farewell to his Senate colleagues and made a last, impassioned plea for peace. Commissioned major general to lead Mississippi's army, he was soon chosen provisional president of the Confederacy by the Confederate Convention in Montgomery, Alabama.

Even now, he continued to seek an alternative to war, sending, shortly after his inauguration on February 18, 1861, a peace commission to Washington, D.C. Unwilling to recognize the Confederacy as a sovereign nation, President Lincoln refused to see the commission. Early in April, when Lincoln sent armed ships to resupply Fort Sumter, Davis, with great reluctance, ordered the bombardment of the fort.

Once the fight began, Davis showed himself a man of iron determination, which meant that he was strong, but also inflexible and, ultimately, brittle. His task was to prosecute a paradox: to carry out a conservative revolution, a rebellion to preserve the status quo. That put one great stress on Davis's iron spine. Another was the necessity of creating an instant government, but not just any government: a government with sufficient central authority to fight a war. The trouble was that states' rights, the doctrine at the very heart of the rebellion, were by definition incompatible with strong central government. Any claim Davis laid to broad wartime powers, however necessary, would be met with a storm of criticism.

Finally, there was the Confederate Cabinet. Davis lacked Lincoln's skill in managing volatile but creative personalities. The result was a mostly undistinguished cabinet, unequal to the task of fighting a war or managing a government.

Of all the cabinet members, only Judah P. Benjamin, former U.S. senator from Louisiana, would show real brilliance, first as attorney general, then as secretary of war, and, most of all, as secretary of state. Benjamin was to serve only briefly as secretary of war, but, then, so did everyone else who tried his hand at that thankless job. No fewer than six men would occupy the post in four years. In modern terminology, Davis insisted on "micromanaging" his cabinet, and in no case was this more true than in the war department. He would shoulder the entire burden of the war, often to the detriment of the war effort.

Jefferson Davis with his first Confederate Cabinet. Seated (left to right): Attorney General Judah B. Benjamin, Secretary of the Navy Stephen R. Mallory, Vice President Alexander H. Stephens, President Jefferson Davis, Postmaster General John H. Reagan, Secretary of State Robert Toombs; standing (left to right): Secretary of the Treasury Charles G. Memminger, and Secretary of War Leroy P. Walker.
(Harper's Pictorial History of the Civil War, 1868)

Grim Realities

In contrast to many of the nations of Europe, the United States shunned the maintenance of a large standing army. In most crises, as in the War of 1812 or the Mexican War, local and state militias, as well as other "irregular" forces, were called on to supplement the tiny "regular" army. Just before the fall of Fort Sumter, the U.S. Army consisted of a mere 16,000 officers and men. Until March 3, 1863 (for the Union), and April 16, 1862 (for the Confederacy), there was no such thing as a military draft. The army was an all-volunteer force.

The Arsenal of 1861

By 1861, the world's weapon makers had significantly advanced the technology of killing, introducing improved high-velocity artillery, and putting smooth-bore muskets on a path to obsolescence as they designed accurate and efficient rifle-muskets.

The most important innovations were the percussion rifle-musket and the *minié ball*. Named after its French inventor, Claude Étienne Minié, who designed it in 1848, the minié ball was not a ball at all but was shaped like a bullet. Smaller than the barrel of the rifle-musket, it was easy to load, in contrast to tight-fitting conventional ammunition, which had to be hammered partway down the muzzle of a rifle. Its hollow base filled with gases when the gun was fired, forcing the minié ball to expand into the rifling (spiral grooves) within the rifle barrel. The rifling imparted a spin to the minié ball, making it far more accurate than a conventional projectile fired from an old-fashioned, smooth-bore musket. Yet because the minié ball expanded only as it was fired, it lost considerable velocity as it left the rifled barrel.

DEFINITION

The **minié ball** was named for its inventor, the Frenchman Claude Étienne Minié, who designed it in 1848. The bullet-shaped projectile was a great advance on conventional, long-arm ammunition. Fired from a rifle-musket, it was highly accurate and was the ammunition of choice in the Civil War.

The combination of musket-rifle and minié ball greatly improved the speed and accuracy of fire, but the reality was that, in 1861, American arsenals were stocked not with state-of-the-art weapons, but obsolescent firearms of Mexican War vintage.

The same was true of artillery. Most that was immediately available was outmoded even though, just before the war, two important innovations had been introduced.

The "Napoleon" was a 12-pounder (meaning that it fired a 12-pound projectile), smooth-bore weapon originally developed by the French and named after Emperor Napoleon III. The American-made Napoleon was developed in 1857 and had a range of 1,619 yards. Production of Napoleons proceeded apace on both sides, and by 1863, this weapon made up some 40 percent of the artillery used by the Union as well as the Confederacy.

The ordnance rifle, patented by weapons maker John Griffen in 1855, was used mainly by the Union army and featured a wrought-iron barrel, which was stronger than conventional cast iron and could therefore be loaded with a bigger, more powerful charge without risk of exploding. Unlike the Napoleon, the ordnance rifle had a rifled bore, which imparted a spin to the projectiles, giving them greater accuracy.

The ordnance rifle was lighter than the third important piece of Civil War artillery, the Parrott gun (or Parrott rifle), which was patented in 1861 by Robert P. Parrott. Manufactured in 10- and 20-pound versions, the Parrott Gun featured a breech reinforced with wrought iron, rather than made entirely of it. This made the gun cheaper to manufacture than the ordnance rifle, but also made it more vulnerable to explosion.

Both sides rushed to manufacture or import all these new weapons, but, in the early months of the conflict, they had to rely on whatever obsolescent artillery was available.

The Art of War, 1861

A battle typically consists of attackers and defenders. In the course of the Civil War, weapons technology consistently gave the advantage to the defenders. Improved rifles, including breach-loading repeating rifles, enabled increasingly rapid and accurate fire, making it easier to defend a position and, conversely, harder to attack it. Advances in heavy artillery likewise gave the advantage to those who occupied fortified positions, again making the attacker's task more difficult and costly.

One of the great and tragic paradoxes of the Civil War was that the art of war—strategy and tactics—failed to keep pace with the technology of the war's weapons. Although that technology gave the edge to defenders, the most widely accepted tactics were those born of the age of Napoleon I, which West Point–trained officers studied primarily for their application to the attack rather than defense. Surely this is in part responsible for the terrible toll the Civil War exacted on both sides. Commanders repeatedly ordered foolhardy, futile, even suicidal attacks against defensive weapons of terrible destructiveness. Gradually more appropriate tactics were adopted, though some commanders never learned. By the end of the war, soldiers on both sides, when in proximity to the enemy, usually occupied extensive entrenchments and hugged cover whenever possible. Gone were the days when men stood in the open in serried ranks and exchanged volleys.

The Armies

To fight the great wars of the twentieth century, the federal government enlisted or drafted vast numbers of men directly. During the Civil War, however, the central governments of the North and the South relied on the individual states to raise the necessary forces. This was often a cumbersome and unreliable process, though it improved as the war ground on.

WAR NEWS

The Army of the Confederate States of America was established by act of the Confederate Provisional Congress on March 6, 1861, but never actually came into existence. The war was fought with volunteers of the Provisional Confederate Army, established by acts of February 28 and March 6. In April 1862, the Confederate government passed a conscription act, which inducted soldiers into the Provisional Army through the individual states.

Taking Command

If mustering rank-and-file soldiers into the army was a difficult process, finding the officers to command them was even harder. The U.S. Army made for a thankless career. Promotion proceeded at a glacial pace, and opportunities were severely limited. Good officers were always in short supply and, as the Southern states seceded, many resigned to join the Confederacy.

It was not just an issue of inexperience, but of politics. So-called *political generals*—commanders appointed for reasons of political patronage rather than for proven military accomplishment—infested the armies of both sides, but were especially notorious in the Union army. President Lincoln made the appointments in an effort to enlist the enthusiastic support of various ethnic and political groups for the cause.

DEFINITION

Political generals were inexperienced commanders taken from civilian life and given high military rank as a reward for political services.

Worst and Best

We shall meet some of the commanders, good, bad, and indifferent, in the pages that follow. But what of the soldiers in the ranks? Overwhelmingly, they were ordinary citizens, not professional hirelings of a warlike state. In the North, African Americans, whom Justice Taney's Dred Scott Decision had excluded from citizenship, nevertheless agitated from the very beginning of the war for the right to fight. It was not until the autumn of 1862 that African American troops were admitted into the Union army, in wholly segregated units commanded by white officers. (In the South, during the final, desperate months of the war, the Confederate Congress authorized the recruitment of 300,000 black soldiers, but only two companies were raised and the public raised such an outcry that no African American Confederate soldiers were ever committed to battle.)

The typical soldier on either side was a white Protestant, farmer, unmarried, age 18 to 29. Most men on both sides were native born, although one out of four Northern soldiers was a first- or second-generation immigrant, mostly of German or Irish origin. Three brigades of Cherokees, Choctaws, Chickasaws, and Seminoles fought for the Confederacy, whereas one brigade of Creeks enlisted in the Union army.

The boys of war: An unidentified member of an Ohio regiment (left) and Private Edwin Francis Jamieson, Second Louisiana Regiment (right). Jamieson would fall in the Seven Days' Battles during June 1862.
(Library of Congress)

In April 1862, the Confederacy enacted a draft law, and the Union followed the next year. On both sides, the laws were unjust and unpopular. In the South, those who owned or oversaw 20 or more slaves were exempt from service, which meant that the well-to-do need not fear becoming cannon fodder. As if that wasn't enough, one could pay a cash "commutation fee" in lieu of service, or could hire a substitute to serve in one's stead. Both alternatives required wealth beyond that of the common working man. In the North, the commutation fee was $300—at a time when unskilled labor earned about a dollar a day. Substitutes could also be hired. The inequity of the Northern draft law sparked a series of riots across the country, including an especially bloody one in New York City. During July 13 to 16, 1863, a paroxysm of looting, arson, and murder was carried out there by poor Irish immigrants who were outraged by the notion of being drafted, fearing free black slaves would then come up north to "steal" their jobs. We will return to this bloody episode in Chapter 16.

WAR NEWS

Civil War soldiers, mostly laborers and farm boys, were unaccustomed to handling firearms. Once mustered in, they were poorly trained, doing much marching, but little shooting. As a result, the level of marksmanship was abysmal in both armies. It has been calculated that some 900 pounds of lead and 240 pounds of powder were consumed for each enemy killed.

Commanding officers on neither side valued conscripts highly, describing them with such epithets as "depraved" and "degenerate." But even the best soldiers, the volunteers, stubbornly resisted military discipline. Contrary to the myth that most Civil War recruits were frontiersmen accustomed to firearms, shooting was so alien to most young men of the period that, despite the extraordinarily poor rations issued to the armies of the North and the South, few men seized the obvious alternative of hunting one's supper.

COUNT OFF!

By the end of the war, 2,128,948 men had served in the Union army (359,528 are known to have died). Of those who served, 75,215 were "professional" soldiers—soldiers by vocation. An even smaller number, 46,347, were draftees, and 73,607 were substitutes. (The conscription laws of both the North and the South permitted a draftee to hire a surrogate soldier to serve in his place.) The average strength of the Union army was probably a little over 1.5 million.

The Union's staple ration was hardtack (half-inch thick, three-inch square crackers), salt pork (called salt horse or sowbelly), and coffee beans (which the men crushed and boiled). Fabled for its staleness, it was rumored that hardtack—the troops called it "sheet-iron crackers" or "teeth dullers"—had been warehoused since the Mexican War. Another fragment of folklore asserted that the initials "B.C.," stamped on crates of hardtack, stood not for "Brigade Commissary," but referred to the date of manufacture.

And it got even worse. "Fresh" meat rations, often hard to come by, were typically flyblown and rotten. Dysentery killed many more soldiers than bullets in the Civil War.

Nonprofessional, undisciplined, poorly trained, poorly fed, often inadequately clothed (especially in the South), sometimes equipped with hopelessly obsolescent firearms, the Civil War soldier would endure disorder, discomfort, disease, and death. Yet he would fight a war bigger than any other fought on the North American continent.

> **COUNT OFF!**
>
> Confederate forces kept poor records, and most of those burned in the fires that consumed much of Richmond toward the close of the war. Estimates of the strength of the Confederate army range from 600,000 to 1,500,000, but the generally accepted figure is a little over a million, of whom at least 200,000 died.

The Least You Need to Know

- At the outbreak of the war, Washington, D.C., was virtually a city under siege, vulnerable to a hostile army from without, and to untold numbers of spies from within.
- Abraham Lincoln sometimes struggled with his cabinet but succeeded in forging a strong administration, and was generally well advised.
- Jefferson Davis, an intelligent but inflexible leader, was faced with creating an instant government, but the states resisted giving up authority to the central government. Davis's cabinet, in contrast to Lincoln's, was weak.
- The armies of both sides were similar in that the overwhelming majority of the soldiers were poorly trained, distinctly unmilitary citizen-soldiers.

The Anaconda and a Picnic Party

In This Chapter

- Winfield Scott and his Anaconda Plan
- The role of international diplomacy
- The *Trent* Affair
- Contest for the "border states"
- First Battle of Bull Run

On the face of it, this war was a simple thing. The Confederate States—by June 8, 1861, there were 11 of them—were fighting for independence, while the Union army was fighting to get them all back into the Union. The South, with a much smaller population, a severely limited economy, and comparatively puny industrial capacity, seemed to many doomed, although there were some who doubted the Union, powerful though it was, could ever successfully subjugate a region as vast as the South.

But the situation wasn't as simple as it seemed. The North was hardly unified in its will to fight. Lincoln needed to keep the focus on preserving the Union, even though his powerful, radical, Republican colleagues wanted it to be a war against slavery. Lincoln knew that the majority of Northerners were not radical Republicans and, he believed, were likely not willing to fight a war to end slavery. Moreover the border states, slave states that had not chosen to secede, would almost certainly flock to the Confederacy if the war were proclaimed a struggle for abolition. Finally, while Abraham Lincoln knew he had a constitutional obligation to protect the Union, he was also persuaded that this same Constitution protected slavery. He did not want to put the war on an unconstitutional footing, and the idea of amending the Constitution to ban slavery was too much of a leap to proclaim as an aim of the war.

In contrast to the North, the South enjoyed more unity—at least in the beginning. When the war broke out, most Southerners saw themselves as defending their homeland against political, moral, and economic domination by the North, which had been translated into military invasion. (Even today, some Southerners refer to the Civil War as the "War of Northern Aggression.") This sense of fending off a multidimensional invasion gave the South an early strength and advantage beyond what the region's population and economy would otherwise suggest. The bottom line, though, was this: neither side was really prepared to fight a major war.

Old Fuss and Feathers

No one, North or South, had more military experience than Winfield Scott (introduced in Chapter 5). Born in 1786 in Petersburg, Virginia, he was commissioned a captain of artillery in 1808. He fought in the War of 1812, in which his insistence that American soldiers look, act, and dress like professional soldiers earned him the epithet of "Young Fuss and Feathers." He performed heroically in the War of 1812, afterward rose rapidly to major general, and in 1841 was named general-in-chief of the U.S. Army. Already sixty when he led the landing at Veracruz in the U.S.-Mexican War (1846–1848) and the subsequent invasion that brought about the fall of Mexico City and American victory, his persistent adherence to all military formalities transformed his nickname into *"Old* Fuss and Feathers."

Seventy-five years old at the outbreak of the Civil War, pained by gout and much too fat even to mount a horse—let alone ride into battle—Scott was nevertheless the leader of the Union army.

The Anaconda Plan

Scott knew the U.S. Army had bumbled into both the War of 1812 and the U.S.-Mexican War poorly prepared and—although the public and politicians alike clamored for a dashing campaign that would bring the war to an instant end, teaching the rebels a lesson in the process—he was insistent on the necessity of buying time to train and equip an army capable of making a full-scale invasion of the South. He proposed a plan intended to gain time while also offering a long-range strategy for the defeat of the Confederacy.

Winfield Scott, "Old Fuss and Feathers," general-in-chief of the U.S. Army, was a hero of the War of 1812 and the Mexican War.
(Harper's Pictorial History of the Civil War, 1866)

Scott defined two objectives preparatory to a final invasion. First was obtaining control of the Mississippi River and the major Atlantic and Gulf ports; next came occupying Atlanta, the overland transportation hub of the South. Once these objectives had been obtained, the South would strangle and would readily succumb to invasion. Scott likened his plan to an anaconda's constriction of its prey, and from this comparison the press dubbed it "Scott's Anaconda."

The Anaconda Plan had a serious defect in that the U.S. Navy could not possibly furnish enough ships and firepower to blockade the entire southern coast. Scott countered by pointing out that the Anaconda was a good start and would become increasingly effective as the navy built more ships. Totally unrealistic, he said, was the delusion that the war could be ended with a single decisive battle.

The press, politicians, public, and even many of his fellow officers, resisted his plan, scorning the Anaconda as a dishonorable and timid alternative to glorious combat in the field. Still, it *was* a plan, and Abraham Lincoln endorsed and announced it on April 19, 1861.

> **COUNT OFF!**
>
> In April 1861, the Union navy consisted of 42 ships mounting 555 guns and manned by 7,600 sailors. (Only three of these vessels were modern steam-powered craft.) By year's end, after a crash shipbuilding program, purchases of commercial vessels, and an enlistment drive, the navy had grown to 264 ships mounting 2,557 guns and manned by 22,000 sailors—still hardly adequate to patrol so much southern coastline and so many southern ports.

Blockade of Chesapeake Bay

Initially, Union forces focused on seizing the waterways leading into Virginia. For their part, the Confederates aimed to choke off access to Washington, D.C., via the Chesapeake Bay and the Potomac River.

Union gunboats bombarded Confederate shore batteries—who returned fire—at Sewell's Point, near Norfolk, Virginia, during May 18 and 19, 1861, and then, during May 29 to June 1, at Aquia Creek. Following this action at sea, Union regiments fought at Big Bethel (or Great Bethel), Virginia, on June 10. Poorly led, the Union forces became confused and soon withdrew. "Friendly fire" was a major problem because uniforms had not been standardized, and many Union troops wore gray, which drew fire from their own side. Immediately following Big Bethel, Union gunboats accomplished what they could to patrol Chesapeake Bay, but it was the Confederate artillery that seized the initiative and did a creditable job impeding Washington-bound traffic on the Potomac.

What the World Thought

Despite initial disappointments in and around Chesapeake Bay, time would prove the soundness of Scott's Anaconda Plan. To survive a war, let alone fight and win one, the South now needed even more of everything it used to get from the North. Because its own manufacturing capacity was limited, the Confederacy would have to import goods, especially arms, ammunition, and warships, from abroad. To do this, it needed money. A prime source was the export of such raw materials as cotton, which the

Anaconda blockade would significantly curtail. Another source was foreign credit. But that required either international allies or, failing that, at least international recognition as a sovereign nation. Yet what stake did Europe have in this American struggle?

The most important of the European powers, France and England, viewed the South as a trading partner. British cloth manufacturers, in particular, needed Southern cotton. But having intoned the mantra of "King Cotton" for so many years, Southerners forgot that the English and the French also traded with the North, and that the grain produced on the Northern plains had become, for the English, just as important an American import as cotton.

There was also something more than trade at stake. England and France were monarchies existing in a part of the world that had been swept by waves of republican revolution, most recently in 1848. On the face of it, this should have prejudiced them against rebellion in North America; however, the Confederacy, though ostensibly democratic, presented itself as a conservative "empire" actually ruled by a landed aristocracy. Moreover, the very fact that the Union had been dissolved could be pointed to as an object lesson proving that a republican government could not succeed. Of course, for this lesson to stand, the Union had to *remain* dissolved. Supporting the Confederacy would help to ensure that the Union remained broken.

Dixie Diplomacy

There was one huge obstacle to alliance. Even conservative European governments could not bring themselves to condone slavery. Fortunately for the South's new diplomats, Abraham Lincoln, cleaving to the Constitution, had stipulated that the preservation of the Union, not the abolition of slavery, was the issue of this war, and Congress formally backed him in asserting just that with the Crittenden Resolution. Southern emissaries therefore had some ground on which to persuade the English and French governments that they could come to the aid of the Confederacy without becoming involved in a fight to perpetuate slavery.

The English Question

Jefferson Davis was quick to appoint James M. Mason of Virginia minister to England, and Louisiana's John Slidell minister to France. They slipped out of Charleston harbor on a *blockade runner* (a ship that specialized in evading the Union naval blockade) early in October and made for Havana, Cuba, via Nassau, Bahamas. In Havana, they boarded the British mail packet *Trent*.

As fortune would have it, the USS *San Jacinto*, returning from a tour of duty along the African coast, touched port at Cuba during this time in search of intelligence concerning the activities of Confederate *commerce raiders* (private, civilian vessels that intercepted U.S. merchant ships and seized their cargo). But Captain Charles Wilkes received far more momentous intelligence than he had counted on. Learning that Mason and Slidell had set sail on the *Trent*, he steamed out to the Bahama Channel, intercepted the British craft on November 8, and fired two shots across her bow.

> **DEFINITION**
>
> A **blockade runner** was a vessel—or captain—specializing in evading the Union naval blockade of the South. A **commerce raider** was a civilian vessel authorized by the Confederate government to intercept U.S. merchant ships and seize their cargo.

"What do you mean by heaving my vessel to in this way?" the *Trent*'s skipper called through a speaking trumpet. Wilkes made no answer, but dispatched a boarding party in two boats under the command of Lieutenant D. MacNeill Fairfax.

Slidell manfully introduced himself to the lieutenant, and Mason followed. Acting on the orders of Wilkes, who reasoned that if a nation at war had the right to remove enemy dispatches from neutral ships, it also had the right to remove human emissaries from them, Fairfax took Mason and Slidell back with him to the *San Jacinto*. The American ship delivered the pair to Fort Warren in Boston harbor.

Wilkes was hailed as a national hero and even given the official thanks of Congress. But the British government, outraged and already inclined to sympathize with the Confederate cause, sent 11,000 British soldiers to Canada, put its fleet on alert, and demanded an apology as well as the release of the prisoners.

"One War at a Time"

As secretary of state, it was up to William Seward to advise President Lincoln on how to respond to the British demands. Far from rushing to apologize, Seward counseled that war with Britain might furnish a common enemy against which North and South could reunite. To this dubious scenario, Lincoln replied, "One war at a time."

Seward ordered the release of Mason and Slidell and composed a note of apology, thereby averting a major crisis for the beleaguered Union. Still, the United Kingdom continued to lean toward the Confederate cause and, although officially neutral, turned a blind eye toward English munitions works and shipyards that were selling war materials to the American Confederate south. On May 13, 1861, the British government recognized the Confederacy as a "belligerent," which lent a degree of international legitimacy to the cause.

States on the Border

Closer to home, another kind of diplomacy was called for. The border states—Delaware, Kentucky, Missouri, Maryland, and the mountain counties of Virginia that would become West Virginia—were slave states, but had not voted to secede. For the Union, losing them might well mean losing the war before it had hardly begun; for the Confederacy, gaining the border states would mean a great advantage won.

Although slavery was legal in Delaware, secession was never a significant issue there, and the small state's loyalty to the Union was certain. Kentucky, however, sat on the fence. Its governor was inclined to secede, but its legislature was solidly Unionist. The result was the state's declaration of neutrality enacted on May 16, 1861, and neither Lincoln nor Davis wanted to risk disturbing this delicate situation. Although both the Union and the Confederacy unofficially raised troops in Kentucky, officially they left the state alone.

Civil War in Missouri

Missouri was another matter altogether. As in Kentucky, the legislature favored the Union, while the governor, Claiborne F. Jackson, was a secessionist. Shortly after the fall of Fort Sumter, Jackson attempted to seize the federal arsenal at St. Louis. When an aggressive Union army captain named Nathaniel S. Lyon blocked this effort, the governor's troops set up Camp Jackson on the outskirts of the city and bided their time. Authorities in Washington, D.C., deciding that the Union general in command of the area, William A. Harney, was far too passive about the continued threat the pro-Confederate troops posed, put Lyon in temporary command of Harney's brigade. He soon jumped in rank to brigadier general of volunteers.

On May 10, 1861, Lyon moved against Camp Jackson, arrested the state militiamen, and, as he marched his prisoners through St. Louis, suddenly found that he had incited a riot. After one drunken St. Louisan wounded an officer with a random pistol shot, the Union troops returned fire, killing more than 20 civilians.

Carthage and Wilson's Creek

General Harney's policy had been to maintain something between a standoff and a truce with the governor's pro-Confederate forces. As in Kentucky, neither side wanted to take action that might propel Missouri into the opposite camp.

There was a clash at the town of Carthage, on July 5, 1861, when Claiborne Jackson himself—who had defied the state legislature by setting up a breakaway Confederate state "government" at the town of Neosho—led a ragtag group of rebels against the forces of Brigadier General Franz Sigel. Sigel prudently withdrew, and it wasn't until the impetuous Lyon decided to march into southwestern Missouri to confront Confederate forces under Ben McCulloch, that genuine combat took place.

Outnumbered more than two to one, Lyon nevertheless attacked at Wilson's Creek on August 10 and fought an incredibly intense battle, which resulted in his death and the retreat of his army.

While the Confederates remained in control of southwestern Missouri, the state never seceded, although it was plagued throughout the war by an especially bitter and brutal brand of murder and mayhem that military commanders chose to call guerrilla warfare.

> **COUNT OFF!**
>
> The Battle of Wilson's Creek (August 10, 1861) accomplished nothing, but cost both sides much. The Union fielded 5,400 men against the Confederacy's 11,600. Among the Federals, 223 were killed, 721 wounded, and 291 went missing. The Confederates lost 257 killed, some 900 wounded, and 27 missing. Although the Union forces lost the engagement, they fought more effectively than the rebels. For every 1,000 Union troops engaged, 241 Confederates were killed or wounded; whereas for every 1,000 Confederates engaged, only 81 Union soldiers became casualties.

Montani Semper Liberi

The Latin motto adopted by the state of West Virginia, *Montani semper liberi* ("Mountaineers are always free"), expresses the attitude of backwoods western Virginia toward coastal Virginia more than it proclaims any love of the Union. The struggling frontier people of the state's mountainous western counties had long been hostile to relatively prosperous tidewater Virginia, the seat of a government (the Westerners felt) that cared little for them. Secession presented an opportune time for the western counties to break away and seize their own destiny.

As we shall see in the next chapter, the dashing young Major General George B. McClellan won a small but significant victory against the Confederates at Philippi (June 3, 1861) and Rich Mountain (July 11) in western Virginia, thereby securing the region for the Union. On June 20, 1863, West Virginia was admitted to the Union as a new state.

Brawl in Baltimore

On April 19, 1861, the Sixth Massachusetts Regiment, commanded by Colonel Edward F. Jones, was on the rails, heading toward Washington to garrison the besieged capital. When the troops changed trains in Baltimore, they were mobbed by Confederate sympathizers called plug uglies, who hurled stones and bricks at them, killing four of their number. The soldiers opened fire, killing 12 Baltimoreans and wounding others. Three days after this, a citizens' committee called on President Lincoln to protest the "pollution" of Maryland soil.

On April 19, 1861, Baltimoreans rioted against the Sixth Massachusetts Regiment, which was passing through Baltimore on the way to garrison Washington, D.C. Four soldiers and twelve civilians were killed.
(Harper's Pictorial History of the Civil War, 1866)

"Our men are not moles, and cannot dig under the earth," Lincoln replied to the committee members. "They are not birds, and cannot fly through the air. There is no way but to march across, and that they must do." In response, Baltimoreans cut telegraph lines, sabotaged railroad tracks, and destroyed bridges. For a time, Washington was cut off from communication with the North.

Habeas Corpus Held Hostage

Lincoln responded by ordering General Benjamin F. Butler to occupy the city, empowering him to arrest and jail all prosecessionists, including nine members of the state legislature, Mayor William Brown, and the city's chief of police.

In Baltimore, Abraham Lincoln effectively suspended one of the most cherished democratic rights of Americans: *habeas corpus*, the basic protection from imprisonment except as a result of due course of law. For this, some, in the North as well as the South, condemned the president as a tyrant, although it must be noted that Confederate President Jefferson Davis did precisely the same thing.

The Battle of Bull Run

In the wake of Fort Sumter's fall, Northern newspapers, spearheaded by Horace Greeley's *New York Daily Tribune*, called for the kind of decisive action Scott's Anaconda failed to provide. Yet, as the weeks ground on, more states left the Union: Virginia, April 17; Arkansas, May 6; North Carolina, May 20; and Tennessee (though deeply divided over secession), June 8.

At last, in July, with an army of some 35,000 men massed in Alexandria, Virginia, General Irvin McDowell was directed to make a major move. He was to attack a Confederate force of about 23,000 men under P. G. T. Beauregard at Manassas Junction, on a creek called Bull Run, squarely athwart the best direct route to Richmond.

McDowell was a West Pointer who had also been educated in France and had a fine command of the classical texts on military tactics but was unproven in battle.

McDowell enjoyed a significant numerical advantage over Beauregard, but he was also aware that an additional 9,000 rebels under the command of Joseph Johnston were near Harpers Ferry, facing 16,000 Federals under 69-year-old General Robert Patterson. McDowell understood that if Johnston somehow evaded Patterson so that he could reinforce Beauregard, the Union's superiority of numbers would vanish. Patterson was accordingly ordered to maintain vigilant pressure on Johnston.

.While McDowell was a trained soldier, few of his enlisted men were. As they marched to battle in the oppressive July heat, many broke ranks to rest or to pick blackberries.

McDowell's skylarking troops made their first contact with the enemy on July 18. One Union division was driven back in the resulting skirmish. Worse, while these preliminaries were going on near Bull Run, Johnston, in the Shenandoah Valley, managed to give Patterson the slip so that, when the battle finally took place on July 21, some 35,000 Union troops were pitted against reinforced Confederate forces of 32,000 to 34,000. On either side, however, no more than 18,000 would become actively engaged in the battle.

The Rebel Rose

Unknown to the Union commander, the Confederates had a secret weapon at Bull Run—a weapon that had come into play before a shot had been fired. In 1854, after the death of her husband, Department of State official Dr. Robert Greenhow, Rose O'Neal Greenhow became a kind of merry widow, ingratiating herself with any number of influential Washington men in the government and the military. When the war began, rebel spymaster Thomas Jordan recruited Greenhow as a spy.

She did consider herself "a Southern woman, born with revolutionary blood in my veins," and set about her new profession enthusiastically. She obtained a fair amount of information about Union plans for the Bull Run battle, which she transmitted via a female courier, Betty Duvall, a comely Washingtonian who hid Greenhow's enciphered messages in, what Confederate General M. L. Bonham called, "the longest and most beautiful roll of hair I have ever seen."

Thanks to Greenhow's intelligence, General Beauregard deployed his forces advantageously behind Bull Run Creek.

WAR NEWS

The espionage career of Rose O'Neal Greenhow, whom the tabloids of the time would later dub "The Rebel Rose," was cut short by no less a figure than Allan Pinkerton, who ran her to ground on August 23, 1861. She was held under house arrest and then consigned to the Old Capitol Prison—originally built after the War of 1812 as temporary quarters for Congress until the original Capitol, burned by the British, was rebuilt—but was ultimately paroled to the South. On September 1, 1864, she drowned in the wreck of the ship *Condor*, running the Union blockade off the coast of North Carolina. She was smuggling gold for the Confederate cause, and the weight of one of the bags she carried pulled her under the waves.

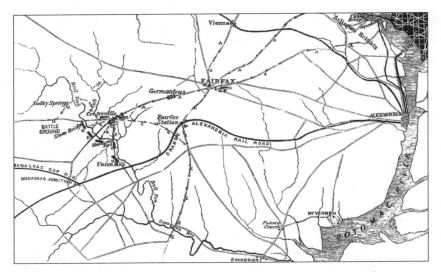

A map of the vicinity of Bull Run. The battleground is just to the west of Centreville, which is west and slightly south of Washington.
(Harper's Pictorial History of the Civil War, 1866)

Cheers

The morning of the battle, flocks of fashionably dressed Washingtonians rode out to Centreville, Virginia, 18 to 20 miles from the city, in carriages filled with picnic baskets and bottles of champagne to view, through their field glasses and opera glasses, the action some three miles off.

McDowell's forces at first drove the Confederates from their defensive positions and even managed to turn the Confederate left flank. The picnic parties cheered.

Like a Stone Wall

Then something extraordinary happened. The Confederate Beauregard was a good soldier, but overly fond of tactics too complex for his indifferently trained and untested men to execute. Union General McDowell was knowledgeable but uninspired. But Confederate Brigadier General Thomas J. Jackson was made of stuff from another world altogether, it seemed. Anyone who looked into his gimlet-blue eyes—"Old Blue Light," his men called him—would attest to the otherworldly power of his presence.

While men stumbled over one another in confusion or ran off in panic, Jackson materialized with his brigade of unwavering Virginians.

WAR NEWS

General Bee might have actually expressed himself more mundanely: "Yonder stands Jackson like a stone wall; let's go to his assistance." It is also possible, according to some witnesses, that Bee did not intend the "stone wall" remark as a compliment, but thought that Jackson should be on the move rather than just standing "like a stone wall."

General Barnard Bee, destined to sustain a mortal wound later in the battle and die the next day, saw Jackson and his stalwarts hold their ground against the Federal onslaught. "There's Jackson standing like a stone wall!" Bee shouted. Then, grandly gesturing with his sword, Bee called out, "Rally behind the Virginians!" And so they did. As for Jackson, he was known as "Stonewall" from that day on, and his command earned the nickname "Stonewall Brigade."

Pursued by Furies

For the rest of the afternoon, the fighting seesawed. Finally late in the day, the Confederates, hitherto fighting mainly a defensive battle, massed for a decisive counterthrust.

"Yell like furies," Jackson ordered his men as they charged, and, for the first time on any battlefield, friend and foe alike heard the "rebel yell"—a high-pitched keening that seemed to come from the same otherworldly place as the eerie blue of Old Blue Light's eyes. The effect was electric. The Federal lines broke, crumbled, then dissolved, and panic-stricken soldiers fled the enemy along roads choked with erstwhile picnickers, now as panic-stricken as the soldiers.

Anyone searching for a symbol of "civil war" would have found it that afternoon: dust, death, terror, confusion, and chaos. Yet if McDowell's army had fallen apart in defeat, the army of Beauregard and Johnston was not much better organized. Jefferson Davis, always the micromanager, arrived on the scene to supervise. It crossed his mind to order a pursuit of the routed Union forces, but over the fruitless urgings of Jackson, he did not. Instead the rebels settled into camp, feeling now that the war might be over quickly. For its part, the Union started looking around for a new general.

COUNT OFF!

Union losses at Bull Run were 2,896 killed, wounded, and missing. Confederate casualties amounted to 1,982.

The Least You Need to Know

- Winfield Scott planned to strangle the South with land operations along the Mississippi River and a naval blockade.
- International diplomacy was a crucial aspect of the war, as was control of the border states.
- The First Battle of Bull Run, or First Manassas, was a contest of amateur armies, but nevertheless deadly; for most of the battle, the fighting was indecisive, until "Stonewall" Jackson rallied the Confederates and triggered a rout of the Union troops.

McClellan and Grant

In This Chapter

- McClellan's victories in western Virginia
- The Ball's Bluff disaster
- Lee's and Grant's maiden battles
- Grant takes Forts Henry and Donelson
- The bloody battle at Shiloh

The Civil War names we think of as the greatest—Grant and Lee—belonged to more or less obscure figures during the opening months of the war, with Grant even more obscure than Lee. In the early months of the war, the names of Winfield Scott and George B. McClellan were on every lip in the North, and, in the South, it was Pierre Gustave Toutant Beauregard and Albert Sidney Johnston—the latter active in Tennessee and considered by many to be one of the most promising Confederate commanders. The South looked to the recent victory at Bull Run for encouragement, while the North could only cling to the future, hoping that it would deliver a heroic general to rescue the Union in its darkest hour.

This chapter focuses on the maiden battles of McClellan, Lee, and Grant, ending with Grant's bloody trial at Shiloh.

A Saddle and Small Victories

From the Union's confused and shamefaced post–Bull Run perspective, no man appeared more competent than George Brinton McClellan. He'd graduated from West Point in 1846, second in his class, and was thrice *breveted* (promoted for bravery) in the U.S.-Mexican War. Assigned as an official observer during the Crimean War (1853–1856), McClellan introduced a number of innovations in uniforms, tents, and drill, and in 1856, designed a European-style cavalry saddle that was adopted by the army. Bright though he was, like other young officers, he had advanced only to the rank of captain after 10 years' service and resigned his commission in 1857 to become a railroad executive. In this capacity, he first met Abraham Lincoln, who was a lawyer retained by the Illinois Central.

> **DEFINITION**
>
> A **brevet** is a promotion for conspicuous bravery or meritorious service. The promotion usually comes without an increase in pay and is often of an honorary or temporary nature.

Philippi

When the war started, Pennsylvania-born McClellan returned to the army as a major general of the Ohio volunteers and was quickly promoted to major general of regulars, with command of the Department of the Ohio. Dispatched to western Virginia, McClellan attacked a Confederate camp at the mountain settlement of Philippi. Forewarned by local secessionists, the rebels fled in what some newspapers derisively called the "Philippi races." Although fewer than 10 Confederates became casualties, McClellan was credited with having routed some 1,500 on the night of June 3, 1861.

Rich Mountain

McClellan's next victory, at Rich Mountain, on July 11, was more important. His subordinate, Brigadier General William Rosecrans, skillfully advanced through an unguarded mountain trail, cut off a Confederate unit, seized more than 500 prisoners, then opened the way for deeper Union penetration. Although the battle involved small numbers, for the Union it secured the region that would break away from Confederate Virginia to become the loyal state of West Virginia.

While Rich Mountain was a significant gain, both it and Philippi were on a small scale. Nevertheless, in the gloom of the Bull Run disaster they glowed, and Lincoln gave McClellan command of the Department (later Army) of the Potomac. At the time, this army functioned only to guard Washington, D.C., but McClellan set about transforming it from something of a ragtag garrison into a fighting force. He proved himself a brilliant administrator, quickly earning respect and affection from his men and admiration from the press. At five foot eight he was not tall, but at 35 years old (young for a general) he cut a youthful and dashing figure. The papers called him the "Young Napoleon."

Death Leap

In late October, McClellan sent a reconnaissance force under Brigadier General Charles P. Stone across the Potomac River to Ball's Bluff, a steep, wooded hill about 30 miles upriver from Washington. Pressing the reconnaissance heedlessly, the Federals got trapped on the top of the bluff. Among the first to fall in the fighting on October 21 was Colonel Edward D. Baker, a U.S. senator and a close personal friend of Lincoln. In part demoralized by the sight of the colonel's body being carried from the front, a knot of inexperienced Union soldiers panicked and commenced an unauthorized retreat.

The only path to safety was down the bluff and into boats that would take the men across the Potomac to the Maryland shore. The retreat became a panicked rout as, under intense fire from the Confederates, the Federals backed up to the top of the bluff, all wanting desperately to get to the boats. Bunching together, the soldiers made an obscenely opportune blue-coated target.

COUNT OFF!

Federal losses at Ball's Bluff were 49 killed, 158 wounded, and 714 captured or missing. Confederate losses were 33 killed, 115 wounded, and 1 missing.

"A kind of shiver ran through the huddled mass upon the brow of the cliff," one Confederate soldier later recalled. "It gave way; rushed a few steps; then, in one wild, panic-stricken herd, rolled, leaped, tumbled over the precipice."

Men jumped down, one on top of another, some skewering themselves on the bayonets of those who had leaped first.

A grandson of Paul Revere was captured; a son of Dr. Oliver Wendell Holmes Sr., wounded; a nephew of celebrated author, James Russell Lowell, killed—all were casualties at Ball's Bluff. But it was the death of Senator Baker that sent shock waves through Washington. Congress created the Joint Committee on the Conduct of the War, which would look over Lincoln's shoulder throughout the rest of the conflict, and immediately looked for a scapegoat. General Stone was imprisoned for 189 days with neither charge nor trial.

> **SITES AND SIGHTS**
>
> Ball's Bluff Regional Park (Ball's Bluff Road, Leesburg, Virginia) surrounds the
> Ball's Bluff National Cemetery and preserves the battlefield. The park is open
> year-round from dawn to dusk and is staffed by volunteer battlefield interpret-
> ers (Phone: 703-737-7800).

Congress did not dare touch the "Young Napoleon," George McClellan. Emerging
from Ball's Bluff blameless, he was named in November general-in-chief of the Union
armies, replacing the aged and infirm Scott.

A Granny and a Tannery Clerk

Before the Civil War, few people knew Robert E. Lee and far fewer knew Ulysses S.
Grant. Both men had served with distinction in the U.S.-Mexican War, but the public
had a short memory. Lee rose quietly in the peacetime army, and Grant settled into
a dreary assignment at Fort Humboldt, California, where he acquired a reputation
for little more than heavy drinking. He resigned his commission in 1854 to take up
farming and then real estate. Failing miserably at both, he became a clerk in a leather
goods business owned by his father and operated by his brothers in Galena, Illinois.

Lee Retreats from Cheat Mountain

Though little known by the public, Robert E. Lee was so highly regarded in professional military circles that Winfield Scott offered him an important command in
the Union armies before the Virginian, pleading that he could not take up the sword
against his native "country" (meaning Virginia), resigned his commission to join the
Confederate army.

Jefferson Davis made Lee his personal military advisor. But Lee's first field command,
in western Virginia, proved worse than disappointing. Saddled with unruly subordinates and operating amid a hostile local populace, Lee nevertheless mounted an assault
on Cheat Mountain, a position that controlled a major turnpike and several mountain
passes. On September 11, 1861, he attacked a Union position, only to be tricked by
some Federal prisoners of war, who persuaded him that the Cheat summit was held by
4,000 Federals, far outnumbering his force.

In fact, only 300 Union soldiers held the summit, but Lee was suckered; he hesitated,
lost the element of surprise, and soon found himself facing all-too-real Union reinforcements. After a two-day skirmish, Lee withdrew. His casualties were light, but it

had been an inauspicious maiden battle for the general, whom the Richmond papers derided as "Granny Lee" and "Evacuating Lee."

Robert E. Lee, commander of the South's Army of Northern Virginia and, by the end of the war, general-in-chief of the Confederate armies. No commander, North or South, was more respected or beloved than Lee.
(National Archives and Records Administration)

Grant Retreats from the Battle of Belmont

Ulysses S. Grant's first Civil War battle was also unimpressive. Leading some 3,000 troops in boats out of Cairo, Illinois, across the Mississippi to Belmont, Missouri, he defeated Confederate forces under General Gideon Pillow.

So far so good, but Grant allowed his men to revel in their achievement by looting the abandoned Confederate camp. At this point, Confederate General Leonidas Polk trained his artillery against Grant's distracted men, then massed some 10,000 troops below Belmont in an attempt to cut Grant off from his river transports.

Ulysses S. Grant, a business failure rumored to be a hard drinker, became the brilliant commander of the Union forces. He understood the essential nature of the Civil War: the populous North could afford to lose men, while the more thinly populated South could not. Some would call Grant a butcher; others would say he saved the Union.

(National Archives and Records Administration)

It was a tight spot, but if Grant had blundered in his first engagement with the enemy, he demonstrated a remarkable presence of mind in recovering from it. To a subordinate who bellowed that they were surrounded, Grant calmly replied, "Well, we must cut our way out as we cut our way in." Although Grant yielded the camp, he preserved his forces.

COUNT OFF!

Grant suffered 607 casualties out of 3,114 engaged at Belmont, while the Confederates lost 642 (killed, wounded, and missing) out of some 4,000 engaged.

Hope for the Young Napoleon

As 1861 drew to a close, Southerners tried to bask in what was left of Bull Run's glow, while Northerners had little or nothing tangible to base their hopes on. They did have, however, the prospect and promise of the "Young Napoleon."

Little Mac Takes Command

In the demoralized wake of Bull Run, McClellan reorganized and trained the units that became part of the newly designated "Army of the Potomac." McClellan was a superb organizer, and also a good strategist. But he was a hapless field commander who, always handicapped by his fears, was unable to implement his plans. As the final months of 1861 dissolved into 1862, McClellan did nothing but train and drill. As he repeatedly delayed committing it to combat, Lincoln began to doubt his general.

The "Young Napoleon," George Brinton McClellan, posed for this imperial portrait with his wife, Ellen Marcy McClellan. Lincoln and the North pinned their hopes on him as general-in-chief of the army. This old photograph is badly stained and streaked.

(National Archives and Records Administration)

Triumph at Fort Donelson

The attention of most Americans, North and South, was fixed on the East Coast. Being assigned to an army command in and about Virginia was prestigious, whereas leading soldiers into battle in the war's western theater—that is, west of the Appalachians—was regarded as something of a backwater assignment.

In the opening months of the war, the Union entrusted command of operations in the area to John Charles Frémont, a Western explorer who had fought in the U.S.-Mexican War, but who was at best a marginally competent commander. Frémont was sufficiently savvy to order the construction of a *gunboat* fleet—invaluable in a region watered by the Mississippi, Tennessee, and Cumberland rivers—and he also elevated Grant, at that point a brigadier, to command the key position of Cairo (pronounced *Kay-ro*), Illinois (where the Ohio River joins the Mississippi).

> **DEFINITION**
>
> In the Civil War era, a **gunboat** was a squat, shallow-draft vessel. Often clad in iron plates to deflect cannonballs, it was designed mainly for use on rivers as a floating artillery platform.

In September 1861, Kentucky ended its neutrality, declaring itself for the Union, whereupon Confederate General Polk invaded the state and occupied Columbus, situated on commanding bluffs above the Mississippi. Grant answered by taking Paducah, which controlled the mouths of the Tennessee and Cumberland rivers.

Also in September, Davis appointed Albert Sidney Johnston (no relation to Joseph E. Johnston, the ranking Confederate officer at First Bull Run), at the time considered the most capable of the Confederate army's officers, to command in the West. Johnston secured the Mississippi by reinforcing Columbus, and he fortified the Cumberland and Tennessee rivers, which he figured to be principal highways of potential Northern invasion. He built Fort Henry on the Tennessee and Fort Donelson on the Cumberland.

In November of 1861, the Union made some command changes of its own. Frémont was fired, and his command divided between two other generals. Major General Henry Wager Halleck—known as "Old Brains" because back in 1846, he had written a textbook called *Elements of Military Art and Science*—was put in charge of the area west of the Cumberland, and Brigadier General Don Carlos Buell was given command east of that river. Between them, Halleck and Buell commanded more men than Johnston, but the two men were professional rivals who consistently refused to coordinate their plans and movements.

Albert Sidney Johnston, whom Jefferson Davis among others considered the South's ablest commander, headed the Confederate army's Western Department until his death at the Battle of Shiloh.
(Harper's Pictorial History of the Civil War, 1866)

Nevertheless, the first assault on Johnston's army went well as Union General George H. Thomas defeated Confederates under the command of George B. Crittenden at Mill Springs, Kentucky, on January 19, 1862. After this, Halleck dispatched Grant with 15,000 men and a squadron of ironclad gunboats under navy Flag Officer Andrew Foote against Fort Henry on the Tennessee. That bastion fell quickly, on February 6.

Wasting no time, Grant turned sharply east and marched to the Cumberland to attack Fort Donelson, again coordinating his attack with Foote's gunboats. Johnston did not wish a repeat of Fort Henry, so he had reinforced the Cumberland River position with some 15,000 troops pulled out of Bowling Green, Kentucky. Fort Donelson held out against the Union onslaught for three days, until Grant received reinforcements and was able to pound the position with artillery.

U.S. Navy Flag Officer Andrew Foote was Ulysses S. Grant's collaborator in the capture of the Confederate forts on the Tennessee and Cumberland rivers.
(Harper's Pictorial History of the Civil War, 1866)

When Confederate General Simon Bolivar Buckner penned a note to Grant proposing the "appointment of commissioners to agree upon the terms of capitulation of the forces and fort under my command," Grant replied, "No terms except an unconditional and immediate surrender can be accepted. I propose to move immediately upon your works."

The Union commander's given name was Hiram Ulysses, but Congressman Thomas L. Hamer had nominated him to West Point under the name "Ulysses S. Grant." When Hiram arrived at the Academy and pointed out that this was not his name, the adjutant replied that it was now—at least as long as he stayed in the U.S. Army.

Since Hamer hadn't specified what the *S* stood for, Grant wrote in his mother's maiden name, *Simpson*. He soon learned to enjoy having the initials "U. S.," which quickly invited his classmates to call him Uncle Sam. After Fort Donelson, however, the Northern press insisted jubilantly that the initials stood for "Unconditional Surrender."

Place of Peace

Grant and Foote had won a significant victory. With the fall of the river forts, General Johnston was forced to evacuate Nashville, leaving behind supplies the Confederacy could ill afford to lose. The strongly fortified and strategically critical position at Columbus was also abandoned. P. G. T. Beauregard transferred from Virginia and arrived as Johnston's second in command; his first assignment was to take the Columbus garrison south to join up with Johnston's troops at Corinth, Mississippi, a key rail connection. With luck, Johnston and Beauregard would be able to field about 50,000 men.

Of course, it was the Union army's job to meet this combined force with overwhelming numbers. And they *could* do it. If Halleck and Buell managed their movements swiftly and efficiently, they could hurl some 70,000 troops against the Confederate's 50,000. Grant, though now a major general, was still subordinate to Halleck. He urged "Old Brains" to press the pursuit of the retreating rebels, but Halleck and Buell not only failed to cooperate with one another, they moved slowly, giving Beauregard and Johnston ample time to meet and regroup at Corinth.

Grant's Mistake

Grant established his camp with some 42,000 men at Savannah, downriver from Pittsburg Landing, Tennessee, on the west bank of the Tennessee River, just northeast of the Confederate position at Corinth, Mississippi. Nursing a badly sprained ankle, Grant set up his headquarters tent next to a log-built Methodist meeting house called Shiloh Chapel (after the Canaanite town mentioned in the Old Testament as the place where the Tabernacle and the Ark of the Covenant were lodged). The Hebrew name means "place of peace."

And that is precisely what Grant expected. Believing that most of the Confederate force would stay in Corinth for the present, Grant did not adequately defend his camp: no entrenchments, no cavalry patrols, and no remote *pickets*. On Sunday morning, April 6, Albert Sidney Johnston and P. G. T. Beauregard attacked.

DEFINITION

During the Civil War, **picket** was another name for sentry, and a **picket line** was an outer perimeter, usually around a camp, which was patrolled by sentries.

Carnage at Shiloh

Panic shot through Pittsburg Landing as violently as Confederate bullets. Many of the disorganized Union troops sought places to hide rather than fight. For its opening 12 hours, the battle was a one-sided pounding by Confederates against Federals, and by the end of Sunday, the army in gray had captured the key position of Shiloh Chapel and nearly pushed the Federal lines into the river.

Sherman Emerges

Union defeat seemed certain but William Tecumseh Sherman rallied and regrouped his forces, proving that Grant was right to admire Sherman, even though others had their doubts. After First Bull Run he served as commanding general of the Department of the Cumberland in Kentucky, he feuded savagely with his superiors and the press, protesting that they did not understand that this war would assume a terrible magnitude. Sherman was so vehement that he was accused of insanity. Shiloh and subsequent battles proved him all too sane and his appraisal chillingly accurate. His conduct at Shiloh, and throughout the rest of the war, revealed Sherman as among the nation's fiercest and most skillful warriors.

Despite their initial triumph, the Confederates suffered one loss that Jefferson Davis among others deemed more damaging than all the others. About 2:30 on Sunday afternoon, Albert Sidney Johnston sustained a wound in the leg. He ignored it at first. Then his aide saw him reel in the saddle.

"General, are you hurt?"

"Yes, and I fear seriously," Johnston replied.

The aide saw that his right boot had filled with blood. A bullet had severed his femoral artery. Albert Sidney Johnston bled to death from a wound that needn't have been fatal had a tourniquet been applied in timely fashion.

SITES AND SIGHTS

Shiloh National Military Park, located 22 miles northeast of Corinth, Mississippi on TN 22, is a beautiful spot. All the major sites are well marked, and the Shiloh Methodist Church has been reconstructed. The park is adjacent to the Shiloh National Cemetery. The park is open every day except Christmas. For information, call 731-689-5696.

Sunday night, General Beauregard was left alone to telegraph the devastating news of Johnston's death, albeit tempered with a report of Southern victory at Shiloh.

That report proved premature. Unlike most Union generals at the time, Grant did not give up. As darkness fell, William Tecumseh Sherman observed, "Well, General, we've had the Devil's own day," to which Grant responded, "Yes. Lick 'em tomorrow, though." The reinforced Union army counterattacked on Monday morning, and Beauregard, after a 10-hour fight, withdrew his army to Corinth.

The Battle of Island Number 10

Tactically, Shiloh was either a narrow Union victory or a draw—and one that was bloody beyond all precedent on the North American continent. Strategically, however, it was the beginning of the Confederate defeat in the western theater.

In part, this was because of the ingenuity and initiative of another of Halleck's generals, the surly and arrogant John Pope. He had begun methodically attacking the Mississippi River defenses in March. The toughest of these was Island Number 10, at the extreme northwestern edge of Tennessee at the Kentucky line, which bristled with 50 guns and occupied a seemingly unassailable double-hairpin turn of the river. Flag Officer Foote thought it suicide to run past Island Number 10's batteries with ironclad gunboats, let alone with unarmored troop transports.

Pope was not stymied for long, however. He had his engineers dig a shallow canal connecting the Mississippi to a Kentucky stream called Wilson's Bayou, which joined the river *below* Island Number 10. This enabled Pope's transports simply to bypass the Confederate defenses, which they did on April 7. The canal was too shallow for the ironclad gunboats Pope still needed as artillery support for his land force. Fortunately, he finally succeeded in talking Foote into allowing one of his captains, Henry Walker, to attempt a run past the island. He did so on April 4 and was followed two days later by another gunboat, thus supported from the river, Pope cut off the Confederate line of retreat from Shiloh at Tiptonville, Tennessee, capturing 3,500 men. By neutralizing the Mississippi defenses, he also opened the river downstream to Fort Pillow, destined to fall in June. A big piece of the big river was now under Union control.

> **COUNT OFF!**
>
> Of 62,682 Union soldiers engaged at Shiloh, 1,754 were killed, 8,408 wounded, and 2,885 went missing. Confederate losses were 723 killed, 8,012 wounded, and 959 missing out of 40,335 men engaged.

He Fights

The success of the Battle of Island Number 10 notwithstanding, Shiloh had been the bloodiest battle fought to that date in North America, and Abraham Lincoln was pressed by many to remove Grant from command. The president, burdened with generals who moved slowly and failed to pursue the enemy, pushed back. "I can't spare this man," he said. "He fights."

The Least You Need to Know

- The Union, depressed by defeat at Bull Run, looked to George B. McClellan, a dashing young general, as the commander who would win the war.
- Lee and Grant, destined to emerge as the central military figures of the war, began the war obscurely and inauspiciously with defeat and near disaster.
- Grant's and Pope's capture of forts on the Tennessee, Cumberland, and Mississippi rivers began the ultimate defeat of the Southern cause in the war's western theater.
- At the time it was fought, Shiloh, a strategic Union victory, was the largest and bloodiest battle ever seen on the North American continent.

Ocean, Valley, and River

In This Chapter

- McClellan's failure to act
- Clash of the *Monitor* and the *Merrimack*
- Stonewall Jackson's Shenandoah Valley campaign
- Farragut takes New Orleans for the Union
- "Beast" Butler occupies New Orleans

"I can do it all," McClellan assured Lincoln when the president named him general-in-chief of the Union armies. Never a shrinking violet, the "Young Napoleon" then wrote to his wife, "Who would have thought, when we were married, that I should so soon be called upon to save my country?"

But as weeks dragged into months without a decisive campaign from McClellan, Lincoln's hopes for his general turned to doubt. On March 11, 1862, Lincoln formally relieved McClellan as general-in-chief of the armies, returning him to command of the Army of the Potomac only. But when the president urged him to lead this now drilled and polished force from Washington to Richmond, McClellan proposed a plan at once more ambitious and less direct. Lincoln, grudgingly, agreed.

This chapter begins with this plan and McClellan's hesitations, and then focuses on actions that are more decisive at sea, in the Shenandoah Valley, and on the great Mississippi River leading to the Crescent City, New Orleans.

"What Are You Waiting For, Tardy George?"

A song lyric of the day said—or sang—it all. By early 1862, the vaunted "Young Napoleon" had, for many, become the comical "Tardy George." "What are you waiting for?" the song asked. Lincoln asked, too.

Instead of driving directly overland from Washington to the rebel capital, McClellan proposed to transport his army by ship down the Chesapeake Bay to the Rappahannock River. By moving to a position below General Joseph E. Johnston's lines, he would thus outflank him by sea, force the Confederates to pull back, and, in the process, avoid a major battle—or at least fight the battle closer to Richmond than to Washington. It was not a bad plan, but by the time "Tardy George" got underway, Johnston had left his position at Manassas (site of the First Bull Run battle) and moved south to the Rappahannock River, closer to Richmond.

McClellan had delayed his advance because he believed that the Confederate army outnumbered him. In part, his grossly exaggerated estimate of enemy troop strength was a product of his own pathologically overcautious nature, but intelligence reports from Allan J. Pinkerton's detectives-turned-spies were also wildly inflated, furnishing McClellan with figures too large—by factors of two, three, and even more.

Oh, well. If the enemy had moved south, so would McClellan. He decided to ferry his troops down to Fort Monroe near Newport News and Hampton Roads, in the southeastern corner of Virginia, well below the rebel capital. His revised plan was to land and proceed north toward Richmond via the Yorktown Peninsula separating the York and James rivers. That geographical feature gave the operation its name: the Peninsula Campaign. It was the largest amphibious operation in American history to that time, and, although skillfully planned, would produce tragically disappointing results.

WAR NEWS

"What Are You Waiting For, Tardy George?" was one of some 9,000 songs to emerge from the North during the Civil War. In the South, where facilities and materials for publishing sheet music were scarce, some 750 war songs appeared between 1861 and 1865. "Battle Hymn of the Republic," "When Johnny Comes Marching Home," "Tenting Tonight," and "Battle Cry of Freedom" are among the period's most enduring songs.

Flesh and Iron

The Army of the Potomac landed on April 4 under rainy, miserable conditions. Some 90,000 men slogged through a soupy, low-lying, coastal mudflat as Johnston's Confederates withdrew up the Yorktown Peninsula. Instead of immediately attacking the Confederate entrenchments at Yorktown—where George Washington and the count de Rochambeau had won *the* decisive battle of the American Revolution— McClellan set up a static siege. On April 9, a disgusted Abraham Lincoln penned a sarcastic note: "If McClellan is not using the army, I should like to borrow it for a while." But he tucked it into a desk drawer and never sent it.

Tweaking the Anaconda

While McClellan dithered and delayed on land, at sea the Confederate blockade runners were very active. Thinly spread, the Union's "Anaconda" blockade succeeded in capturing perhaps one in ten rebel vessels. (By the conclusion of the war, the numbers were closer to one in three.) Nevertheless, the blockade was making a major impact on Southern economy and morale, and the embryonic Confederate navy was not content with merely *running* the blockade. Its officers wanted to destroy it.

A Resurrection

On the south shore of Hampton Roads was the Gosport Navy Yard, evacuated by Union forces at the beginning of the war. Before they left, they scuttled the *frigate Merrimack* rather than let it fall into rebel hands. Not that Northern naval officials thought the Confederates could do much with the USS *Merrimack* anyway because vessels of the Union fleet were blockading the Roads, thereby sealing off the water route to Richmond.

DEFINITION

In the mid-nineteenth century, a **frigate** was any high-speed, medium-size warship.

In fact, Confederate engineers refloated the *Merrimack*. The Tredegar Iron Works in Richmond, employing slave labor, turned out a large order of iron plates with which the engineers clad the hull of the resurrected ship, the "ironclad" result was rechristened the CSS *Virginia*.

The prospect of an ironclad was terrifying. In the 1860s, the world's navies were making a slow transition from sail to steam-powered craft. Most modern ships were hybrids, rigged for sail, but also equipped with steam engines driving side paddle wheels or aft screws (propellers). But even these hybrids were based on *wooden* hulls vulnerable to naval artillery and to being rammed by vessels equipped with special iron ramming gear mounted on their prows. An ironclad vessel could withstand bombardment and ramming while delivering a lethal pounding.

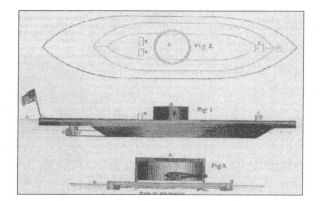

The USS Monitor *is illustrated in plan and elevation: a "cheesebox on a raft." The CSS* Virginia—*born the USS* Merrimack—*didn't look much prettier. Together, they changed the course of naval warfare forever.*
(Harper's Pictorial History of the Civil War, 1866)

Tin Can on a Shingle

Fortunately for the Union navy, word of the *Merrimack*'s rebirth and conversion did leak out. In response, a contract was let to John Ericsson, a Swedish-born

New Yorker, to build a ship capable of killing an ironclad. Ericsson designed an ugly, flat raft of a vessel, equipped with his own invention, a revolving armored turret sporting two 11-inch guns. Importantly, unlike the *Merrimack* conversion, the USS *Monitor* (as Ericsson's ship was called), was not merely clad in iron and steel, it was built of it, through and through, from keel to superstructure.

DEFINITION

The name **monitor** was soon applied generically to all steel-built or ironclad vessels with gun turrets, especially those designed for coastal bombardment.

Construction was put on a 100-day rush schedule, which Ericsson failed to meet. But when news came (from a Union sympathizer in Norfolk) that the *Merrimack/Virginia* was nearing completion, Ericsson redoubled his efforts, and the *Monitor* was launched on March 6. Clumsy and barely seaworthy, she looked, with her protruding turret, like a "tin can on a shingle" or a "cheesebox on a raft."

At about this time, Franklin Buchanan, the former commandant of the Brooklyn Navy Yard, was now made skipper of the *Merrimack/Virginia*. On March 8, he took her out to meet the wooden-hulled Union fleet blockading Hampton Roads.

CSS *Virginia* was no more attractive than the USS *Monitor*, looking (according to one Union sailor) "like the roof of a very big barn belching … smoke," and to another, like "a huge half-submerged crocodile." She had no turret; instead, her guns were fixed in rows poking out through narrow ports cut into her sloping ironclad sides. Mounted on her prow was a stout iron ram.

The blockading vessels and the Union shore batteries opened fire on the *Virginia*, but as the USS *Cumberland*'s pilot, A. B. Smith, recalled, the cannonballs bounced "upon her mailed sides like India-rubber." The Confederate craft opened up on the *Cumberland*, killing five marines, and then rammed the ship, sending her to the shallow bottom just outside the Roads. The masts protruded from the water, the Stars and Stripes still flying.

WAR NEWS

"Brother against brother" is the hoariest cliché associated with the Civil War. Nevertheless it was often all too true. On board the USS *Congress* was McKean Buchanan, brother of the CSS *Virginia*'s skipper, Franklin Buchanan.

The USS *Congress*, which had run aground and was immobilized, was the next to take *Virginia*'s fire. After the Union vessel burst into flame, it struck colors and surrendered. Chivalrously, Franklin Buchanan dispatched a boarding party from another Confederate ship to rescue the Union's wounded, but when the Union shore batteries fired on the rescuers, an enraged Buchanan seized a rifle and shot back. Sustaining a bad leg wound in this exchange, he turned over command of the *Virginia* to Lieutenant Catesby ap Jones.

Jones broke off the engagement at the end of the day, having forced the USS *Minnesota* and USS *Congress*, a smaller frigate aground. He intended to finish these off the next day.

In the meantime, as word of the battle traveled north, panic shot through Washington. People whispered that the invincible *Virginia* would sail up the Potomac and train her guns on the capital. Lincoln's cabinet convened for an emergency meeting and could think of nothing better to do than pray.

Duel at Hampton Roads

Perhaps that was for the best. For on March 9, the brand-new *Monitor*, having barely managed to avoid being swamped by ocean waves, arrived at the Roads and took up a position athwart the disabled *Minnesota*.

At 9:00 in the morning, the *Virginia* opened up on the *Monitor*, and the two vessels pounded one another for the next three hours. While both vessels dealt and endured the ceaseless pounding, the toll on their crews was brutal. Cannonballs might bounce off these ships like "India-rubber," but to the human beings onboard, each impact was a mighty blow. The shock of iron against iron sent knees buckling. The soles of the sailors' feet bled—and many of their eardrums burst from the incessant concussions.

Encased within the *Monitor*'s iron pilothouse was skipper Lieutenant John L. Worden who, at about noon, put his face to one of the narrow observation slits in the pilothouse wall. At that moment, a shot exploded against the pilothouse, temporarily blinding him. The *Monitor* suddenly drifted out of control and Jones, on the *Virginia*, assumed that his adversary was withdrawing. His own vessel damaged and taking on water, his crew exhausted, and his supply of powder almost gone, Jones withdrew also.

On the deck of the Monitor, *some of the tough men who sailed the new iron and steel warships—black as well as white, for the navy was the only integrated service at the time. The navy also recruited tough boys: the top photograph portrays a "powder-monkey"—a gunner's assistant, who hauled gunpowder, water, and other necessities—aboard a conventional wooden vessel.*

(Library of Congress)

Sails Furled

On balance, the duel of the ironclads at Hampton Roads was a draw—though the *Monitor* had saved the *Minnesota*, had prevented the Confederates from breaking the blockade of Richmond, and had averted yet another Union military disaster. More important, however, the battle changed naval warfare forever, bringing to a close the great age of wooden ships. In the short term, the battle persuaded both the Union and Confederate navies to concentrate on building more ironclads and *Monitor*-class vessels rather than wooden sail craft. With its more developed industrial base, the North could—and would—build far more *Monitor*-class ships than the Confederacy.

WAR NEWS

Neither of the original iron ships enjoyed long careers. *Virginia* ran aground on May 11, 1862, and was set ablaze by its own crew to prevent capture. The *Monitor*, which rode a mere 18 inches above her waterline, foundered in heavy seas while being towed off Cape Hatteras, North Carolina, on December 31, 1862. Sixteen crew members perished. On August 5, 2002, a salvage team under the auspices of the National Oceanic and Atmospheric Administration (NOAA) recovered the *Monitor*'s turret from the bottom of waters off Cape Hatteras. The turret was sent to the Mariners' Museum for preservation work.

Blue Light in the Valley

George B. McClellan's mud-soaked soldiers laid siege against Yorktown, Virginia, on April 5. Lincoln deemed it nothing more than inaction and pleaded with his general to attack the Confederate defenses.

No, McClellan insisted. He would attack only after his big guns had softened up the enemy. His spymaster, Pinkerton, had reported that Yorktown was very heavily defended and that he was outnumbered. McClellan blamed Lincoln for having insisted that he leave behind, to defend Washington, a significant number of the 130,000 men he had originally intended to take with him up the Virginia peninsula.

The fact was that, in withdrawing closer to Virginia, Confederate General Joseph E. Johnston had left only about 15,000 men under General John B. Magruder at Yorktown. McClellan commanded nearly six times that number. By digging in instead of attacking, however, McClellan gave Robert E. Lee, trained as a military engineer, valuable time to create elaborate permanent defenses around Richmond.

Retreat at Kernstown

Robert E. Lee and the other top Confederate military commanders understood Lincoln's intense concern to defend Washington, and they saw in this an opportunity to leverage their relatively small numbers against the superior Union forces. "Old Blue Light," as the intensely blue-eyed Stonewall Jackson was reverently called, was assigned to sweep through Virginia's Shenandoah Valley to persuade the North that an invasion of the capital, from the Valley, was imminent. "Divide and conquer" has been a winning strategy since the days of Caesar. Jackson's Shenandoah Valley campaign was aimed at compelling the Union to divide its comparatively numerous forces, which could then be attacked and defeated in detail (separately).

The first battle of the campaign was fought on March 23, at Kernstown, near Winchester. Jackson thought he was attacking the four-regiment rear guard of Union General Nathaniel Banks, but found himself up against an entire 9,000-man division. Suffering a sharp defeat, Jackson retreated.

Yet this tactical defeat was quickly translated into a strategic triumph: The Kernstown fight persuaded Northern leaders that an invasion was indeed afoot, and 35,000 men under General Irvin McDowell were detached from McClellan's peninsula command to reinforce the defense of Washington. McClellan was left with 90,000 men, which he (mistakenly) thought insufficient to attack Yorktown.

Victory at McDowell

On May 8, Jackson fought another tactically undistinguished battle, managing to repulse Federal forces at McDowell, Virginia, but suffering in the process twice the casualties (498 versus 256) incurred by the attackers.

Front Royal

From his costly but effective victory at McDowell, Jackson deployed his cavalry under Colonel Turner Ashby to deceive Banks into thinking he was moving west, toward Strasburg. However after picking up reinforcements, Jackson marched the main body of his army, now about 17,000 men, to the Federal outpost at Front Royal, Virginia, which he attacked on May 23.

Jackson easily outfought Banks, netting 904 prisoners and, even more important, two cannon and a cache of arms. The Confederates appropriated so much in the way of supplies from Banks's army that they mockingly dubbed him *"Commissary* Banks."

This likeness of Thomas J. "Stonewall" Jackson, one of the Confederacy's greatest tacticians, was probably made well before the Civil War, when Jackson was a young U.S. Army officer.

(Harper's Pictorial History of the Civil War, 1866)

DEFINITION

In the military jargon of the period, a **commissary** was a store from which rations and supplies were drawn, as well as the officer in charge of provisions and supplies.

Attack at Winchester

Banks sent his army into retreat toward Winchester, Virginia, having divided his forces on May 24 after Jackson hit one of his columns at Middletown. It was therefore a reduced army that Jackson attacked at Winchester on May 25. He quickly overwhelmed Banks, sending his army in full retreat back across the Potomac. Jackson gave chase to Harpers Ferry, and then tweaked Union commanders and politicians alike by feigning a Potomac crossing, putting Washington in the crosshairs, before he turned south.

Cross Keys

Banks's army was not the only Union force in the Shenandoah Valley. Some 16,000 men under General John Charles Frémont attacked a Confederate *bivouac* at Cross Keys, Virginia, on June 8. The assault on Confederate Major General Richard Ewell's bivouac was uncoordinated and therefore readily beaten back. Sadly, Frémont, for all his bravery and earnestness, was (in the words of a later writer) "a giddy and fumbling general."

> **DEFINITION**
>
> A **bivouac** is a temporary encampment.

Port Republic

One of Frémont's abler subordinates, Irish-born Brigadier General James Shields, dispatched his vanguard under Colonel Samuel S. Carroll to raid Jackson's position at Port Republic on June 8. The Confederate general narrowly escaped capture by driving Carroll off with artillery and an infantry regiment. The next day, Jackson attacked Brigadier General Erastus Tyler, who had reinforced Carroll to the northeast, at Port Republic. At first Tyler's men seemed to prevail, but, after hand-to-hand combat, the rebels captured an important Federal artillery position, while Frémont and his troops, stranded on the opposite bank of the flood-swollen South Fork, could only watch helplessly.

Despite his victory, Jackson realized that the columns of Shields and Frémont would unite. So he pulled back, as did the Union forces. This ended Jackson's Shenandoah Valley campaign, a display of the most spectacular military maneuvering of the entire war. Jackson had used some 17,000 men to hold and immobilize 50,000 Union soldiers, frightening the politicians in Washington, who feared an attack on the capital, thereby denying to McClellan the overwhelming numbers he felt necessary to attack Richmond. The Confederate capital was spared, and the war prolonged.

New Orleans Falls

Richmond, capital of the Confederacy, may have been saved, but the South's largest city and its most important port would not be so fortunate.

David Dixon Porter, one of the U.S. Navy's senior commanders, planned the assault, invasion, and capture of New Orleans. To lead the operation, he recommended David Glasgow Farragut, age 60, the navy's most experienced sailor.

Farragut assembled a fleet of 2 steam frigates, 7 *screw sloops*, and 9 gunboats, plus 20 *schooners* converted to carry mortars—artillery pieces designed to fire very heavy, 13-inch projectiles in a high trajectory. Mortars were devastating against walled forts. The *mortar* boats were commanded by Porter, who volunteered to serve under the leader he himself had nominated.

DEFINITION

A **screw sloop** was a small armed vessel powered by a steam-driven propeller (screw). A **schooner** was (and is) a fore-and-aft-rigged sailing vessel. A **mortar** was a short, thick-walled artillery piece designed to lob a heavy projectile in a steep, high trajectory; it was most often used against high-walled forts.

Farragut took his fleet into the mouth of the Mississippi and in mid-April, commenced a week-long bombardment of Forts Jackson and St. Philip, which guarded the approach to New Orleans. At 2:00 A.M. on April 24, having sufficiently reduced the forts, he led the Union fleet upriver, successfully dodging the blazing unmanned fire rafts the Confederates had launched. Soon Farragut's fleet broke through all opposition and steamed past the forts, which—now cut off—surrendered.

Union General Ben Butler marched his troops in to take possession of the fallen forts and the now-defenseless city. New Orleans and, with it, the mouth of the Mississippi, belonged to the Union again. The South had now lost control of both the upper and the lower Mississippi.

COUNT OFF!

Farragut took New Orleans and its forts at the cost of a single Union ship sunk and the loss of 37 men killed and 147 wounded.

"Beast" Butler in the Crescent City

Benjamin Butler was not a tolerant man. At the start of the war, he had quelled rioters in Baltimore, and he now brought harsh martial law to New Orleans. When a mob tore down the Stars and Stripes newly raised over the Mint, Butler responded by taking into custody a citizen found wearing a fragment of the flag in his buttonhole. When he boasted about having helped to tear it down, Butler summarily tried him for treason, sentenced him to death by hanging, and hanged him in front of the Mint.

The "Woman Order" and the Will to Fight

If the men of New Orleans were sobered into submission by the hanging, the city's women continued to miss no opportunity to demonstrate their contempt for the "invaders." They boldly wore Confederate insignia on their dresses, held their noses when Yankees passed, and repeatedly forced soldiers off the city's "banquettes" (sidewalks) into the mud by refusing to step to the right when passed.

When one New Orleans belle allegedly took careful aim from her window and emptied a chamber pot on Flag Officer Farragut's head, Butler responded with General Order 28 on May 15, 1862:

> As the Officers and Soldiers of the United States have been subject to repeated insults from the women calling themselves ladies of New Orleans, in return for the most scrupulous non-interference and courtesy on our part, it is ordered that hereafter when any Female shall, by word, gesture, or movement, insult or show contempt for any officer of the United States, she shall be regarded and held liable to be treated as a woman of the town plying her avocation.

For this infamous "Woman Order," citizens and the press of New Orleans dubbed the general "Beast" Butler, and General Beauregard used the outrage as means of renewing the resolve of his troops: "Men of the South! shall [we allow] . . . the ladies of the South [to be treated] as common harlots? Arouse, friends, and drive back from our soil, those infamous invaders of our homes and disturbers of our family ties."

 WAR NEWS

Even after the Civil War ended, chamber pots featuring the face of Benjamin Butler on the inside bottom were popular items in many Southern homes.

Hollow Victory

While the Union enjoyed victory on the Mississippi the "Young Napoleon" was finally ready to move against Yorktown. To his acute embarrassment however, the Confederates, under General John Bankhead Magruder (nicknamed "Prince John," for his regal manner), had by this time withdrawn to join the main Confederate force closer to Richmond. Confederate cavalry, commanded by General Jeb Stuart covered the withdrawal. On May 4 and 5, McClellan's subordinates, General Edwin V. Sumner and General Joseph Hooker, engaged Johnston's rear guard at Williamsburg, the colonial capital of Virginia, but now no more than a sleepy little village.

The battle was inconclusive, but McClellan claimed victory. He had chased Magruder out of Yorktown, hadn't he? Then he had chased Stuart out of Williamsburg, right?

The Northern press bought Little Mac's interpretation and congratulated him. Lincoln, however, fretted. And McClellan himself would soon reap the harshest reality of his Peninsula Campaign in a series of meatgrinder battles that would be remembered simply as "The Seven Days."

The Least You Need to Know

- George McClellan was a brilliant administrator and organizer, but he lacked the initiative and resolve to be an effective combat leader.
- The duel of the USS *Monitor* and the CSS *Virginia* (formerly USS *Merrimack*), although inconclusive, ushered in a new era in naval warfare.
- Stonewall Jackson's Shenandoah campaign was one of the most sweeping and brilliant shows of military maneuvering of the entire war.
- David Farragut's triumph at New Orleans deprived the Confederacy of its most important port city.

Blue, Gray, and Red

In This Chapter

- Drain of soldiers from the West to the East
- Guerrilla warfare in Missouri
- The "Gettysburg of the West"
- The fight for Texas
- The role of the "Indian Wars" in the Civil War

As you read in Chapter 7, when Civil War soldiers and politicians talked about the "war in the west," they usually meant the action in Kentucky, Tennessee, and elsewhere along the Mississippi River. But the Civil War was also fought in what most of us, today, think of as the American West: in Missouri, Arkansas, Kansas, Texas, New Mexico, and Arizona.

Out West, no great cities were lost or won, and few decisive strategic ends were achieved. Nevertheless, as in the East, men fought, and men died.

This chapter turns from the East to the far-flung, small-scale, intensely bitter combat in the West.

An Army Without Officers

The first shots of the Civil War might have been fired on the Carolina coast, but they made a deep impact in the West. By Sumter's fall, 313 officers, one third of the Army's officer corps, had left their commands to join the Confederate forces. "We are practically an army without officers," one Federal soldier in the West complained. And of the soldiers and officers who remained at their posts, many would be transferred to the East, where most of the war's action was unfolding.

Missouri's Misery

If the U.S. Army in the West was depleted and troubled at the beginning of the war, Missouri, like its neighbor Kansas, had been wallowing in it since the 1850s. We saw in Chapter 6 how the state was torn between its pro-Confederate governor and its mostly pro-Union legislature, and how the impetuous Union firebrand captain-turned-general Nathaniel Lyon attacked Confederate forces encamped at Wilson's Creek on August 10, 1861.

The ambitious but inept Union General John Charles Frémont had been involved in the Wilson's Creek debacle. Because General William A. Harney lacked aggressiveness, Abraham Lincoln relieved him of command in Missouri on May 29 and temporarily elevated Lyon to his post. On July 3, Lincoln put Frémont in "permanent" command of a newly created Western Department. He arrived in St. Louis on July 25, 1861, and promptly found himself overwhelmed by the complex military situation in Missouri. When Lyon asked for reinforcements to fight Confederate General Sterling Price at Wilson's Creek, Frémont ordered him to *avoid* combat. Lyon ignored the order, lost the battle, and was killed.

Despite this defeat, on August 30, Frémont declared martial law in Missouri and proclaimed the emancipation of Missouri's slaves—something Lincoln had not yet even contemplated and Frémont had no authority to do. Frémont also began confiscating property of known Confederate sympathizers. These actions drove many undecided Missourians off the fence and straight into the Confederate camp. Guerrilla war, always simmering in Missouri, now boiled over. General Sterling Price won another victory at Lexington, Missouri, on September 13, and Frémont's brief reign as commander of the Western Department came to an end. He was transferred to West Virginia.

Pea Ridge

In October 1861, a pro-South rump minority of the Missouri legislature convened in October 1861 at Neosho and voted to secede. Although the Neosho group was not the legally constituted legislature and the majority of the elected legislature remained loyal so that the state never seceded, Jefferson Davis made a show of welcoming Missouri into the Confederacy.

But now it was Davis's turn to suffer a lapse in judgment. The Confederate president was suspicious of General Sterling Price, who had been a close personal friend of the former Union Commander Harney. Davis, therefore, declined to commit troops to

Price, who was now confronted by forces under Brigadier General Samuel R. Curtis. Curtis had been ordered by the new commander of the Western Department, Henry "Old Brains" Halleck, to drive the Confederates out of the state. Without support, Price had no choice but to withdraw into Arkansas.

Henry Wager Halleck, called (none too affectionately) "Old Brains," was commander of the U.S. Army's Western Department at the time of Pea Ridge.
(Harper's Pictorial History of the Civil War, 1866)

He wanted to join forces there with a contingent under General Ben McCulloch, but General Earl Van Dorn intercepted Price and McCulloch and joined them to reinforcements that included several thousand Indians led by Cherokee General Stand Watie. With a combined, albeit motley, army of 17,000 men, Van Dorn proposed to attack Curtis, whose forces numbered only about 11,000.

WAR NEWS

Stand Watie (1806–1871) was a mixed-blood Cherokee tribal leader from Georgia who became a Confederate general. At Pea Ridge, his troops captured vital Union artillery positions, and then effectively covered the retreat of Confederate forces. At the end of the war, General Stand Watie was the last Confederate general to surrender his troops, in June 1865.

Alerted to the Confederate buildup by his scout, James Butler Hickok (who, after the war, as "Wild Bill" Hickok, would become one of the West's legendary gunfighters), Curtis took a strong defensive position at Pea Ridge, on high ground overlooking Little Sugar Creek. At dawn on March 7, skirmishing broke out near Elk Horn Tavern. This soon developed into heavy fighting.

COUNT OFF!

Of 11,250 Union troops engaged at Pea Ridge, 1,384 were killed, wounded, or missing. Of some 14,000 Confederates, 800 were casualties.

The Federals held their ground against Van Dorn on the 7th, but the Confederate general renewed his attack on the 8th, whereupon the Union forces were able to seize the initiative and drive Van Dorn's forces from the field in complete disarray. Ordered to assist in the doomed defense of the Mississippi River, Van Dorn left Arkansas.

Guerrillas

After Pea Ridge, the rump legislature hightailed it out of the state, and the fighting in Missouri became a sporadic and bloody contest between *jayhawkers* (pro-Union raiders), and pro-Confederate guerrillas called *bushwhackers* in addition to sporadic warfare between neighbors. This combat continued throughout the war.

DEFINITION

Jayhawkers were self-appointed abolitionist guerrillas active in the Kansas-Missouri border region. The most aggressive of them were called "Red Legs," after the red leggings they often wore as their only uniform. **Bushwhacker** was the generic term for pro-Confederate guerrillas active in the same area.

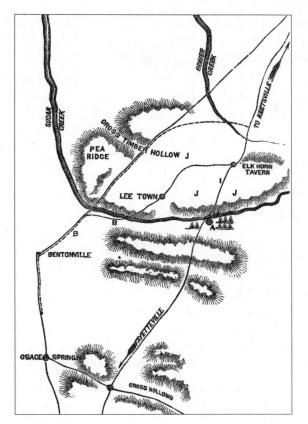

Map of Pea Ridge, Arkansas, and vicinity. The fighting centered near the Elk Horn Tavern. (The Confederates called Pea Ridge the Battle of Elk Horn Tavern.)
(Harper's Pictorial History of the Civil War, 1866)

Most notorious of the Confederate bushwhackers was 24 years old, William Clarke Quantrill (1837–1865). Son of a schoolmaster and himself a former teacher, Quantrill had been an abolitionist, but unaccountably changed sides once war broke out. He was commissioned a captain in the Confederate army and, with William C. "Bloody Bill" Anderson, wreaked havoc on Kansas border patrols and Missouri's Union militia.

On August 14, 1862, Union General John M. Schofield, who had replaced Halleck, approved a plan to "remove" everyone in Missouri known to have aided or abetted Quantrill and company. The wives, mothers, and sisters of suspected bushwhackers were rounded up and deposited under lock and key in a tumble-down, three-story building in Kansas City. The improvised prison collapsed from overloading, severely injuring a number of the women and killing five, including Anderson's sister.

For this outrage the guerrillas craved revenge, and, with 450 men, Quantrill attacked much-beleaguered Lawrence, Kansas, on August 21. The raiders killed more than 150 unarmed civilians and put the town to the torch.

Indeed, Quantrill recognized no morality in guerrilla warfare. At Baxter Springs, Kansas, on October 6, 1863, he and his men donned Union uniforms to deceive a detachment of Federal troops into ambush. Sixty-five men in a troop of 100 soldiers were gunned down, many of them disarmed prisoners who were simply and summarily executed.

WAR NEWS

Bushwhacker William Clarke Quantrill was killed by Union guerrillas on May 10, 1865, as he traveled through Kentucky, supposedly on a self-assigned mission to Washington, D.C., where he had planned to assassinate President Lincoln. By that time, John Wilkes Booth had beaten him to it.

Schofield's subordinate, General Thomas Ewing Jr. next issued the notorious General Order Number 11, giving everyone living within one mile of Union military posts in Jackson, Cass, Bates, and the northern half of Vernon counties 15 days to leave their homes. The order also required them to take all grain and hay from their farms to the local military post. Any other crops and foodstuffs would be destroyed.

Federal troops then swept through the Missouri-Kansas border country, burning everything in their path. For decades after the war, this area would be called the "Burnt District."

The Yankees' depredations garnered renewed support for General Sterling Price, who, in January 1864, led a last invasion of Missouri. He ordered "Bloody Bill" Anderson and other bushwhackers into action. Anderson raided Centralia, and while he presided over the torture and murder of a number of civilians, a train happened through town. The raiders intercepted it, robbed the passengers, and, finding 25 unarmed Union soldiers headed home to Iowa on furlough, ordered them to strip off their uniforms. Each was executed at point-blank range.

The Centralia Massacre was the last major guerrilla action in Missouri.

COUNT OFF!

Counting all the guerrilla actions and skirmishes, 1,162 engagements took place in Missouri, 11 percent of all the engagements in the Civil War, the third highest number in a single state.

Confederate Arizona

Confederate Lieutenant Colonel John Robert Baylor took advantage of the Federal army's weakness in the Southwest to sweep through the southern New Mexico Territory all the way from the Rio Grande to California. By July 1862, Baylor grandly proclaimed the Confederate Territory of Arizona, which encompassed all of present-day Arizona and New Mexico, south of the 34th parallel.

Sibley's Invasion

Baylor's almost-unopposed advance was followed during the winter of 1861 through 1862 by a larger Confederate invasion led by General Henry Hopkins Sibley (no relation to Union General Henry *Hastings* Sibley). The Confederate Sibley's mission was to take the rest of New Mexico and to seize the silver mines of Colorado, which would greatly enrich the Southern war chest. If possible, Sibley was to press the invasion all the way to Southern California.

Sibley advanced up the Rio Grande. His first objective was Fort Union, along the strategically vital Santa Fe Trail. The best-provisioned Union post in the Southwest, it was the headquarters of Colonel Edward R. S. Canby, commander of the Department of New Mexico.

Even as Sibley's invaders menaced, Canby had his hands full fighting Navajo raids in New Mexico and dealing with unauthorized citizen counterraids, which only made the Indian violence worse. Although the Confederates had their own Indian troubles, Sibley pressed the attack on Canby, engaging him at Valverde, New Mexico, on February 21, 1862, and emerging victorious. From here, he was able to take Santa Fe, and then he advanced to Fort Union.

The Battle of La Glorieta Pass

The route to Fort Union lay through La Glorieta Pass, at the apex of the climb through the Sangre de Cristo Mountains. There, on March 26, 1862, Union troops under Colonel John Slough, reinforced by Colorado volunteers commanded by Major John M. Chivington, opened battle with Sibley's Texans. For the next two days, through the 28th, they fought it out on harsh desert mountain terrain.

By Eastern standards, the Battle of La Glorieta Pass was a mere skirmish, and both sides, exhausted, declared victory. But the advantage was clearly with the North. The Confederates lost 121 men to the Union's 31, and Sibley retreated back to Texas. After the war, some would call this encounter the "Gettysburg of the West" because it turned the tide against the Confederates in the Southwest.

Arizona Rangers

If Union General Canby had to fight Indians as well as Confederates, Confederate Colonel Baylor also had his own problems with the Indians. Chiricahua and Mimbreño Apaches freely raided the newly proclaimed Confederate Territory of Arizona. Baylor responded by creating units of Arizona Rangers and Arizona Guards. When this failed to halt the raids, Baylor sent the Guards' commander a letter announcing that the Confederate Congress had "passed a law declaring extermination of all hostile Indians." This was untrue, yet Baylor continued: "… persuade the Apaches or any tribe to come in for the purpose of making peace, and when you get them together, kill all the grown Indians and take the children prisoners and sell them [as slaves] to defray the expense of killing the Indians." The letter was leaked, dooming Confederate efforts to win allies among the tribes.

California Column

At about the time Slough and Chivington were battling Sibley, Colonel James H. Carleton, led the First California Regiment of Infantry, called the "California Column," into New Mexico Territory. The sweep pushed the Confederates out of the present-day state of Arizona, and on April 15, 1862, the Battle of Picacho Peak (New Mexico), the westernmost action of the Civil War, ended the brief existence of the Confederate Territory of Arizona.

Texas Troubles

At the outbreak of the war, Texas was another western trouble spot for the Union. Governor Sam Houston, leader of Texan independence, confounded his fellow Texans by supporting the Union and resisting secession. In February 1861, however, his state seceded out from under him, and he resigned office. General David E. Twiggs, commander of the U.S. Army's Department of Texas, surrendered all Federal property to the Confederates—without firing a shot.

In October 1862, the U.S. Navy took the important Texas port city of Galveston, which was occupied by Union troops in December. The Confederates retook Galveston on January 1, 1863, after a four-hour fight. But the Union kept up a naval blockade, which almost completely closed the port.

By late 1863, the Mississippi River was firmly in Union hands, and Texas was cut off from the rest of the South. But there was still fighting to be done. President Lincoln understood that, perhaps ironically, the North needed cotton for its war effort. For that reason, he winked at a certain limited Northern trade with Southern cotton planters. When this led to outrageous gouging by unscrupulous Northern speculators, Lincoln ordered General Nathaniel Banks to raid Texas for the cotton the Union needed.

Banks's Red River Campaign spanned from March to May 1864. The objective was the capture of Shreveport, Louisiana, which would give the Union control of East Texas. A joint U.S. Army-Navy action ran afoul of treacherous river waters, giving Confederate General Edmund Kirby Smith's troops time to evade the Northern pursuers and to set fire to their cotton stores rather than let them fall into Yankee hands.

Kirby Smith's troops then routed Banks's forces at the battles of Sabine Cross Roads (April 8, 1864) and Pleasant Hill (April 12). The Union troops piled into their river-borne transports and beat a hasty retreat.

The Real Conflict

The late action in Texas hardly mattered to the fate of the Confederacy in the West. With the loss of New Mexico and Arizona by the end of 1862, and the loss of the Mississippi River by late 1863, the entire West was lost to the Confederate cause.

Still, Union supporters worried that the Confederates would cajole, or even buy, Indian allies and turn them against Union soldiers and civilians. It is true that the Confederacy recruited from among the Caddos, Wichitas, Osages, Shawnees, Delawares, Senecas, and Quapaws, and that both the North and the South recruited from other tribes that had been "removed" by act of Congress to Indian Territory (present-day Oklahoma) during the 1830s and 1840s (Cherokees, Chickasaws, Choctaws, Creeks, and Seminoles). Confederate agents also supplied arms to some Comanches and Kiowas on the southern plains. Yet, for the most part, the Western Indians sided with neither the North nor the South. They either remained neutral or fought against both sides in the early phases of what the U.S. Army dubbed the Indian Wars.

The "Indian War" most directly relevant to the Civil War broke out in the remote village of New Ulm, in south-central Minnesota, in 1862.

The Santee Sioux (a division of the Sioux often called the Dakota, consisting of the Mdewakantons, Wahpekutes, Sissetons, and Wahpetons) at first accepted the policy of "concentration" that the Apaches and Navajos in the Southwest had so vigorously resisted. But resentment smoldered among them as they suffered crop failures and were increasingly hemmed in by growing numbers of Scandinavian and German immigrants.

Worst of all, the corrupt federal Indian agency system consistently diverted the funds and supplies promised by treaty. During the summer of 1862, Santees repeatedly petitioned for the release of their rations and funds. Repeatedly, they were rebuffed.

Little Crow, chief of the Mdewakanton villages, put his case to those in charge of the local Indian agency: "We have no food, but here are these stores, filled with food. We ask that you, the agent, make some arrangements by which we can get food from the stores, or else we may take our own way to keep ourselves from starving. When men are hungry they help themselves."

To this, a local trader, Andrew J. Myrick, replied, "So far as I am concerned, if they are hungry, let them eat grass."

Shortly after this encounter, on August 17, four young Mdewakanton men were returning from an all too typically fruitless hunting trip. One of them stopped to steal eggs from the nest of a hen belonging to a white man. When another of the young hunters cautioned against the theft, the others called him a coward. He declared that he was not afraid to kill a white man, whereupon the four impulsively murdered the farmer and his family.

Andrew Myrick was the very next white to die. Attacked in his store on August 18, he tried to run and was shot down. Into his dead mouth, the Indians stuffed a tuft of grass.

Then war spread throughout a region very short on soldiers. The immigrant village of New Ulm fell under siege on the afternoon of August 20 and, again, on the 23rd. Thirty-six townspeople died, and another 23 were wounded. Most of the town lay in ruins, and its 2,000 citizens evacuated to Mankato.

They were not alone in their flight. By August 27, it was clear that the entire Sioux nation in Minnesota was on the warpath. Between 350 and 800 settlers had been killed, horrible atrocities were committed, and about half the state's population were refugees from Indian wrath. Unfounded rumor held that the Indians had been provoked by Confederates.

If abuse and starvation, not the Confederacy, was the real cause of the Santee Sioux Uprising, the bloody episode did indirectly benefit the South. Minnesota governor Alexander Ramsey asked President Lincoln for permission to delay sending his state's quota of enlistees to fight the Civil War in the East. Lincoln replied by telegraph: "Attend to the Indians. If the draft cannot proceed of course it will not proceed. Necessity knows no law."

The orgy of raiding ended on September 23, 1862, at the Battle of Wood Lake. Little Crow fled west and did not return to Minnesota until the following year. On July 3, 1863, he was picking raspberries with his 16-year-old son when he was ambushed and killed by settlers seeking to collect a $25 bounty on Sioux scalps.

The Least You Need to Know

- Although no great battles were fought in the far West, chronic guerrilla and Indian warfare affected the war effort of both sides by draining manpower that might have been used elsewhere.
- Of all states, Missouri suffered the ravages of guerrilla warfare most severely.
- For a short time during 1861 and 1862, the Confederacy maintained the Confederate Territory of Arizona in the Southwest until the Battle of La Glorieta Pass (the "Gettysburg of the West") turned the tide toward the Union.
- The demands of the Civil War greatly reduced the military presence in the West and gave rise to widespread Indian hostilities in the Southwest and in Minnesota.

Seven Days and Another Bull Run

Chapter 10

In This Chapter

- Jeb Stuart's ride around McClellan
- The Seven Days' Battles
- McClellan temporarily loses command
- The Second Battle of Bull Run
- Civil War nursing

George McClellan, driven by a fear of losing rather than a passion for victory, had divided his army in an unsuccessful effort to counter Stonewall Jackson's Shenandoah Valley Campaign. This meant that, at the end of June 1862, more than a quarter of his strength, about 25,000 men, remained isolated north of Virginia's Chickahominy River. With the broad flank of the rest of the Federal army now exposed and vulnerable, McClellan was about to reap the consequences of his faulty troop dispositions. He would face a new adversary, Robert E. Lee, who was leading some 65,000 soldiers. Always afraid of being outnumbered, McClellan had created the very circumstances he most feared.

This chapter chronicles some hard times for the Union's Army of the Potomac and its commander.

Fair Oaks Prelude

Let's go back, briefly, to the *beginning* of June. At that point, most of McClellan's army was north of the Chickahominy, except for a corps commanded by General Erasmus Darwin Keyes. Confederate General Joseph E. Johnston was quick to recognize the vulnerability of Keyes's isolated position, and he decided to attack. On May 31, 1862, he hit Keyes at Fair Oaks and Seven Pines.

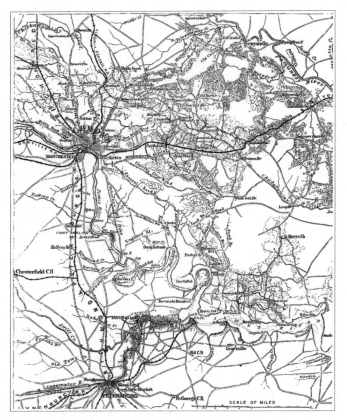

Map of Richmond, Virginia, and vicinity. The Chickahominy River is east of Richmond, and Mechanicsville (focus of one of the early Seven Days' Battles) may be seen to the northeast.
(Harper's Pictorial History of the Civil War, 1866)

A series of Confederate errors and misunderstandings followed, however, resulting in delays that gave other elements of McClellan's forces time to join the fray. The result was an inconclusive and bloody two-day battle, one of the costliest of the war thus far (only Shiloh was bloodier), fought between almost equally matched forces.

An inconclusive battle, but not one without consequence.

In the course of the fight, General Johnston was severely wounded and would have to drop out of the war for a time. His replacement was Robert E. Lee.

COUNT OFF!

Of 41,797 Union troops engaged at Fair Oaks and Seven Pines, 5,031 were casualties; of 41,816 Confederates, 6,134 became casualties.

Jeb and the Gray Ghost

Thus far in the war, Lee's career had lacked luster. After faring poorly in western Virginia combat, he performed important but unexciting work improving coastal fortifications, and he had served behind the lines as President Jefferson Davis's personal military advisor. In this capacity, he had given Stonewall Jackson the idea and impetus for his Shenandoah Valley Campaign. But it was Jackson's campaign, and Jackson got the glory for it.

Other Confederate commanders were getting glory at this time, too. There was James Ewell Brown Stuart—Jeb Stuart—who, not yet 30, was a brigadier general cavalry commander decked out in an ostrich-plumed hat, a cape lined in red, and gold spurs at his heels. Come evening, he busied himself writing dispatches, not to Confederate headquarters but to the London newspapers, which made him an international celebrity.

In military tactics of the mid-nineteenth century, the cavalry was the "eyes" of the army. Its chief function was rapid reconnaissance. For all his preening, Jeb Stuart was a highly skilled and daring tactician, as he demonstrated, between June 12 and 15, 1862. With 1,200 cavalrymen, he performed a reconnaissance that completely circled the Union positions in Virginia—he rode around the army. He was guided in this by his scout, First Lieutenant John Singleton Mosby, who would soon gain renown equal to Stuart's as the "Gray Ghost of the Confederacy," the leader of the Partisan Rangers, a remarkably bold, stealthy, and effective band of guerrillas.

James Ewell Brown "Jeb" Stuart (left) and John Singleton Mosby, with his "Partisan Rangers" (right), were the two great guerrilla leaders of the Civil War. As Confederate cavalry commanders, their tactics were swift, shrewd, and stealthy. Mosby, known as the "Gray Ghost of the Confederacy," stands fifth from left.
(Image of Stuart from Harper's Pictorial History of the Civil War, 1866; image of Mosby courtesy Library of Congress)

Seven-Day Duel

Stuart's ride made the young brigadier a legend. For McClellan, it was just one more embarrassment. But it was also a wake-up call. The Federal commander realized that he had put his army in a vulnerable position. He began, therefore, to move it, except for a single corps, south of the Chickahominy. It seemed that he was now finally resolved to begin his drive to Richmond in earnest.

Resistance at Oak Grove

On June 25, at Oak Grove, near Mechanicsville, right along the Chickahominy River, McClellan's forces met stiff resistance. At first driven back, McClellan was able to bring up reinforcements, who used *canister shot* to drive back the Confederate troops. This accomplished, the Union forces were able to occupy positions around Oak Grove. But, as night began to fall, operations were halted.

> **DEFINITION**
>
> **Canister shot,** or just canister, was a type of artillery shell designed to explode upon firing, spraying out the lead or iron shot that was packed within the canister. It was a cruelly effective antipersonnel weapon, generally used at close range.

Mechanicsville

As it turned out, Oak Grove was just a curtain-raiser to seven days of intense combat. Lee's strategy was to bring the bulk of his army—65,000 troops—to the north bank of the Chickahominy and overwhelm the 25,000 Union troops under General Fitz-John Porter, who were left, isolated, on that side of the river. Had the plan worked, Porter's corps would have been cut to ribbons.

But it didn't work. Jackson, so dazzling in the Valley, inexplicably decided to bivouac (make a temporary camp) on June 26 instead of attacking Porter. Confederate General A. P. Hill, impatient with Jackson's failure to arrive, attacked alone and without Lee's orders. The result: Mechanicsville was a bloody repulse for the Confederates, and Porter withdrew safely to the south bank of the Chickahominy.

Reprieved, McClellan nevertheless gave in to the usual fears of being outnumbered. He suddenly ordered the withdrawal of his army to a new supply base on the James River, below and *away from* Richmond. His subordinate officers protested, but to no avail.

> **COUNT OFF!**
>
> Armies were the largest operational units and contained several corps, each consisting of two or more divisions and commanded by a major general in the Union army and a lieutenant general in the Confederate army. A standard Union division consisted of about 6,200 officers and men, a Confederate division, 8,700, but the actual numbers varied widely throughout the war. A division was two or more brigades. A brigade comprised two or more regiments, which was two or more battalions. A battalion consisted of two or more companies or (in the case of an artillery battalion) batteries.

Gaines's Mill

Lee wasn't about to let McClellan off so easily. He hounded and attacked mercilessly throughout the remaining seven days. While McClellan was rarely personally present to supervise his troops, his corps commanders executed skillful rearguard actions and counterattacks that made McClellan's retreat costly for Lee as well.

After Jackson's brilliance in the Shenandoah Valley, Lee put much faith and reliance in "Old Blue Light." Uncharacteristically, however, Jackson disappointed him, failing to attack on time not only on June 26, but also on three more occasions during the series of the Seven Days' Battles. Lee formulated plans to isolate and defeat in detail the elements of McClellan's vulnerable army, but the plans were overcomplex and asked too much of inadequately trained subordinates, causing the plans to fail in the execution.

At the Battle of Gaines's Mill, on June 27, Jackson was again tardy, which gave the beleaguered Union corps commander, Fitz-John Porter, time to reinforce his outnumbered position. The fighting, when it finally began in earnest, was severe. The Federal line held until shortly before dark, but once the Confederates at last fully coordinated their attack, the Union began a bloody retreat.

WAR NEWS

The Union typically named its armies after rivers: the Army of the Potomac, the Army of the Mississippi, and so on. The Confederacy typically named its armies after states or regions. Sometimes, this could be confusing; the Union had an Army of *the* Tennessee (the river), while the Confederacy had an Army of Tennessee (the state). The most famous Confederate army was the Army of Northern Virginia, led by Robert E. Lee.

Savage's Station

McClellan's order to withdraw to the James River was issued to the corps commanders immediately following the retreat from Gaines's Mill. Lee, eager to renew the attack on the retreating Union army, nevertheless bided his time until he was certain of McClellan's direction. Lee's plan of attack was complex, however, and beyond the ability of his corps commanders to carry out effectively. The attack came late on June 29 and was highly spirited, but not well coordinated.

COUNT OFF!

At Gaines's Mill, the bloodiest of the Seven Days' Battles, 34,214 Union troops were engaged—of whom 893 died, 3,107 were wounded, and 2,836 were reported missing. Although the Confederates forced a Union retreat, their casualties were heavier, numbering 8,751 killed and/or wounded.

Once again, Lee had missed an opportunity to deal a decisive, damaging blow to the Army of the Potomac. Federal rearguard actions and counterattacks cost him heavily, but it was the breaking of a violent thunderstorm that finally cut the battle short and saved the Union rear guard from ultimate defeat. Still, the withdrawing Union forces left behind a large quantity of supplies, as well as 2,500 wounded men (victims of Savage's Station and previous battles) in a field hospital.

COUNT OFF!

Losses in the engagement at Savage's Station were 1,590 killed and/or wounded on the Union side and 626 on the Confederate side.

Frayser's Farm

Having withdrawn from Savage's Station, McClellan concentrated his forces behind White Oak Swamp and in a line to Malvern Hill to protect the Union supply trains on their way to Harrison's Landing on the James River.

Lee again formulated a plan for a coordinated attack designed to pummel McClellan's army, but, yet again, the coordination failed in execution. Although Lee pushed McClellan back, the Confederates sustained heavier losses than the Federals.

COUNT OFF!

At Frayser's Farm (also called Glendale), Union casualties were 2,853 killed and/or wounded; Confederate losses were 3,615 killed and/or wounded.

Malvern Hill

After Frayser's Farm, McClellan withdrew his entire army to Malvern Hill, a low, two-mile-wide ridge alongside the James River. Having reached Malvern Hill meant the failure of McClellan's Peninsula Campaign. At great cost, McClellan had failed to take Richmond and, at the end of the Seven Days, was farther from the rebel capital than he had been at the start.

Yet all was not lost. The Union general had positioned his army on the high ground and could not be flanked (attacked on a vulnerable side), which put Lee at a great disadvantage. Nevertheless, recognizing that this was his last opportunity to destroy the Army of the Potomac, Lee attacked Malvern Hill on July 1.

By now, the results were all too predictable. Poor coordination was combined with terrain that made it impossible to bring more than a fraction of the Confederate artillery up to support the piecemeal attacks. By deadly accurate Union artillery fire—the massed cannons were almost wheel to wheel—Lee was repulsed and two of McClellan's field officers, Porter and Colonel Henry J. Hunt, urged their commander to seize the initiative now, hold Malvern Hill, and order a counterattack. But McClellan was thoroughly intimidated by his adversary. Instead of fighting, he completed the withdrawal to Harrison's Landing.

Success and Glory; Disaster and Shame

With the completion of McClellan's retreat, the vaunted Peninsula Campaign was over. Tactically, perhaps, McClellan had been successful. Commanding the larger army, he had sustained during the Seven Days a total of about 16,000 casualties (killed and/or wounded), whereas Lee's smaller force suffered nearly 20,000 casualties. Strategically, however, Lee clearly won. He had kept McClellan from taking Richmond.

Pope Takes Command

One victim of the Seven Days wasn't on any casualty rolls. George Brinton McClellan, entrenched at Harrison's Landing, protesting that Lee's army numbered near 200,000 (a wild overestimate due to McClellan's overcaution and spymaster Pinkerton's miscalculation), continually appealed for reinforcements. Lincoln had had enough. He called on General John Pope, who had shown such leadership as commander of the Army of the Mississippi, to take command of the new Army of Virginia (a consolidation of several forces).

This catch-all force was supposed to operate in coordination with McClellan's Army of the Potomac, its initial mission to draw Confederate forces away from Richmond, so that McClellan could finally assault the rebel capital. Pope believed his mission was doomed, and hightailed it back to Washington as soon as possible, devoting himself to a combination of public relations and political lobbying while he left his army to fend for itself in the field.

Hoping to gain control of the Army of the Potomac, Pope filled President Lincoln's ears with poison against McClellan, suggesting that the "Young Napoleon's" chronic tendency to an excess of caution was not so much a matter of military philosophy as it was a function of politics. As a Democrat, Pope told Lincoln, McClellan was in no hurry to win a war that would bring an end to slavery. As for McClellan, he took an inordinately long time to start the Army of the Potomac marching back down the peninsula to board steamers to take them up the Chesapeake Bay to join Pope.

Union General John Pope, victorious in the West, was summoned to take command in the East. His arrogance earned him hatred from the South and resentment from the North.
(Harper's Pictorial History of the Civil War, 1866)

Just before he left for Washington, however, Pope, perhaps the most obnoxious general ever to lead an army, found time to address the men of the Army of Virginia only to scold them for their failure to win victories. He also gave orders to treat the citizens of Virginia as a conquered people, freely seizing their food when he needed it and threatening to execute as traitors Southern civilians and soldiers alike. Pope's policy provoked Robert E. Lee to label the Union general a "miscreant," who "should be suppressed."

At the beginning of August, Pope shuttled back and forth between northern Virginia and Washington while most of McClellan's Army of the Potomac remained dug in on the peninsula. Henry Wager Halleck, now officially the Union army's general-in-chief (McClellan's old job) gave McClellan a direct order to hasten to northern Virginia to join his army to Pope's.

McClellan's delay provided Lee an opportunity. He ordered Stonewall Jackson to attack part of Pope's army at Cedar Mountain, near Culpeper, Virginia, on August 9, before it could be reinforced by any of McClellan's men. In itself, this battle was of slight consequence, but it was only the opening move in what would prove Pope's undoing.

Lee maneuvered Pope into retreat north of the Rappahannock River. Knowing that speed was of the essence, Lee boldly violated a cornerstone of military tactics: he divided his army in the presence of the enemy.

Separated from Pope by only the shallow Rappahannock, Lee put half his forces under the command of Major General James Longstreet to occupy Pope's front while he sent the other half under Stonewall Jackson on a roundabout march to the northwest—to make a surprise attack on the rear of Pope's army.

In the meantime, in a quick raid, some of Pope's troops captured Jeb Stuart's adjutant. Stuart himself managed to escape, but the raiders snatched his fancy plumed hat and scarlet-lined cloak. By way of retaliation, Stuart, on August 22, raided and overran Pope's headquarters camp at Catlett's Station and made off with $35,000 in payroll greenbacks, Pope's personal baggage (including *his* dress uniform coat), 300 prisoners, and papers that gave Lee critical information about Pope's battle plans.

To add to Pope's consternation, Jackson destroyed his supply depot at Manassas Junction, Virginia—near the site of the Bull Run battle—on August 26, cutting off Pope's rail and telegraph communications. Pope turned to pursue Jackson, but was unable to find him until Jackson showed himself by attacking Brigadier General Rufus King at Groveton on August 28. It was a fierce battle in which the Union's "Black Hat Brigade" (or "Iron Brigade," as it was later called) demonstrated incredible heroism, suffering a 33 percent casualty rate.

Alerted to Jackson's position, Pope concentrated his main force near Groveton, intent on destroying Jackson once and for all. The *Second* Battle of Bull Run was about to begin.

Slow March to Freedom

While Jackson and Lee were (sometimes literally) running rings around Union commanders, the U.S. government marched slowly toward making emancipation and abolition issues of the war. On July 17, 1862, Congress passed a second Confiscation Act, which authorized the "confiscation" of slaves owned by supporters of the "rebellion." This was a stronger, broader, and more forthright measure than the first Confiscation Act, of August 1861, which merely conferred "contraband" status on slaves whose labor had been used directly in the war effort.

On July 22, 1862, Lincoln showed his first draft of an "emancipation proclamation" to the cabinet. He heeded their advice, however, to keep it under wraps until the Union army had achieved a significant victory. To proclaim emancipation now (the cabinet argued), in the shadow of defeat, would at worst appear like an act of desperation and, at best, would be a hollow gesture.

Second Bull Run

Pope faced the culmination of the Second Bull Run campaign with confidence. No longer fighting rearguard actions, it was he who launched the attack on August 29, 1862, boasting that he would "bag the whole crowd," meaning Jackson, Lee, and all the subordinate Confederate generals.

Pope seized and held the initiative on the first day of the battle, hammering at Jackson's Confederates, who nevertheless refused to yield. Having repulsed Pope's repeated attacks, Jackson did not attempt to hold his ground, but made a tactical withdrawal. Confused or falling victim to wishful thinking, Pope interpreted this as a full-out retreat. Proclaiming himself victorious, he vowed a hot pursuit—in 24 hours.

WAR NEWS

A story buzzed throughout the Union army in 1862 that Major General John Pope made it a practice to preface all his written orders with the phrase "Headquarters in the Saddle." In response to this extraordinary piece of pomposity, some wag—no one knows who for sure—remarked that this precisely described the general's main deficiency: he had his headquarters where his hindquarters should be.

Pope was utterly unaware that the other half of Lee's divided army, under General Longstreet, had arrived about 11:00, but hadn't yet joined the battle. Longstreet did not fail to fight the next day, August 30, and instead of launching a hot pursuit, Pope found himself on the receiving end of a battle even hotter than the day before. Five rebel divisions under Longstreet stormed into the Union flank along a two-mile front.

Pope suffered a very costly tactical defeat, and again a shattered Union army was humiliated at Bull Run. However, the exhausted Confederates didn't give chase, allowing Pope's troops to retreat intact.

COUNT OFF!

Second Bull Run was a bigger and costlier battle than First Bull Run. Pope commanded 75,696 Union troops against the Confederates' 48,527. The Union lost 1,724 killed, 8,372 wounded, and 5,958 missing—a staggering 21 percent casualty rate. The Confederates lost 1,481 killed, 7,627 wounded, and 89 missing—an almost equally devastating 19 percent casualty rate.

Just three days after Second Bull Run, a deflated John Pope was relieved of command in the East and was exiled to the U.S. Army's Department of the Northwest to fight the Sioux in Minnesota. McClellan, who had never been officially relieved of command of the Army of the Potomac (but had been ordered to turn much of it over to Pope), was once again put in full charge of that army.

Dragon Dix and the Angel of the Battlefield

A Civil War soldier was far more likely to be wounded than killed. Unfortunately, as Union Surgeon General William A. Hammond remarked years after the war, "the Civil War was fought at the end of the medical Middle Ages." This meant that a wounded soldier was eight times more likely to die from his wounds than a World War I doughboy, who fought 60 years later. He was even more likely to succumb to disease than to be wounded or killed in battle.

It was not just that medical science was far less advanced in the 1860s than in the 1910s, but that so few resources were devoted to even the most basic care of the wounded and the most fundamental issues of sanitation. A handful of dedicated men—and especially women—sought to improve this horrific situation.

Dorothea Lynde Dix was born in 1802 in Hampden, Maine. She left her schoolteacher's position in 1836, traveled, and became a passionate advocate for the improvement of conditions in American prisons and institutions for the mentally ill. She earned an international reputation as a reformer, and soon after the commencement of the Civil War in 1861, she was appointed Superintendent of Women Nurses for the Union army.

Enter the Nurses

Dix created the foundation of what would become the Army Nursing Corps, and more immediately, introduced a level of basic sanitation and humanity into the care of those wounded in a war that had taken weaponry to a new level of destructiveness.

Determined and deliberately overbearing, she ruled her nursing corps with an iron hand—"Dragon Dix," they called her—but she made the profession respectable for women, eased unspeakable suffering, and saved untold lives.

But relief for the wounded was never solely the work of the government or the army. The U.S. Sanitary Commission was formed by prominent private citizens to improve conditions for the sick and wounded, and Clara Barton (1821–1912), for 18 years a schoolteacher in Massachusetts and New Jersey and then a clerk in the U.S. Patent Office in Washington, D.C., almost single-handedly organized an agency to obtain and distribute supplies for wounded soldiers. She personally visited the battlefields and field hospitals, carrying supplies in a wagon she drove herself, and her kind demeanor, the opposite of Dix's steely sternness, won her the soldiers' grateful affection.

Called the "Angel of the Battlefield," Clara Barton was a former teacher and patent clerk who took it upon herself to bring supplies and comfort to the Union wounded. Some years after the war, she founded the American Red Cross.
(Library of Congress)

They called Barton the "Angel of the Battlefield." Later in the war, she would set up a bureau of records to try to identify the unknown dead on both sides. After the war, in 1881, she established the American National Red Cross.

Walt Whitman Among the Wounded

Dix, Barton, and the professional women associated with them were not the only nurses in the war. Relatives of soldiers and concerned volunteers also pitched in to assist soldiers who had been assigned as nurses. One such was Walt Whitman, a self-published poet from Long Island, New York, who, in 1862, went to Fredericksburg, Virginia, to tend to his wounded brother, a soldier in the Union army. Whitman remained in camp for a time, caring for his brother and other wounded soldiers, and then he took a temporary job in the paymaster's office in Washington. In his off-hours, he visited the wounded and dying in the Washington hospitals. He spent his meager salary on treats for the young men, to whom he read or with whom he spoke, always in an effort to cheer them as best he could.

Best known for such poems as *Song of Myself* and "When Lilacs Last in the Dooryard Bloom'd," Whitman also wrote unblinking prose descriptions of his work among the wounded (in *Specimen Days*, 1882) and fine, honest, war verse (in *Drum-Taps*, 1865, and *Sequel to Drum-Taps*, 1866). These lines are from "The Dresser" of 1865:

> Returning, resuming, I thread my way through the hospitals;
> The hurt and wounded I pacify with soothing hand,
> I sit by the restless all the dark night—some are so young;
> Some suffer so much—I recall the experience sweet and sad;
> (Many a soldier's loving arms about this neck have cross'd and rested,
> Many a soldier's kiss dwells on these bearded lips.)

The Least You Need to Know

- McClellan's chronic hesitation caused him to bungle the Peninsula Campaign, greatly prolonging the war.
- The Seven Days' Battles were tremendously costly. Although McClellan was the tactical victor, Robert E. Lee won the all-important strategic objective of fending off an invasion of Richmond, the Confederate capital.
- Union General John Pope's defeat at the Second Battle of Bull Run was even more disastrous than the defeat suffered at the First Battle of Bull Run.
- Dorothea Dix, Clara Barton, and Walt Whitman were among the sympathetic civilians who provided nursing care for wounded soldiers.

Die to Make Men Free

In this part, you'll understand how the war took on a deeper moral dimension for the North after Lincoln's preliminary Emancipation Proclamation of September 22, 1862. But this hardly made for a shortcut to victory, as you'll see when you read about the Union disasters at Fredericksburg and at Chancellorsville.

The Confederate military victories continued to come, but always at great cost. Southern civilians suffered from ever-worsening shortages of food, goods, and cash as, behind the lines, the Confederacy faltered.

In this part, you'll see the ruthless toll the war exacted on both the North and South, becoming a contest not merely of military superiority, but, on both sides, of national will.

In Blood Proclaimed

In This Chapter

- Lincoln and emancipation
- Lee invades Maryland
- The Battle of Antietam
- The true effects of the Emancipation Proclamation

George Washington was called the "Father of His Country," Andrew Jackson "Old Hickory," and Abraham Lincoln "the Great Emancipator." Yet when General John Charles Frémont had taken it upon himself to liberate Missouri's slaves, Lincoln promptly annulled the order. When General David Hunter—commanding the U.S. Army's Department of the South—took Fort Pulaski, Georgia, in April 1862, and freed slaves living within the reach of his military jurisdiction, Lincoln annulled that order as well.

This chapter explains "the Great Emancipator's" cautious position on slavery and how the Civil War finally did become a fight "to make men free."

The Prayer of Twenty Million

Abraham Lincoln did not relish annulling the emancipation orders his generals had issued. He was no lover of slavery ("If slavery is not wrong, nothing is wrong," he famously remarked). Nevertheless, in 1862, he understood that most Union soldiers were not fighting the war to end slavery, but to preserve the Union. He feared that defining *emancipation* (the freeing of slaves) as the purpose of the war would alienate many soldiers and turn volunteers away. He also feared that the border states would fly to the cause of the South if he suddenly announced that the goal of the war was to end slavery.

> **DEFINITION**
>
> To **emancipate** is to free from bondage or involuntary servitude.

Yet throughout the North, the voices calling for emancipation grew more numerous and more strident. On August 19, 1862, Horace Greeley, influential editor of the *New York Tribune*, published in his paper an open letter to Abraham Lincoln on behalf (he said) of the 20 million citizens of the loyal states. He took the president to task for annulling his generals' orders of emancipation, for failing to enforce the Confiscation Acts (discussed in Chapter 10), and for refusing to understand that "no loyal person [could be] rightfully held in Slavery by a traitor." Greeley called for immediate emancipation.

The president replied, by "open" letter, just three days later:

> … My paramount object in this struggle is to save the Union, and is not either to save or destroy Slavery. If I could save the Union without freeing any slave, I would do it; and if I could save it by freeing all the slaves, I would do it; and if I could do it by freeing some and leaving others alone, I would also do that. What I do about Slavery and the colored race, I do because I believe it helps to save this Union; and what I forbear, I forbear because I do not believe it would help to save the Union ….

Even as he denied any motive to end slavery, Lincoln continued to polish his draft of the Emancipation Proclamation, awaiting only the right time to make it public.

"Again I Have Been Called Upon to Save the Country"

That time was not now. Not after the disastrous defeat of Pope and the Union forces at Second Bull Run (see Chapter 10), which produced Union casualties *five times* what they had been at the first humiliating Bull Run defeat. In desperation, Lincoln restored full command of the Army of the Potomac, augmented by the troops Pope had led, to George McClellan, believing that, for all his grave faults as a combat commander, McClellan commanded the love and loyalty of his troops.

"Again I have been called upon to save the country," McClellan wrote to his wife.

Invasion Plans

On September 5, 1862, Robert E. Lee dramatically changed the conduct of the war. He led his Army of Northern Virginia across the Potomac into Maryland, thereby invading the North with about 60,000 men.

Shifting from defense to offense was yet another of Lee's astoundingly bold moves. The army he led, however, looked like anything but an army of invasion. Many of his men lacked shoes, not to mention ammunition. But Lee understood that the South could not win a long war of attrition. The North, with far more men, money, and munitions, would surely prevail if the struggle went on long enough. Lee believed that the best hope for the South was to win over the border states—of which Maryland was the most important—gain international credibility and, in the process, destroy the North's morale and its will to continue the fight.

This, at least, was Lee's intention. Historical hindsight suggests the South might have fared better with a defensive strategy punctuated by opportunistic counteroffensives. Considering the outcome, Lee's invasion of the North was a strategic blunder.

The Lost Order

Then something incredible happened. Lee drew up Special Order Number 191, which detailed his plan for opening the invasion of the North. He distributed copies to his generals, including Stonewall Jackson, who in turn copied a set for General Daniel Harvey Hill. Hill, who may have already received the order from Lee, either carelessly discarded the copy or it may have been lost before reaching him. In any case, on September 13, Union troops occupied the campground Hill had just vacated. There, Union Private W. B. Mitchell, 27th Indiana, found the discarded or dropped document wrapped around some cigars. Mitchell coveted the cigars, but he also realized that he had something more important, and he passed the paper to his superiors, who sent it to McClellan.

McClellan must have rubbed his hands together with glee when he announced: "Here is a paper with which, if I cannot whip Bobby Lee, I will be willing to go home."

Yet McClellan also hesitated—prompted by an equally fretful Henry Wager Halleck—he believed Lee had twice the number of men he actually commanded and feared that the "lost order" might be a lure to a trap. So instead of boldly exploiting the intercepted order, McClellan sent forces to timidly probe three gaps in South Mountain on September 14. Stiff resistance from Hill bought Lee enough time to establish the main part of his army west of Antietam Creek, near the town of Sharpsburg.

The Battle of Antietam

After Shiloh and the Seven Days, no one would have thought that fighting could be harder or more fierce. But Antietam would be the scene of the hardest fighting yet.

The Blast of a Thousand Bugles

McClellan seems to have planned an attack to strike at both of Lee's flanks, and then attack the center with his reserves. However, when it came on April 17, the attack was an uncoordinated series of piecemeal assaults. Union General Joseph "Fighting Joe" Hooker drove back Stonewall Jackson's corps so far, so quickly, that Lee was forced to order up reserves. Daniel Harvey Hill's and James Longstreet's rebels joined the battle in the East and West Woods, in Farmer Miller's cornfield, and around a church belonging to a German pacifist sect called the Dunkards.

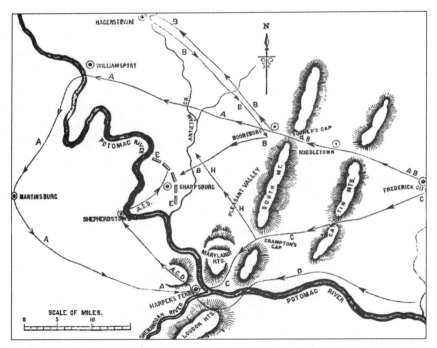

The Antietam battlefield and vicinity. Sharpsburg, the focal point of the fighting, is between the Potomac (to the west) and Antietam Creek (to the east).
(Harper's Pictorial History of the Civil War, 1866)

Bloody Lane

By midday, the fighting shifted to the center, along a sunken farm road ever after called the "Bloody Lane," which was held by Confederate General D. H. Hill. It took three divisions of Union Major General Edwin "Bull" Sumner's corps and five horrific hours to drive Hill out of this position.

By mid-afternoon, the Union left wing, commanded by General Ambrose Burnside, broke through the Confederate line after many delays, which had been caused largely by Burnside's insistence on capturing a bridge instead of immediately fording shallow Antietam Creek. By the time Burnside broke through, however, A. P. Hill, whose troops had just arrived from Harpers Ferry, made a surprise counterattack that pushed him back.

"McClellan's … infantry fell upon the left of Lee's lines with the crushing weight of a landslide," Confederate Brigadier General John Brown Gordon recalled. But when Lee approached the line, the troops "re-formed … and with a shout as piercing as the blast of a thousand bugles, rushed in countercharge upon the exulting Federals [and] hurled them back in confusion."

Despite McClellan's erroneous intelligence reports, his troops far outnumbered the Confederates, and the sheer weight of this superiority, coupled with the grit of the fighting men, finally drove the rebels back to the outskirts of Sharpsburg. Yet McClellan persistently refused to accept that he indeed held the advantage. In the days following the battle, he did not pursue the withdrawing Confederates, who escaped back across the Potomac and into Virginia. Once again, an opportunity to destroy a Confederate army had been lost.

Before the Battle of Antietam, this was a sunken road. During the battle, it became infamous as "Bloody Lane."
(Library of Congress)

Slow Road to Emancipation

Historians call Antietam the "single bloodiest day of the war." Union casualties numbered about 12,000, while Confederate losses may have been close to 14,000, if the missing are included.

Tactically, the battle was a draw. Strategically, it was both a Union victory and tragedy. McClellan drove Lee out of Maryland, but he missed an opportunity to destroy the Army of Northern Virginia and, perhaps, end the war.

COUNT OFF!

The Union threw 75,316 young men into the Antietam meat grinder. Of these, 2,108 were killed, 9,549 were wounded, and 753 went missing. The Confederates engaged 51,844, losing some 2,700 killed, 9,024 wounded, and approximately 2,000 missing.

Preliminary Proclamation

Whatever was and was not accomplished at Antietam, Lincoln judged it enough of a victory to issue a preliminary Emancipation Proclamation on September 23, 1862. In hindsight, this seems a timid document, its rhetoric more legalistic than inspiring, because Lincoln wanted to define what he was doing as an act of "military necessity," and thus within his power as president. He was at pains to ensure that the proclamation could not be challenged later as unconstitutional.

The preliminary proclamation stated that "all persons held as slaves within any State or any designated part of a State, the people whereof shall be in rebellion against the United States, shall then [i.e., on January 1, 1863], thenceforward, and forever be free ...." It further stated that on January 1, 1863, the executive would designate the states and parts of states that were in rebellion, and that this would be determined by whether the state, or part of a state, was duly represented in the Congress of the United States. Tennessee was exempted altogether from the proclamation, as were the counties slated to form the new state of West Virginia.

Forever Free

By the end of the year, three congressional districts occupied by Union troops—two in southeast Louisiana and one in eastern Virginia—had elected representatives to the U.S. Congress; these areas were deemed no longer in rebellion and thus their slaves remained enslaved. Slaves were immediately freed in all other areas occupied by the Union army, including northern Arkansas; various parts of northern Alabama, Mississippi, and Virginia (Jefferson County, the lower Shenandoah Valley, and the area around Alexandria); northeastern North Carolina; coastal enclaves in South Carolina, Georgia, and Florida; and Baton Rouge, Louisiana (captured December 20, 1862). It is likely that at least 20,000 slaves were immediately freed, and as the war progressed and the Union armies advanced, more and more were liberated.

Congress Acts

Tentative as the Emancipation Proclamation might seem from our perspective, it was a momentous document and probably just right for its time and circumstances. It gave the war new moral force. For those who chose to see the Civil War as a war to make men free, the document officially made it such a struggle.

The proclamation was sufficiently temperate to avoid inflaming the occupied South and the border states, but reaction from the Confederacy was violent. Richmond stated that black soldiers and their white officers would be executed upon capture, as indeed later many were. General Beauregard went so far as to say that, after January 1, 1863, *all* Union prisoners should be executed, and the means of execution should be strangulation by garrote.

Before the war ended, Congress would take action beyond the proclamation. The 13th Amendment to the U.S. Constitution was passed by the Senate on April 8, 1864, and by the House (after a fight) on January 31, 1865. By December 18, 1865, the measure was ratified by the states. The amendment is brief: "Neither slavery nor involuntary servitude, except as a punishment for crime whereof the party shall have been duly convicted, shall exist within the United States, or any place subject to their jurisdiction."

The Least You Need to Know

- Lincoln moved cautiously on the issue of emancipation to avoid alienating his soldiers and officers (most of whom were not abolitionists), and to avoid losing the tenuous loyalty of the border states.

- Because of General John Pope's terrible defeat at the Second Battle of Bull Run, Lincoln reinstated General George B. McClellan to command of the Army of the Potomac.

- Antietam saw the "bloodiest single day of the Civil War." While McClellan achieved a narrow victory for the Union, he tragically missed an opportunity to destroy Lee's Army of Northern Virginia and perhaps bring the war to an end.

- The Emancipation Proclamation freed slaves immediately in parts of nine of the seceded states that were occupied by Union forces. Slaves living in the border states of Maryland, Kentucky, Missouri, and Tennessee were not liberated by law until the 13th Amendment was ratified in December 1865.

A Worse Place Than Hell

Chapter 12

In This Chapter

- McClellan is permanently relieved of command
- Burnside assumes command
- Burnside's blunders
- General Joseph Hooker takes command

Before Antietam, the Confederacy had reached what historians call its "high-water mark." It had invaded the North, Great Britain was on the verge of recognizing it as a sovereign nation, and the Union seemed incapable of doing anything about either of these things. But the narrow Federal victory at Antietam began the ebbing of that Southern tide. Lee blamed his defeat on the loss of Special Order Number 191. However for failing to pursue and crush Lee, George McClellan had no one to blame but himself. (Nevertheless, he blamed Lincoln for having failed to give him the endless reinforcements he thought he needed.)

The president's patience was growing short. To friends and colleagues, he complained that McClellan suffered from a bad case of the "slows." In contrast, Lee, strategically defeated at Antietam, simply refused to act as if he had been beaten. This chapter chronicles the next step in Lincoln's desperate search for a commander to match the Confederacy's greatest general.

A Second Ride Around

Abraham Lincoln was a patient man, but the blood of Antietam weighed heavily on him. McClellan had purchased little with all that carnage. The battle was over on September 17. The rest of that month passed without action from McClellan. On

October 1, Lincoln ordered McClellan to "cross the Potomac and give battle to the enemy."

McClellan did nothing.

A week later he wrote his general demanding to know why he had not attacked, McClellan replied that his cavalry was exhausted and the horses fatigued. At this the president's patience finally snapped: "Will you pardon me for asking," he wrote in reply, "what the horses of your army have done since the battle of Antietam that fatigues anything?"

In the meantime, Lee sent Jeb Stuart back into the North. This time it was not into Maryland, a contested border state, but into Pennsylvania, a solid nonslavery state. Having famously ridden around McClellan's army before the Battle of Mechanicsville at the start of the Seven Days (see Chapter 10), Stuart rode around him a *second* time, during October 9–12, 1862, to raid the Pennsylvania town of Chambersburg.

The raid was of no great military significance—500 horses were captured and a machine shop was wrecked, along with several stores—but it tweaked the collective noses of the North. Stuart's cavalry troopers had camped openly in the very streets of a Union town in a Union state!

On October 26, McClellan finally began to march south, to Warrenton, Virginia, but so slowly that Lee was able to interpose his army between the Federal forces and Richmond. On November 7, 1862, General-in-chief Halleck sent the Young Napoleon a telegram:

> General: On receipt of the order of the President, sent herewith, you will immediately turn over your command to Major General Burnside, and repair to Trenton, N.J., reporting your arrival at that place, by telegraph, for further orders.

George Brinton McClellan had been fired.

Popular, Reluctant, Hapless: Burnside

A native of Liberty, Indiana, and a West Point graduate, Ambrose Everett Burnside (1824–1881) cut a handsome military figure. His trademark mutton-chop whiskers became a popular fashion and have been known by an inversion of his name ever since: *sideburns*. Like McClellan, he was popular with his troops, whose affection and respect he readily returned.

Ambrose E. Burnside (seated, arms folded), pictured here with some of his Rhode Island regimental staff, reluctantly accepted command of the Army of the Potomac. (Library of Congress)

Unlike McClellan, Burnside was modest, with little confidence in his own capacity for leadership. He twice declined Lincoln's offer of command of the Army of the Potomac before accepting, with great reluctance, the president's third entreaty.

Slaughter at Fredericksburg

Burnside marched his army just north of the Rappahannock River at Warrenton, Virginia—30 miles from Lee's army, which consisted of just two corps, commanded by James Longstreet and Stonewall Jackson. Jackson's corps had been stationed in the Valley, and was under orders from Lee to rejoin him. Briefly, Burnside had an opportunity to *defeat* the Confederates *in detail*. Instead, overly eager to please, he yielded to congressional demands for a quick, decisive victory and advanced toward Richmond to attack well south of Warrenton, at Fredericksburg.

General Sumner's division arrived at a position across the Rappahannock from Fredericksburg on November 17. Confederate General Longstreet would not reach the town until the next day. Burnside should have ordered Sumner to cross the river immediately, but he insisted instead on waiting for the arrival of five *pontoon bridges* (transportable temporary bridges) that had somehow gone astray, and ordered

Sumner's troops to make camp on the river's north bank. This gave Longstreet ample time to entrench defensively in the hills south and west of Fredericksburg.

DEFINITION

To **defeat in detail** is the time-honored tactic of attacking the spread-out elements of an enemy force one by one before they have time to unite in a single, more powerful unit. A **pontoon bridge** is a transportable temporary bridge resting on floating pontoons or pontoon boats rather than on permanent piers or pilings.

Burnside's tragic delay stretched into days, and each day, Lee fortified his defensive positions even more strongly. On December 11, 78,000 Confederates were securely dug in on the south bank of the Rappahannock, with the town between them and the river. At last, on December 11, Burnside's bridges were in place, and the Union crossing began. But with Lee entrenched, the conditions necessary for Union success had vanished, the crossing was senseless, and the attack doomed.

Confederates destroyed the bridges across the Rappahannock, photographed in April 1863 by Union Captain A. J. Russell. The figures on the far side are soldiers of Barksdale's Mississippi Brigade. It is believed that this is the only photograph of active Confederate soldiers taken by a Union photographer.
(Library of Congress)

With Stonewall Jackson, General James Longstreet was a principal Confederate commander at Fredericksburg.
(Harper's Pictorial History of the Civil War, 1866)

"A Chicken Could Not Live"

The main phase of the Battle of Fredericksburg took place on December 13, 1862. Despite some success against Jackson on the Confederate left, the Union effort fell apart when Burnside made a series of hopeless assaults on the Confederates' impregnable hilltop positions. Even as the Federal dead piled up before a stone wall in front of a sunken road below the Confederates' chief position at Marye's Heights, Burnside continued to order one assault after another.

One Federal officer described the battle as "murder, not warfare," and an artillery officer of Longstreet's corps remarked, "a chicken could not live on that field when we open[ed] on it."

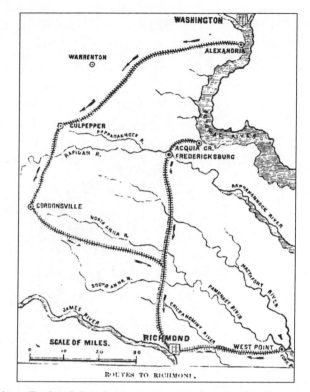

This map shows Fredericksburg's strategic position between Washington, to the north, and Richmond, to the south.

(Harper's Pictorial History of the Civil War, 1866)

COUNT OFF!

The Battle of Fredericksburg stands as one of the worst defeats in the history of the U.S. Army. It is estimated that 106,000 Union soldiers participated in the attacks; 12,700 were killed or wounded. Confederate losses were 5,300 killed or wounded out of some 72,500 engaged.

"I Am Responsible"

Burnside ordered 14 charges, each of them a virtual suicide mission. At dusk he announced, weeping, that he would lead the final attack personally. Instead, he at last allowed himself to be persuaded to withdraw back across the Rappahannock. He heard his aide call for three cheers as he rode past his men. The men responded with a silence as dead as the dead soldiers below Marye's Heights.

Burnside reported to his superior, Henry Wager Halleck: "For the failure in the attack I am responsible .... To the families and friends of the dead I can offer my heartfelt sympathies, but for the wounded I can offer my earnest prayers for their comfortable and final recovery."

"Heartfelt Sympathies ... Earnest Prayers"

To be killed in battle was the hard fate that awaited many young men of the North and the South, but to be wounded was often even harder. "Earnest prayers" were typically about all that could be offered a wounded soldier.

Modern Weapons, Medieval Medicine

Civil War weapons could inflict far more damage than doctors could repair.

For abdominal or head wounds, next to nothing could be done, and the best a surgeon might offer a man wounded in the leg or arm was a quick amputation. Chloroform, the only anesthetic, was widely used but (especially on the Southern side) was often in short supply. The practice of *antisepsis*—the destruction of infection-causing bacteria—would not emerge until the British physician Joseph Lister discovered the work of Louis Pasteur in 1865, the closing year of the American Civil War.

In field hospitals, wounds were often poorly cleaned and dressings were not sterile. To stanch the flow of blood, wounds were packed with lint, material obtained from scraping linen cloth. Surgeons did perform complex operations, but even if an operation or procedure was successful, relatively minor wounds routinely became infected—causing fever, illness, and often death. Nor did one have to be wounded to contract a dread disease. More men died of disease in the Civil War than of wounds sustained on the battlefield.

Mary Edwards Walker, M.D.

As we saw in Chapter 10, such tireless reformers as Dorothea Dix and Clara Barton struggled to bring skilled nursing care and a decent level of sanitation to the battlefield. If female nurses were accepted grudgingly by the military medical establishment, women doctors were all but unheard of.

Mary Edwards Walker, born in Oswego, New York, on November 26, 1832, bucked the male-dominated medical establishment by earning admission to, and graduation, from Syracuse Medical College. During the 1840s and 1850s, she struggled to survive in her Cincinnati, Ohio, practice and gained little professional acceptance from either gender.

Mary Edwards Walker, M.D., was finally allowed to practice field surgery in 1864, and was the first woman awarded the Medal of Honor.
(National Archives and Records Administration)

With the outbreak of the war, Walker volunteered her medical services in the only capacity the Union army would allow: as a nurse. Early in 1864, however, an Ohio regiment hired her as a "contract surgeon" for six months and, in October of that year, the Union army at last commissioned her as an assistant surgeon. During her tour of duty, she saw service not only as a physician, but, reputedly, also as a spy. Walker, who was known for looking after wounded on both sides, was captured by Confederates when she stopped to treat a wounded rebel. She spent four months in a Southern prison camp.

Walker was the first woman to be awarded the Medal of Honor. However in 1919, the Board of Medals revoked the award because she was not an official member of the armed forces. "You can have it over my dead body," the 87-year-old physician told federal authorities. Six days later, she died. The medal was not officially restored to her until 1977.

Shoddy Goods: A Soldier's Life

It was not only the sick and wounded soldier who suffered during the Civil War. Weather and exposure are ever-present adversaries that take no sides and give no quarter, especially to men who are ill-equipped. And Civil War soldiers, both North and South, were about as ill-equipped as any troops of the nineteenth century.

Corruption and war profiteering were rampant in the North. The soldiers' rations, poor at best, were sometimes downright deadly, as purveyors foisted condemned meat on military commissaries.

Even the proud blue uniforms fell apart as government contractors started making them of what came to be called *shoddy*, made up of waste fabric that was not woven but compounded and glued together. It looked good enough when brand new, but would disintegrate and dissolve on exposure to the weather.

 DEFINITION

The word **shoddy** is derived from the Civil War, meaning a kind of cloth made from scraps of material compounded and glued rather than woven together and, therefore, subject to disintegration. Today, it's an adjective applied to anything cheap or poorly made.

Bad as all this was, conditions were even worse for the Confederates. True, they had won a great victory at Fredericksburg, but the men faced the onset of winter even more poorly clothed and meagerly fed than the Northern soldiers. This was not due to corruption and profiteering, but to lack of money. Scott's Anaconda—the naval blockade of the South so roundly mocked at the beginning of the war (see Chapter 6)—was gaining in effectiveness with each passing week. Worse, recognition by the great European powers was not forthcoming. Despite the Southern victory at Fredericksburg, the failure of the Confederate invasion of the North at Antietam, coupled with the moral high ground seized by the Union with the Emancipation Proclamation, turned France and Britain away from any thought of active alliance with the Confederacy.

North and South, soldiers shivered miserably around their campfires during the dreary winter of 1862 into 1863.

The Mud March

After the useless bloodshed of Fredericksburg, Burnside was determined to cross the Rappahannock again to renew the fight. He started to turn back to cross the river downstream from Lee's strong position, but some of Burnside's alarmed subordinates alerted President Lincoln, who vetoed this movement.

So the Army of the Potomac huddled in winter quarters until January 20, 1863, when Burnside began to execute what looked like a much sounder strategy. He would envelop Lee's army via a river crossing called Banks's Ford. But a two-day torrent of icy rain transformed the scarred landscape into a quagmire, and the movement became known as the "Mud March."

The all-too-symbolic spectacle of an entire army bogged down in impassable mud, its morale at rock-bottom, was too much for the Union and for Abraham Lincoln to bear. On January 26, 1863, the president relieved Ambrose Burnside as commander of the Army of the Potomac and replaced him with Joseph "Fighting Joe" Hooker.

 WAR NEWS

Relieved of command in November 1862, George B. McClellan resigned from the army and, in 1864, ran against Lincoln as the Democratic candidate for president. In contrast, Burnside accepted responsibility for Fredericksburg and selflessly volunteered for a series of subordinate commands. He proved himself an able subordinate until the Battle of the Crater (see Chapter 19), when his mismanagement contributed to a tragic defeat. Found culpable by a court of inquiry, he resigned from the army in April 1865.

Give Us Victories

Fredericksburg had been hell for the Union soldiers who fought there. For Abraham Lincoln, unable to find a winning general, it was almost worse: "If there is a worse place than hell, I am in it."

To Hooker, Lincoln wrote: "What I now ask of you is military success …. Beware of rashness, but with energy and sleepless vigilance go forward and give us victories."

Fighting Joe

Joseph Hooker (1814–1879) was born in Hadley, Massachusetts, and graduated from West Point in 1837. He served in the Second Seminole War (1835–1843) and in the Mexican War, fighting alongside Robert E. Lee and Thomas J. Jackson (long before anyone called him "Stonewall"). Hooker fought well and bravely, but was inclined to be disloyal to his commander. During the U.S.-Mexican War, there was a dispute between General Gideon Pillow and Hooker's commanding officer, General Winfield Scott. Hooker took Pillow's side, and Scott never forgave him. When the Civil War broke out, Scott snubbed Hooker when he, having earlier resigned from the army, sought an officer's commission.

"Fighting Joe" Hooker, hard-drinking and full of bluff and bluster, always ready to speak ill of a superior officer, replaced Burnside after Fredericksburg.
(Harper's Pictorial History of the Civil War, 1866)

At the First Battle of Bull Run, Hooker was just one of the many civilians who watched the fighting. He pestered Lincoln with unsolicited advice, and when he finally obtained an audience with the president, he told him: "I was at … Bull Run … and it is neither vanity nor boasting in me to declare that I am a damned sight better general than you, sir, had on that field."

Lincoln personally commissioned Hooker a brigadier general of volunteers. He fought well under McClellan, but his disloyal streak surfaced when he mocked his commander as an "infant among soldiers." Little wonder then that the army's senior officer corps did not welcome Hooker's appointment as commander of the Army of the Potomac.

As for his nickname, "Fighting Joe," Hooker hated it. It had been attached to him by accident when newspapers all over the country printed the headline of an Associated Press article covering Hooker during the Seven Days' Battles, "Fighting—Joe Hooker," without the dash: "Fighting Joe Hooker."

Of Cavalry and Balloons

Whatever senior officers thought, the common soldier greeted the advent of Joseph Hooker with great excitement. He roused the Army of the Potomac out of its despair and restored its morale. He greatly upgraded the quality of rations and clothing—insisting fresh-baked bread be issued instead of the hated hardtack—and he mercilessly pursued and prosecuted corrupt *commissary* officers.

> **DEFINITION**
>
> The **commissary** was the store from which rations were drawn, as well as the officer in charge of provisions.

Hooker also gave the Army of the Potomac something the Confederates had long used effectively: a revised and expanded role for the cavalry. Whereas McClellan had employed infantry at cavalry's expense, Hooker saw the cavalry as a vitally important instrument of reconnaissance. Nor was Hooker content with men on horses to perform the reconnaissance mission. He also liked the idea of men in balloons.

Since the fall of Sumter, a handful of balloonists had tried to interest the army in their services. The army purchased a single balloon for observation use at the First Battle of Bull Run, but it was wrecked before reaching the battlefield. By January 1862, the army had seven balloons—the nucleus of the first air branch of the U.S. military—and, in contrast to the overwhelming majority of his military contemporaries, Hooker was enthusiastic about the possibilities of the balloon in reconnaissance, in artillery spotting, and even for directing battles from aloft. He personally made an ascent in a tethered balloon.

"The Finest Army on the Planet"

By the early spring of 1863, Hooker was in high spirits, and not just because he had been up in a balloon. His troops were better fed, better clothed, better armed, and better trained than they had ever been before. Declaring that he was now in possession of the "finest army on the planet," he swore: "May God have mercy on General Lee, for I will have none."

The Least You Need to Know

- Lincoln replaced George McClellan with Ambrose Burnside as commander of the Army of the Potomac, over Burnside's own self-doubts.
- Burnside conducted his first campaign, at Fredericksburg on December 13, 1862, disastrously, bringing the U.S. Army the worst single defeat in its history.
- Whereas the Confederate army was short on food and supplies because it was strapped for cash, the Union army, though well funded, was plagued by corrupt and inefficient suppliers and supply officers.
- Burnside was replaced by General Joseph "Fighting Joe" Hooker. He did much to restore and improve the battered Army of the Potomac, and he confidently faced the prospect of battle against Robert E. Lee.

Bread and Bullets

In This Chapter

- Trouble on the Confederate home front
- Wartime inflation
- The problem of desertion
- The Confederates invade Kentucky
- The Vicksburg Campaign

If New Year's 1863 was not happy for the North, it was downright miserable for the South. True, Robert E. Lee had out-generaled Northerners in the East, but in the West the Union had enjoyed an almost unbroken succession of victories.

Behind the lines, the Confederacy was becoming what in modern parlance we would call a "failed state"—with whole areas given over to civil violence, widespread desertion, hyper-inflation, and severe shortages of essential goods.

Yet if Confederate morale was on the wane, so was morale in the North. Twenty months of bloody war and repeated setbacks in the East led many to wonder if it was possible to overcome the secessionists—and if doing so was even worth the cost.

"Gone are the proud hopes," a Union soldier named William Thompson Lusk wrote to his mother after Fredericksburg. "Once more unsuccessful, and only a bloody record to show our men were brave …. [The army] has strong limbs to march and meet the foe, stout arms to strike heavy blows, brave hearts to dare—but the brains, the brains! Have we no brains to use the arms and limbs and eager hearts …?"

In the South, people saw that their soldiers were going without enough food and decent clothing. And now civilians were feeling the pinch and going hungry as well.

This chapter looks at the home front in the South and the suffering of the Southern civilian. After a few words on reporting the Civil War, the discussion returns to combat west of the Appalachians.

"Bread! Bread!"

At the outbreak of the war, Richmond was neither a sleepy little Southern village nor a great metropolis, but a middling city. When the town was suddenly proclaimed the capital of the Confederacy, its population doubled almost overnight. In the best of times such instant growth would have put a strain on the food supply and other necessities. But these, of course, were hardly the best of times. The Union blockade was increasingly effective, and although McClellan and Burnside had both failed to occupy Richmond, the major fighting in Virginia had taken place on the outskirts of the city—on the farms and fields that were supposed to supply it with food.

If there is a popular image of the Southern home front, it is of a homogenous people fiercely loyal to their land and thoroughly convinced that their way of life was worth fighting for. The truth is that there was a wide spectrum of commitment—from total devotion to those who wanted a negotiated settlement, to others favoring immediate unconditional surrender and reunification, and to those who were pro-Union in the first place. Under the pressure of privation, even the most loyal Confederates were liable to snap.

On April 2, 1863, a mob of Richmond women started a riot. With shouts of "Bread! Bread!" they smashed store windows and looted all the food, as well as jewelry, clothing, and whatever other goods they could find. Richmond's mayor called out the militia, ordering them to fire on the rioters (never mind that they were Southern women) if they failed to disperse.

> **COUNT OFF!**
>
> In 1863, a Richmond newspaper estimated that the cost of feeding a small family in the city was $68.25 per week. During the year before the war, that cost had been only $6.55. This was at a time when an unskilled laborer could expect to earn a little more than a dollar a day.

That's when Jefferson Davis himself appeared. As his wife, Varina, tells it (the story is otherwise uncorroborated), Davis mounted a wagon and, after scolding the rioters for stealing trinkets and finery while crying for bread, he called out: "You say you are hungry and have no money—here is all I have!" With that, he dug into his pockets and threw out money. Neither history nor Varina Davis records whether this was gold and silver coins (worth something) or Confederate notes (worth almost nothing).

Having distributed his largesse, Davis next pulled out his pocket watch and declared that he would order the militia to open fire on the crowd if it failed to disperse within five minutes.

Similar riots broke out in other towns and cities across the Confederacy.

Paper War

Paper. By 1862, that's pretty much all Confederate money was. The Anaconda naval blockade (see Chapter 6) reduced the flow of goods in and out of the South, which was bad enough, but the Davis government made the situation even worse by failing to discourage a voluntary grassroots embargo on the export of cotton. Various local "patriotic" groups urged the embargo as a means of coercing France and England into an alliance. The coercion was resented and rejected abroad, and both the British and the French found alternative suppliers of cotton.

And yet the government had to finance the war somehow. It offered bonds paying 8 percent interest, but as early as the end of 1861, inflation in the Southern states topped 12 percent *a month*. Stiff taxes were also imposed on everything manufactured or grown, but few could afford to buy much, so the levies generated little revenue.

Nothing was left for the government to do but print more Treasury notes. The predictable result was inflation so severe that Confederate money was practically worthless as soon as it was issued.

COUNT OFF!

A Confederate paper dollar was worth:

80 cents	December 1, 1861
60 cents	February 1, 1862
20 cents	February 1, 1863
8 cents	June 1863
4.5 cents	November 1864
2.5 cents	January 1865
1.5 cents	April 1, 1865

After this, up until the surrender at Appomattox on April 9, it took approximately $1,000 in Confederate currency to buy one U.S. gold dollar.

The Draft and Desertion

Southerners liked to believe that the Confederate fighting man was superior to the Union common soldier in every respect. But the enlisted men on both sides, although sometimes poorly disciplined and inadequately trained, showed equally remarkable courage, endurance, and resourcefulness.

The Confederate "Johnny Reb" did have the morale-lifting advantage of defending his homeland rather than fighting on "foreign" soil, but as the families of these warriors suffered, it became increasingly clear to many of them that fighting and dying had less to do with protecting their wives, mothers, sisters, and children than it did with preserving the feudal world of the South's wealthy landowners—the 1,800 or so planters wealthy enough to own more than a hundred slaves.

WAR NEWS

In February 1865, the Confederate Congress authorized conscription of free blacks and slaves for auxiliary (noncombat) military service. Despite resistance, on March 13, 1865, the "Negro Soldier Law" permitted the recruitment (not conscription) of slaves for combat. Such soldiers could remain slaves or, with the "consent of the owners and of the States," could be marginally emancipated. A few companies of African American Confederate soldiers were enrolled, but the war ended before any saw combat.

Significant numbers of Southern men chose to join the Union army, and as the war ground on, these numbers increased. Even more critical were problems with enlistment and desertion. On October 6, 1864, *The Richmond Enquirer* reported President Davis's announcement that, "two-thirds of the Army are absent from the ranks." Thus, at this time, there were more deserters than fighting men.

The Confederacy claimed to be fighting to end the tyranny of a government that trampled the rights of states and individuals, yet the Davis government passed a conscription law on April 16, 1862, almost a full year before the Union did. All white males between 18 and 35 who were not legally exempt were conscripted for three years' service. In September 1862, the upper age limit was raised to 45, and in February 1864, to 50 (with the lower limit pushed down to 17).

As explained in Chapter 5, Confederate conscription laws, like those later enacted in the North, were grossly unjust. Anyone with enough money could pay a commutation fee or hire a substitute to avoid being drafted. In the South, men who owned or oversaw 20 or more slaves were automatically exempt.

Combat Journalism

The nineteenth-century European military theoretician Carl von Clausewitz famously wrote of the "fog of war," the great veil of confusion surrounding battle on the field and off. The public as well as politicians and soldiers were desperate for a glimpse of what a later generation of Americans at war would call "the big picture" and turned to newspapers and illustrated weekly magazines.

Journalists and Artists

Every major newspaper, North and South, sent reporters and correspondents into the field to cover battles. They also often reported on general troop movements—much to the chagrin of commanders, who wanted to keep such things secret.

For the most part, reportage in the daily newspapers was undistinguished and, more often than not, grossly inaccurate. Given the relatively slow pace of communications during the period, the illustrated weeklies had an advantage over the daily papers. Not only did the weekly format allow writers to gain a degree of perspective on the events reported, but also there was sufficient time to prepare often elaborate engravings of battle scenes.

The weeklies employed a small legion of artists and artist-correspondents. The most famous of the Civil War artist-correspondents was Winslow Homer (1816–1910), who worked for *Harper's* and became celebrated for his depictions of ordinary soldiers in battle and in camp. He also worked behind the scenes—for example, portraying the grim work of Union surgeons. After the war, Homer went on to a brilliant career as a fine artist and is considered one of the very greatest of America's late nineteenth- and early twentieth-century painters.

The Photographers

At the outbreak of the Civil War in 1861, the art and science of photography was less than three decades old. Joseph Nicéphore Niépce and Louis-Jacques Mandé Daguerre created the Daguerreotype process in France in the 1830s, and by the 1860s, photography was sufficiently advanced to enable both studio portraiture and on-the-scene coverage. Cameras, photographic plates, and the necessary on-the-spot processing equipment were too cumbersome, and photographic emulsions too "slow" (insufficiently light sensitive), to enable genuine battle-action photography, but scenes of encampments, marches, and aftermaths were within the state of the art. Civil War photographers made an estimated one million wartime images.

Although the technology for directly reproducing photographs in illustrated news-papers did not exist in the 1860s, photographs were used as the basis of many widely reproduced engravings. However, much Civil War photography was sold directly to the public, and even more was intended strictly for personal use. Soldiers visited photo studios to have portraits made for their parents, wives, and sweethearts. Those images that survive are among the most compelling and emotionally powerful arti-facts of the war.

By far the most celebrated Civil War photographer was Mathew B. Brady (c. 1823–1896), who opened a New York City photo studio in 1844 and was very well established by the time of the war. With Scotch-born Alexander Gardner (1821–1882), whom he hired in 1856, Brady organized an army of more than 100 photographers to cover every aspect of the war.

The Confederacy had three prominent photographers. Charlestonians James M. Osborn and F. W. Durbec portrayed the aftermath of the surrender of Fort Sumter; and Julian Vannerson, a Virginian, photographed the South's most important military leaders.

Foreign Affairs

Early in the war, both the British and the French seriously considered recognizing the Confederate States of America as a sovereign nation and even making an alliance with it. But the narrow Union victory at Antietam convinced these governments that the Confederate invasion of the Union would fail, and the Emancipation Proclamation proved so popular with the people of England and France that neither government dared risk recognizing a slaveholding nation, let alone making an alliance with one.

This did not mean, however, that all Confederate-European diplomacy was dead. Just after the fall of Fort Sumter, James D. Bulloch called on Confederate Secretary of the Navy Stephen R. Mallory, offering his services as a naval officer. Georgia-born Bulloch had been a sailor since age 16, when he joined the U. S. Navy as a midship-man. Since 1853, he had been skipper of a commercial mail steamer plying the waters between New York and New Orleans. But Secretary Mallory was less interested in Bulloch's seamanship than in his business sense, knowledge of naval architecture, and discretion. He sent Bulloch to England to buy, or commission to build, six commerce raiders—and to arm them, and recruit the crews to man them as well.

During the opening months of the Civil War, visitors to the industrial and shipbuilding city of Liverpool, England reported seeing as many Confederate flags as British Union Jacks flying. Despite this show of popular support, Britain was officially neutral. Bulloch hired a prominent attorney to find a loophole in Britain's Foreign Enlistments Act, which among other provisions prohibited the arming of ships to be used by foreign combatants. The lawyer declared that the act did not forbid the building of *unarmed* ships in Great Britain—ships that might be *armed* elsewhere. Having found his loophole, Bulloch crawled through it and negotiated for the construction of vessels in England to be fitted elsewhere with guns.

This was the beginning of an international cat-and-mouse game played out in England and other parts of Europe between Bulloch and U.S. diplomats.

Warships weren't the only armaments produced in England for export to the Confederacy. For example, Bulloch purchased the *Fingal*, a blockade runner, which he loaded with "1,000 short rifles, with cutlass bayonets, and 1,000 rounds of ammunition per rifle; 500 revolvers, with suitable ammunition; two $4\frac{1}{2}$-inch muzzle-loading rifled guns, with traversing carriages, all necessary gear, and 200 made-up cartridges, shot and shell, per gun; two breech-loading $2\frac{1}{2}$-inch steel-rifled guns for boats or field service, with 200 rounds of ammunition per gun; 400 barrels of coarse cannon powder, and a large quantity of made-up clothing for seamen." In addition, as many as 14,000 Enfield rifles might have been onboard.

This was typical, and while U.S. officials worked through diplomatic channels to stem the flow of munitions, Union secret agents worked behind-the-scenes to intercept and purchase the supplies out from under the Confederates. Sometimes the Union agents were successful, and sometimes not. The most famous Southern warship built in England and successfully delivered to the Confederate navy was the CSS *Alabama*, which left Liverpool on July 29, 1862, and embarked on a most destructive career (covered in Chapter 20) against Union shipping.

Old Kentucky Home

While McClellan was entrenching on Virginia's James River after the failure of his Peninsula Campaign, and after Ulysses S. Grant had won his victories over the rebel forts on the Mississippi, Confederate Major General Edmund Kirby Smith left Knoxville, Tennessee, to invade central Kentucky on August 14, 1862. Two weeks later, Confederate General Braxton Bragg left Chattanooga to join Kirby Smith in Kentucky. On August 30, Union General Don Carlos Buell ordered the pursuit of these Confederate invaders.

General Braxton Bragg, Confederate States Army (CSA), boldly invaded Kentucky, but was chased out of the state by General Don Carlos Buell.

Friendly Advice

The little town of Munfordville, Kentucky, was hotly contested during September 14 to 17, 1862. A premature Confederate assault on the town was repulsed with heavy losses on the 14th. Then, as the Federals reinforced the town, Bragg mounted a much larger attack and by the 16th, surrounded the Union garrison there. Confederate General Simon Bolivar Buckner formally demanded surrender.

Now the 4,133 men of the Union garrison were led by Colonel J. T. Wilder, an industrialist from Indiana, who had no military experience whatsoever. He knew surrender didn't appeal to him, but he didn't know what else to do. So he responded to Buckner's demand by visiting the Confederate general's headquarters under a flag of truce. Explaining that he was ignorant of military matters, he told Buckner that he understood him to be an officer and a gentleman, who would not deceive him. He then asked Buckner what he should do.

The Confederate commander, taken aback, politely declined to advise his enemy on how to respond to the surrender demand. Wilder replied that he understood, but then asked if he might be permitted to inspect Buckner's forces so that he could count the cannon. To this Buckner consented and after his tour, Wilder turned to the general: "I believe I'll surrender."

Curtain Down: Iuka, Corinth, Perryville

The fall of Munfordville temporarily cut Buell's communications with Louisville, but Bragg did not press this advantage and sought instead to avoid further battle until he united with Kirby Smith. Meaning to occupy Kentucky, he wanted to recruit troops in this border state and to establish supply depots before he engaged in large-scale combat.

In the meantime however, on September 19, Union General William S. Rosecrans, under Grant, had defeated some 17,000 Confederate troops commanded by General Sterling Price at Iuka, Mississippi. Price withdrew southward and Confederate General Earl Van Dorn moved to join him. Believing that Corinth, Mississippi, was lightly defended by a handful of Union troops, Van Dorn attacked the town on October 3. To Van Dorn's surprise, the town was actually held by 23,000 of Rosecrans's troops (versus Van Dorn's 22,000), and Grant quickly reinforced it. Fighting was heaviest on October 4, resulting in a bloody Confederate repulse and Van Dorn's withdrawal to Holly Springs.

The defeat of Van Dorn cut off Bragg in Kentucky from any hope of reinforcement, and Buell maneuvered the now vulnerable Bragg into battle at Perryville, Kentucky, on October 8.

With Buell's combined forces amounting to 36,940 men, and Bragg having only about 16,000 available at Perryville, a glorious Union victory should have followed. A victory it was, but hardly glorious. Buell was unable to bring all of his forces to bear, and although he did push Bragg and Kirby Smith out of Kentucky and into eastern Tennessee, he failed to pursue the retreating Confederates. Buell was replaced as commander of the Department of the Ohio by Rosecrans.

COUNT OFF!

Union losses at Corinth were 2,520 killed, wounded, and missing; Confederate losses were 2,470 killed and/or wounded, with an additional 1,763 missing in action.

General William S. Rosecrans defeated Confederate forces under General Sterling Price at Iuka, Mississippi.
(Harper's Pictorial History of the Civil War, 1866)

Assault at Vicksburg

Yet again the Union found itself victorious, but indecisively so. Following Grant's initial victories against the rebel forts on the Mississippi River, General Henry Wager "Old Brains" Halleck, in overall charge of operations in this theater of the war, had made the mistake of dispersing his forces in order to occupy enemy territory. The effect of this was to forfeit the initiative to the Confederates and to assume a defensive posture. Had Halleck instead consolidated his forces—about 100,000 strong—he could have mounted a powerful offensive deep into Southern territory. Doubtless, the war would have been shortened.

As it was, by the middle of October, the Union had at least beaten back the Confederate invasion of Kentucky, and Grant could turn his attention once again to the drive down the Mississippi. He understood that complete control of the river—and with it, the final isolation of the western from the eastern Confederate states—required the capture of Vicksburg, Mississippi. As his commanding officer

Halleck declared, "In my opinion, the opening of the Mississippi River will be to us more advantage than the capture of forty Richmonds."

But the Confederacy was also well aware of the strategic importance of Vicksburg, nicknamed "the Gibraltar of the West." It was a fortress town, heavily defended by artillery, occupying a high bluff overlooking the river, which made it virtually impregnable. With guns positioned to sweep the river, direct naval assault was difficult, perhaps even impossible. Grant proposed an all-out combined water and land assault.

Holly Springs and Chickasaw Bluffs

In December Grant established an advance base at Holly Springs, Mississippi, preparatory to a planned movement of some 40,000 troops down the Mississippi Central Railroad to link up with 32,000 riverborne troops led by William Tecumseh Sherman. Confederate cavalry under General Van Dorn raided Holly Springs on December 20, catching Colonel R. C. Murphy's 8th Wisconsin Regiment asleep in their tents. After destroying $1,500,000 worth of supplies at Holly Springs, Van Dorn raided one Union outpost after another. In the meantime, the remarkable Confederate General Nathan Bedford Forrest led his cavalry against the railroad, destroying 60 miles of it.

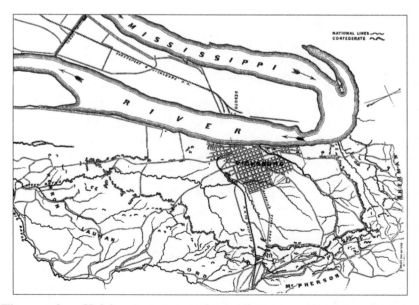

This map shows Vicksburg's strategic and virtually impregnable position on a hairpin turn of the Mississippi.
(Harper's Pictorial History of the Civil War, 1866)

The actions of Van Dorn and Forrest stopped Grant's advance, and Sherman, without Grant's support at Chickasaw Bluffs (just a few miles north of Vicksburg), failed as well. Sherman's summary of the action of December 27 to 29, 1862, was as dry as it comes: "I reached Vicksburg at the time appointed, landed, assaulted, and failed."

Try, Try Again

Grant next took a leaf from John Pope's book and decided to dig a canal to avoid the guns of Vicksburg, as Pope had done, to get behind the guns of Island Number 10 (see Chapter 7). But heavy rains and high water during February 1863 forced him to drop the project in March. Shortly after this, he tried a more ambitious canal at Duckport, and did manage to get a small steamer through the canal-connected bayous. But it soon became clear that the canal approach was impractical on any meaningful scale.

African American laborers did most of the digging of the canals Grant planned to use to get around the guns at Vicksburg.
(Harper's Pictorial History of the Civil War, 1866)

Grant next ordered General James B. McPherson to open up a 400-mile route through Louisiana swamps, lakes, and bayous to a point on the Mississippi below Vicksburg. This incredibly laborious process was successfully under way when in March, it was abandoned in favor of a more roundabout water route through the so-called Yazoo Pass. The Confederates built a fort to block the pass 90 miles north of Vicksburg, and on March 11, the Yazoo Pass expedition was also abandoned.

> **SITES AND SIGHTS**
>
> Vicksburg National Military Park is one of the largest such parks in the nation. It includes an extensive visitor center, as well as a section of reconstructed earthworks and an artillery exhibit. In addition to the park, the town of Vicksburg has many historical buildings to visit. Contact the park at 601-636-0583.

Yet another water route, through Steele's Bayou, was attempted. Admiral David Porter led 11 Union vessels through the difficult waterways, with Sherman's infantry following. On March 19, at Rolling Fork, Mississippi, due north of Vicksburg, Confederate forces stopped Porter's boats and might have destroyed the fleet had Sherman not arrived in the proverbial nick of time. Although the Steele's Bayou expedition was yet another failure, Sherman's rescue was brilliant and daring—his entire unit marching through the swampland at night, their path lighted only by candles inserted in their rifle barrels.

Victory, Slow and Bold

Grant probably had little hope that the preliminary expeditions against Vicksburg would succeed, but he understood the importance of keeping the offensive alive and keeping the enemy guessing.

In May, the vanguard of Grant's army slipped down the western shore of the Mississippi below Vicksburg, looking for a place where the troops could rendezvous with naval transports that would transport them downriver to attack the Confederate strong point of Grand Gulf. On the night of April 16 gunboats and transports ran the gauntlet of Confederate guns at Vicksburg, and linked up with the army. Grand Gulf proved too tough a nut to crack, so the army moved farther south to Bruinsburg. After being ferried across the river, Grant's troops defeated Confederates under Major General John Stevens Bowen outside Port Gibson, then defeated a rebel rear guard and crossed Bayou Pierre.

Grant had been ordered to move south once he had crossed the Mississippi to link up with forces under General Nathaniel Banks for a joint assault on Port Hudson, Louisiana. Learning that Banks was bogged down in his fruitless Red River campaign, Grant boldly decided instead to move immediately against Jackson, Mississippi, where, he knew, Confederate reinforcements were being assembled.

> **COUNT OFF!**
>
> Fighting at Champion Hill was the most severe of the Vicksburg campaign. Of 29,373 Union troops engaged, 410 were killed, 1,844 wounded, and 187 went missing. Of some 20,000 Confederates, 381 died, about 1,800 were wounded, and 1,670 went missing.

On May 14, 1863, Grant used corps under McPherson and Sherman to take Jackson. This paved the way for the bloody Battle of Champion Hill on May 16, which fell to the Union after heavy losses on both sides. Grant pursued the retreating enemy, defeating them the following day at the Big Black River.

Total War

Grant was now in position for an attack on Vicksburg. He ordered a frontal assault on the city on May 19, but was repulsed. He tried again on the 22nd, and was again repulsed with some 3,200 casualties.

After this, he resigned himself to a prolonged siege. From late May through the beginning of July, 200 heavy Union artillery pieces and siege mortars continuously pounded Vicksburg.

The citizens of Vicksburg responded to the siege heroically. They dug caves into the yellow-clay hillsides, and then furnished them with finery dragged out of their ruined houses. Weeks crawled by under the pounding shells. The cave dwellers fought lice, rats, disease, boredom, and despair—eating their emaciated mules, horses, and dogs when food ran out.

Surrender came on July 4, 1863, a day after the Union's victory at Gettysburg (see Chapter 15). With Gettysburg, Vicksburg was the most important victory of the war. The Mississippi River was now in Union hands, and the backbone of the Confederacy was broken.

For the next 81 years, the citizens of Vicksburg would refuse to celebrate Independence Day.

A Union artillery position in the long siege of Vicksburg.
(Harper's Pictorial History of the Civil War, 1866)

The Least You Need to Know

- Southern civilians were plagued by food and other shortages and also by runaway inflation.
- Draft dodging and desertion were major problems in the Confederate army. At times, deserters outnumbered those on active duty.
- The Civil War was covered by a legion of journalists, artist-correspondents, and photographers.
- Although General Don Carlos Buell managed to turn back the Confederate invasion of Kentucky, his failure to pursue the army of Braxton Bragg was yet another missed opportunity for a decisive Union victory.
- Vicksburg, the most arduous campaign of the war, ended on July 4, 1863, after the Confederacy's "Gibraltar of the West" surrendered, thereby yielding the strategically vital Mississippi River to Union control.

Thunderstorm from a Cloudless Sky

Chapter 14

In This Chapter

- Hooker rebuilds the Army of the Potomac
- Lee defeats Hooker at Chancellorsville
- "Stonewall" Jackson dies
- Lee advances to invade Pennsylvania
- Meade replaces Hooker

In plans and on paper, the position of the North always looked good, whereas that of the South appeared dim. The North had so many more men, so much more money, so many more factories, and many, many more miles of railroad. The South, in contrast, was starving; its soldiers dressed in rags, often going without so much as shoes. The Emancipation Proclamation had injected new moral vigor into the war and had won, for the North, as much popular approval as it could expect from Europe.

Yet plenty of Northerners either didn't care about emancipation or downright resented it. The North, for all its advantages, was war-weary. Southerners were fighting to defend their homes; Northerners had to be convinced to fight for concepts, albeit powerful ones: first "union," then "emancipation." Their will to fight could not be sustained on hopes and wishes alone. Lincoln needed results. He desperately needed Hooker to win.

This chapter shows how Hooker tried, and how he failed.

"May God Have Mercy on General Lee ..."

Under General Joseph Hooker, the Army of the Potomac was restored in spirit and strength. Hooker reorganized the army, trained it, and increased it to 130,000 men. He would use this magnificent instrument to strike Robert E. Lee's Army of Northern Virginia at Fredericksburg—scene of Burnside's defeat—and at Chancellorsville. Lee commanded 60,000 men, less than half the number available to Hooker.

"May God have mercy on General Lee," Hooker said, "for I will have none."

Hooker's Plan

Unlike the ill-fated Ambrose Burnside, Hooker decided not to hurl his massive army head-on against the formidable Fredericksburg defenses. Instead, he would deploy about one third of his forces under General John Sedgwick, a capable corps commander, to make a diversionary attack across the Rappahannock above Lee's Fredericksburg entrenchments; while he personally led another third of the army in a long swing up the Rappahannock, coming around to attack Lee on his vulnerable left flank and rear. Except for about 10,000 cavalry troopers under General George Stoneman, who would disrupt Lee's lines of communication to Richmond, the remainder of the Army of the Potomac would be prudently held in reserve at Chancellorsville, ready for use to reinforce either Sedgwick's or Hooker's wings, as needed.

It was an excellent plan, and it seemed certain to send Lee falling back to Richmond in defeat.

Outgeneraled on a Cracker Barrel

The first part of the grand plan unfolded beautifully. By April 30, 1863, Hooker had established about 70,000 men in Chancellorsville and had set up headquarters in a plantation home outside of town called Chancellor House. Hooker then dispatched his cavalry to cut the Richmond, Fredericksburg, and Potomac Railroad.

The trouble with Hooker's plan is that Robert E. Lee came to understand it as well as Hooker did. Maybe even better.

Union soldiers lay a pontoon bridge across the Rappahannock in preparation for General Sedgwick's advance during the Chancellorsville campaign.
(Harper's Pictorial History of the Civil War, 1866)

Largely ignoring Hooker's cavalry, Lee used his own, under Jeb Stuart, to gain control of the roads in and out of Chancellorsville, preventing Hooker from sending patrols out. The Union general was effectively blinded, unable to tell where the Confederates were. Worried, he deployed his men defensively in hastily erected *breastworks* close to Chancellorsville, instead of advancing to his chosen battlefield about 12 miles east of town. In doing so, Hooker passed the initiative to Lee, almost always a fatal thing to do.

DEFINITION

Breastworks are temporary, improvised, defensive barriers, made of earth, stone, wood—whatever materials are available—usually affording protection that is breast high.

In the meantime, having concluded from Stuart's reconnaissance that Hooker intended to attack him from the flank and rear through a tangle of thick second-growth forest known as "the Wilderness," Lee sent 10,000 men under Jubal Early to delay the Union troops at Fredericksburg, while he led the remainder of his army against Hooker at Chancellorsville.

Then General Lee hit on an even bolder and riskier plan. On the night of May 1, he found a scout who could lead Stonewall Jackson's corps through the pathless confusion of the Wilderness to strike at Hooker's exposed flank. Around midnight, Lee invited Jackson to pull up an empty *cracker barrel*, sit down, and listen to his plan.

> **DEFINITION**
>
> Civil War crackers were not the saltines of today, but were synonymous with hardtack, an extremely hard biscuit made with flour and water. Crackers were stored in crates or barrels—in either case called **cracker barrels.**

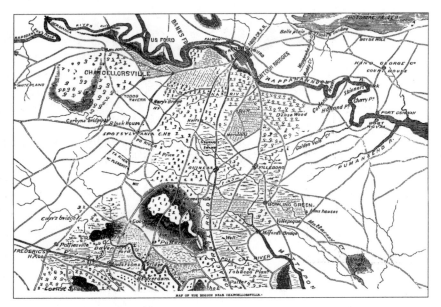

A map of the Chancellorsville area.
(Harper's Pictorial History of the Civil War, 1866)

As he had done against Pope at the Second Battle of Bull Run (see Chapter 10), Lee flouted accepted military doctrine by dividing his army in the presence of the enemy.

He proposed to assign 26,000 men to Jackson for the surprise attack against Hooker's flank, and to retain 17,000 under his own command to make attacks against Hooker's front. Early's troops, meanwhile, would continue to hold the Union troops at Fredericksburg.

Lee's Masterpiece

Even with Hooker in a state of worried confusion, Jackson's maneuver was very dangerous. In broad daylight, he had to move 26,000 men across the Federal front, no more than two and one-half miles away. Indeed, even with Jeb Stuart in control of the roads, pickets with the Union XI Corps under General O. O. Howard saw Jackson's movement. Nevertheless, they were unable to persuade Howard or Hooker that this represented any great danger.

Just two hours before dusk on May 2, Jackson attacked Howard, in command of Hooker's right flank. Most Federals were relaxing, playing cards, and talking, their rifles stacked. One Union soldier recalled that the surprise attack came "like a clap of thunderstorm from a cloudless sky."

The results were devastating. One entire Federal corps panicked and was routed, and then Hooker's entire army was knocked out of its prepared positions.

This was just the beginning of a battle so brilliantly planned that military historians have dubbed it "Lee's Masterpiece." Fighting went on through May 4, by which time Hooker, in full retreat, had withdrawn all of his troops north of the Rappahannock.

"... And Rest Under the Shade of the Trees"

The cost to Hooker was staggering. He had faced an army less than half the size of his—a ragtag army at that: tired, ill fed, and poorly equipped. Against this force he lost 17,000 men as well as, yet again, the chance for a decisive Union victory. But Robert E. Lee also paid a terrible price. He lost 13,000 men—almost one quarter of his strength—at Chancellorsville. And, perhaps worse still, he lost Thomas J. "Stonewall" Jackson.

COUNT OFF!

The Union's 17,000 casualties at Chancellorsville represented 17 percent of the numbers engaged. Lee's 13,000 casualties amounted to a quarter of his forces.

Jackson's assault on Hooker's right flank had begun too late in the day for him to finish it satisfactorily before nightfall. On the night of May 2, Jackson and his staff were in the Wilderness, scouting for a possible night assault. Confusion reigned in that dark woods, and as Jackson returned to the Confederate lines, a line of North Carolina infantry opened fire on him. The general was wounded in the right hand, left wrist and hand, and left arm. None of the wounds were mortal, but infection quickly followed and then pneumonia set in. Stonewall Jackson died on May 10.

"His mind," Jackson's physician, Dr. Hunter McGuire, recalled, "began to … wander, and he frequently talked as if in command upon the field …. A few moments before he died he cried out in his delirium, 'Order A. P. Hill to prepare for action! Pass the infantry to the front rapidly. Tell Major Hawks—' then stopped, leaving the sentence unfinished. Presently a smile … spread itself over his pale face, and he said quietly, and with an expression as if of relief, 'Let us cross over the river and rest under the shade of the trees.'"

"What Will the Country Say?"

Robert E. Lee had once, in a letter, described Jackson as a man "of contrasts … He lives by the New Testament and fights by the Old." Now he said simply, "I have lost my right arm."

Abraham Lincoln had his own grim words in the aftermath of Hooker's total defeat at Chancellorsville: "My God! My God! What will the country say? What will the country say?"

Lee's Bold Offensive

What Lincoln's country said was concisely contained in a phrase often repeated in Union newspapers: "Abraham Lincoln, give us a man!"

As for Jefferson Davis's country, its people declared that Robert E. Lee had won a great victory—never mind the loss of Jackson and a quarter of the forces engaged. Lee heard and heeded the acclaim. He saw that Chancellorsville had raised the spirits of the South. He saw, too, that Chancellorsville had appalled and disheartened the well-fed, populous North. It was, he decided, now or never. He would again invade the North.

SITES AND SIGHTS

The Chancellorsville Battlefield Unit of the Fredericksburg and Spotsylvania Memorial National Military Park includes a Visitor Center located just north of State Route 3 on Bullock Road. Points of interest are well marked throughout the park.

Lee Heads North

Lee knew he could not "conquer" the Union states. But if he could stage a swift, massive, and punishing raid well into Northern territory, he might demolish the Union's will to continue the fight and thereby force a favorably negotiated peace. Although fighting a defensive war held many tactical advantages for the Confederacy, no European power would ally itself with a would-be nation fighting an exclusively defensive war. Moreover, Lee understood that generals do not win wars defensively. Sooner or later, successful offensive action is required for victory.

If Lee's gamble failed, the Confederacy might lose its principal army and with it, the war. Yet such an outcome was possible even without an invasion of the North. Lee could not afford another *Pyrrhic victory*, beating the Union while losing—proportionately—more men than the enemy. He needed the decisive victory a battle on Northern soil might deliver.

DEFINITION

A **Pyrrhic victory** is one that comes at a self-defeating cost. The word derives from Pyrrhus (319–272 B.C.E.), king of Epirus, who defeated a Roman army at the Battle of Heraclea (280 B.C.E.), but lost so many men in the triumph that he remarked, "One more such victory and I shall be lost."

One more factor was pushing Lee to an invasion of Pennsylvania. He recognized the significance of what Grant was accomplishing along the Mississippi. It was now almost June, and Lee understood that Vicksburg, last of the Confederate citadels on the great river, would, in the fullness of time, fall (see Chapter 13). The general's grasp of strategy extended far beyond the borders of his home state—he knew that, soon after Vicksburg fell, many of those western-based Federal troops would be moved east. Time was running out. Lee needed his war-winning victory now.

Beginning on June 3, Lee moved north, dividing his army into three corps. Leading the movement was a corps commanded by James Longstreet, who, of Lee's three lieutenants, was the only one to raise objections to the invasion. He thought it far better to launch offensives within Virginia, while reinforcing Bragg in the menaced area of Chattanooga, Tennessee, and sending troops west in an effort to turn the tables on Grant. But he swallowed his doubts and marched in obedience to Lee's command, pausing with his corps at Culpeper Court House, Virginia, while another corps, under Richard S. Ewell (a sour-tempered man nicknamed "Old Baldy"), advanced against piecemeal Union detachments still in the lower Shenandoah Valley. The third corps, commanded by A. P. Hill, remained at Fredericksburg, eye-to-eye with the Yankees there.

Hooker had a plan for responding to these movements. Stopping his ears to the clamor for his removal as commander of the Army of the Potomac (he had friends in high places willing to take his side, particularly Secretary of the Treasury Salmon P. Chase), Hooker proposed to ignore Lee's move and advance against Richmond. He reasoned that this would soon bring Lee marching back south to defend the capital of the Confederacy.

But the administration that had so long pleaded with McClellan to march to Richmond now refused to approve Hooker's proposed offensive against the rebel capital. Badly shaken by his performance at Chancellorsville, Lincoln and his advisors ordered Hooker to pursue a defensive course only and follow Lee.

Brandy Station

On June 5, obediently and doggedly following Lee, Hooker ordered General John Sedgwick to make a reconnaissance to determine if the Confederates had left Fredericksburg. The result was a skirmish at Franklin's Crossing, Virginia, after which Hooker ordered a full-scale cavalry reconnaissance under Alfred Pleasonton to ascertain the extent and significance of Lee's movements.

The result, on June 9, was the Battle of Brandy Station. Forces under the overall command of Pleasonton surprised the Confederate cavalry under Jeb Stuart, whose own reconnaissance failed to alert him to the Union cavalry's presence. It was the first real cavalry engagement of the Civil War—the largest ever fought in North America, and doubtless an extraordinary spectacle.

In terms of losses, and because Confederate General Jeb Stuart remained in possession of the field after the battle, Brandy Station must be counted as a Union defeat. Yet in an important sense, it was a Union victory. The Federal cavalry, largely neglected by McClellan but brushed up and bolstered by Hooker, more than stood its own against Stuart, who was by now legendary and believed to be unbeatable. Although he had driven the Federals from the field, Stuart had been badly surprised and hadn't prevented them from accomplishing their reconnaissance. Hooker now knew that Lee was leaving Fredericksburg and was heading north.

> **COUNT OFF!**
>
> Some 20,000 horsemen were engaged at Brandy Station, charging and countercharging for a full 12 hours of battle. Union casualties numbered 936 killed, wounded, and/or captured; Confederate casualties were 523.

Disaster at Winchester

But Brandy Station also alerted Lee to the fact that Hooker knew of his movements. With his usual strategic acuity, Lee concluded that Hooker might now turn to advance on Richmond—the very plan Hooker had, in fact, proposed, but which had been overruled. On June 10, Lee dispatched Ewell to attack the remaining Union garrisons in the Shenandoah Valley, which would (Lee hoped) force Lincoln to recall the Army of the Potomac for the defense of the capital.

Ewell's forces clashed with Union troops at Berryville (June 13) and Martinsburg (June 14). Most of the Union soldiers managed to evade capture in these two places, but Ewell's attack on Winchester (June 13 to 15) was a Union disaster. The Confederates bottled up the Union garrison in the forts just west of the town—with the result that 4,443 soldiers became casualties, of whom 3,538 were taken prisoner. Ewell's losses were a mere 269.

Crossing the Potomac

The first units of the Army of Northern Virginia crossed the Potomac into Maryland on June 15. Stuart's cavalry created a *counterreconnaissance* screen to prevent Pleasonton's Union cavalry from discovering Lee's objective—Washington or Pennsylvania. This resulted in a series of cavalry duels at Aldie, Virginia (June 17); Middleburg, Virginia (June 19); and Upperville, Virginia (June 21).

> **DEFINITION**
>
> If cavalry could be used for reconnaissance, an exploration to ascertain military information, it could also be used in **counterreconnaissance,** an effort to foil the enemy's attempt to carry out a reconnaissance mission.

Stuart's Raid

Following these engagements, Stuart, still smarting from his partial humiliation at Brandy Station, hit on a way to redeem himself. While the main body of Lee's army joined the advance detachments in crossing the Potomac, wheeling toward the east, Stuart was to serve as Lee's "eyes," moving along the army's right flank and front to report on the whereabouts of Hooker's forces. Stuart had a choice of taking a short, direct route across the Potomac or a longer route clear around Hooker's rear and flank. He secured Lee's permission to take the longer way around, which, he argued, would give him an opportunity to raid Hooker's supply depots and lines. One cannot help suspecting, however, that Stuart, as vainglorious as he was skilled, wanted yet a third opportunity to make a dashing and spectacular ride around the Union army.

Stuart's "Gettysburg Raid" did allow the cavalryman to cut across and disrupt Hooker's supply lines, and he was also able to capture 125 U.S. Army wagons at Rockville, Maryland, as well as 400 prisoners in skirmishes at Fairfax Courthouse, Virginia (June 27); Westminster, Maryland (June 29); Hanover, Pennsylvania (June 30); and Carlisle, Pennsylvania (July 1). But the ride around the army took much longer than Stuart had anticipated, and for 10 critical days he was out of touch with Lee. Because Stuart's cavalry was Lee's "eyes," this meant that Lee advanced into Pennsylvania blind.

Surprise!

Robert E. Lee rarely allowed himself to be surprised, but without reports from Stuart, he could only assume that Hooker had not yet followed him across the Potomac. Lee, therefore, dispersed his forces in a long line, with the rear at Chambersburg, Pennsylvania, and the front of the army at York, some 50 miles to the east.

The fact was that Hooker *had* crossed the Potomac during June 25 and 26, and not until June 28 did Lee learn that the entire Army of the Potomac was concentrated around Frederick, Maryland, directly south of the 50-mile-long, highly vulnerable flank of the Army of Northern Virginia.

A Used Up Man

Lee learned another thing, too. The Army of the Potomac was no longer under the command of Joseph Hooker. Despite opposition from Chase and others, Lincoln replaced him with Major General George Gordon Meade. Meade was competent, but both irascible and uninspired. Many favored John Fulton Reynolds instead as more charismatic and more temperamentally suited to independent command than Meade. If President Lincoln wanted a hero to lead the Army of the Potomac ("Abraham Lincoln, give us a man!"), surely John Reynolds was it. Lincoln, however, stood by his choice.

Major General George Gordon Meade (1815–1872) was a solid, if uninspired, military man.
(Harper's Pictorial History of the Civil War, 1866)

As for "Fighting Joe" Hooker, he would yet see much action and perform capably, albeit in subordinate roles. Still, in the wake of Chancellorsville, Meade's aide Theodore Lyman described Hooker as "red-faced … with a lackluster eye and an uncertainty of gait and carriage that suggested a used up man."

The Least You Need to Know

- General Hooker revitalized and rebuilt the Army of the Potomac; nevertheless, Lee outgeneraled Hooker and defeated him at Chancellorsville.
- Chancellorsville was a shocking defeat for the Union, but it was also a very costly (though tactically brilliant) victory for Robert E. Lee.
- Lee's decision to invade Pennsylvania was a high-stakes gamble ventured in the hope that it would break the North's will to continue the war.
- Lincoln's choice of the ill-tempered and unpopular George Gordon Meade to replace Joseph Hooker as commanding officer of the Army of the Potomac was controversial at the time and remains so among many historians.

That the Nation Might Live

4

This part begins with the Battle of Gettysburg, July 1 through 3, 1863—one of the most fiercely contested battles in the history of warfare. Along with the fall of Vicksburg the day after the conclusion of the Gettysburg battle, the contest in this Pennsylvania town spelled the beginning of the end for the Confederacy.

Nevertheless, the Civil War was far from over, and as the South contended with acute shortages and increasing demoralization, the North was also wracked with disharmony among those who wanted to fight to absolute victory and those who wanted to negotiate an immediate end to the war. While the South suffered riots over bread, the North was torn by riots protesting the draft and, in some places, the related prospect of fighting to free African American slaves. As if this internal strife were not bad enough, the Midwest learned to live in fear of a Southern-sympathizing faction called the Copperheads, which threatened to bring insurrection to the heart of the North.

Gettysburg

In This Chapter

- Lee hopes to win the war at Gettysburg
- How Jeb Stuart failed Lee
- General Buford seizes the high ground for the Union
- The significance of Gettysburg

History is full of single battles that have turned the tide of entire wars. The very first battle of which we have any knowledge, at Megiddo in Palestine, brought Egypt to the height of its power in 1469 B.C.E. The Battle of Hastings in 1066 ended Saxon rule in England and established the Normans there. The Battle of Yorktown in 1781 heralded America's victory in the Revolution. The Battle of Waterloo, 1815, ended forever Napoleon's dream of dominating Europe. And the Battle of Gettysburg—July 1 through 3, 1863—was the certain beginning of the certain end of the Confederate States of America. This chapter tells the story of the horrific, heroic three-day battle on which many believe the outcome of the Civil War turned.

Legend of the Shoes

The Battle of Gettysburg begins with a legend. Picture a barefoot army in need of shoes. By 1863, Confederate soldiers were chronically in need of everything: food, clothing, and—always—shoes. It is said that, on June 30, 1863, shoeless Confederates of General A. P. Hill's division were foraging in the Pennsylvania town of Gettysburg in search of footgear.

Such a homely task certainly appeals to the imagination as the reason for a momentous battle, just as Gettysburg itself is appealing as the site of that battle. Seat of the Lutheran Theological Seminary and Pennsylvania College (now Gettysburg College), just north of the Maryland state line, home to 3,500, Gettysburg was a genteel, pastoral village, the kind of tranquil place popular printmakers Currier and Ives were already offering as a nostalgic image of American peace and plenty.

The truth is, while Confederates were of necessity always foraging, Hill's men were first and foremost on a mission of reconnaissance, not shoe hunting. It was a mission made necessary by the absence of cavalry intelligence, since Jeb Stuart was still riding around the Union army and had not been heard from for days (see Chapter 14). When the detachment reported that Gettysburg was occupied by Union cavalry, General Henry Heth (pronounced *Heath*) secured Hill's permission to take a brigade into town to clear it out.

The Union cavalrymen in Gettysburg were an understrength division—about 6,000 men—commanded by Brigadier General John Buford. They were the advance guard of the main body of the Army of the Potomac. Yet Robert E. Lee, out of touch with the errant Stuart, was only just now learning how close that enemy army was. Some weeks earlier, Major General James Longstreet had hired a spy, a Mississippian named Henry Thomas Harrison. He now revealed to Lee that the Army of the Potomac was approaching quickly, and that George Gordon Meade was now at its head. After a mere moment's reflection, Lee decided that he must concentrate his army here at Gettysburg.

Although his given name was James, General Longstreet was known affectionately as "Pete" and, even more indulgently, as "Gloomy Old Pete." Lee called him "My Old War Horse." While no one ever questioned his courage—a commodity he had in abundance—Longstreet tended toward pessimism and, true to form, having tried to talk Lee out of invading Pennsylvania in the first place, he now advised against tangling with the Army of the Potomac at Gettysburg.

Lee conceded to Gloomy Pete that Gettysburg was not tactically the ideal place for so important a battle, but he believed he had been presented with a proverbial golden opportunity. Meade's army was spread out. If Lee could quickly concentrate at Gettysburg, he could attack and destroy it piecemeal—in detail. The Army of the Potomac had repeatedly been battered, but never before on its own soil. Make that happen, and the Northern will to fight might well collapse. At the very least defeat at

Gettysburg would cost Lincoln reelection, Lee reasoned, and if a Democrat replaced him, the Confederacy would likely find itself dealing with a president receptive to a negotiated peace. Such were Lee's most compelling reasons for deciding to fight at Gettysburg.

The Union's Brigadier General John Buford led a cavalry division into Gettysburg in advance of Meade's army. Thanks to him, Confederate forces were deprived of the high ground surrounding the town, and thus Gettysburg was not for the Union a repeat of the Fredericksburg massacre.
(Harper's Pictorial History of the Civil War, 1866)

Lee also believed in exploiting a *defensive* opportunity. The Army of Northern Virginia, like the Army of the Potomac, was spread out. If he didn't seize the initiative and concentrate now, Meade would have the opportunity to defeat *him* in detail.

Day One: July 1, 1863

Brigadier General John Buford was a roughhewn Kentuckian who had already shown himself to be an outstanding cavalry commander under Pope and Hooker. When he reached Gettysburg, he immediately grasped the importance of holding the *high ground* called McPherson's Ridge, just west of town. Buford had fought at Fredericksburg and had seen how the Confederates, secure on the heights around that town, had rained-down slaughter upon the Union army of Ambrose Burnside (see Chapter 12). At Gettysburg, he knew that he would be badly outnumbered, but he also knew that he would have the advantage of fighting from the high ground and that his men, equipped with breech-loading carbines, would have a distinct rate-of-fire advantage. Shorter and lighter than the infantry musket, the cavalryman's breach-loading carbine was much faster to reload and fire than the traditional muzzle-loading muskets of the Confederate infantry.

DEFINITION

Soldiers and strategists frequently speak of the **high ground.** This is any elevated ground, such as a hill, on which troops can be placed so as to command clear fields of vision and fire over the ground below. Occupying the high ground always confers a tactical advantage.

The fighting began at 9:00 on the morning of July 1.

The High Ground

Taking up positions on McPherson's Ridge, Buford's cavalry fought dismounted, holding off the first waves of Heth's and William Pender's Confederate infantry divisions while General Reynolds's I Corps and General O. O. Howard's XI Corps rushed to reinforce the Union commander. Reynolds's troops began to arrive by 10:30, but by this time the Confederates were massing and had built up their superior strength. Union I Corps commander John Reynolds took personal command of the celebrated 1,800-man "Iron Brigade" in McPherson's Woods, to the west of the ridge. Within minutes the gallant major general, the man so many thought should have been in Meade's place as Army of the Potomac commander, was shot through the head. He died instantly.

Major General John F. Reynolds commanded the Union's I Corps at Gettysburg and personally led the famed "Iron Brigade" in the field. Cut down early in the battle, he was the highest-ranking officer to die at Gettysburg.
(Harper's Pictorial History of the Civil War, 1866)

By the time O. O. Howard and his XI Corps arrived, shortly before noon, the situation was chaotic. Union forces were repeatedly pushed back, only to rally and counterattack. But when Howard, who assumed overall command in the field following the death of Reynolds, tried to join a division (commanded by Major General Carl Schurz) to the beleaguered brigades of I Corps, the units, in the desperate confusion of combat, failed to link up. Thus the combined strength of Confederate forces under generals Robert Rodes, Jubal Early, and A. P. Hill were able at last to drive the Federals off McPherson's Ridge along with their other positions west and north of Gettysburg. The blue-coated soldiers now retreated into the town proper, fighting hand-to-hand near Pennsylvania College and, ultimately, retreating southeast of Gettysburg down the Baltimore Pike. Meade, who had yet to arrive on the field, sent his most trusted subordinate—General Winfield Scott Hancock—to take charge of the battered and faltering defense.

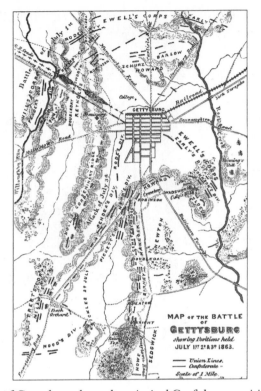

This battle map of Gettysburg shows the principal Confederate position at Seminary Ridge, southwest of town, and the fishhook-shaped deployment of the Union army, directly south of town (at Culp's Hill, Cemetery Hill, Cemetery Ridge and, to the far south, at Little Round Top and Big Round Top).
(Harper's Pictorial History of the Civil War, 1866)

Retreat to a Cemetery

The first day's fighting ended to Lee's advantage, but the battle was not over. The high ground of McPherson's Ridge was lost to the Union, but a catastrophic rout of the Federal forces had been stemmed. Even better, the Federal forces had fallen back to other high ground positions, East Cemetery Hill, Cemetery Ridge, and Culp's Hill, which together ran from due south to southeast of town. The Confederates occupied some high ground of their own, Oak Hill, northwest of town, and Seminary Ridge, due west of Gettysburg.

Thus, toward the end of July 1, the armies were in place on hills separated by a mile of fields and woods that lay to the southwest of town.

"If I Had Stonewall Jackson ..."

Like Ulysses S. Grant, Robert E. Lee is widely remembered as a great general because of his dynamic approach to combat. In contrast to most other generals of the conflict, Lee was more concerned with movement than position. That is why a timid plodder like George McClellan did not stand a chance against him. It was therefore highly uncharacteristic of Lee to leave the situation at Gettysburg in the static state that closed on July 1. In fact he had ordered General Ewell to follow up on his initial progress against the Union army, but appended to his order the phrase "if … practicable." The phrase was also characteristic of Lee. To "follow up" meant to launch an attack on Day One, against Cemetery Hill. But Lee phrased the order less as an urgent military directive than as a request. Apparently, Richard Stoddart Ewell did not judge such an attack to be "practicable." Instead, he gave his men a rest.

Well after the war, Lee reputedly lamented Ewell's decision not to attack: "If I had Stonewall Jackson at Gettysburg, I would have won that fight." And, having won that fight, he might have won the war. The point is, however, that the decision should never have been Ewell's to make.

Day Two: Union Holds the High Ground

While Lee was a formidable strategist and tactician who commanded the love and loyalty of his men, his leadership style more than once invited the kind of fatal error Ewell committed on this occasion. Lee's command problems at Gettysburg were compounded at dawn on July 2 by exhaustion and illness. The commanding general awoke with a bout of dysentery that was endemic to the hard and dirty life of a military field camp. A chronic sufferer from heart disease, he may also have suffered a mild heart attack at this time. In any event, although his mood was bold on the second day of battle, he was far from being in peak condition. Nevertheless, he met with his corps commanders to give detailed orders for an offensive with which he intended to crush the enemy army. Stuart, however, was still absent, and Lee was not fully aware of how many more Union troops were massing at Gettysburg. All he knew for certain was that they *were* massing, and this made him all the more eager to finish what had been started the day before.

Longstreet Advises

As usual, it was "Gloomy Pete" Longstreet who dissented. He believed—correctly, as it turned out—that almost the entire Army of the Potomac would be massing against the Confederates on this day. He feared that the Army of Northern Virginia would be overrun and overwhelmed. His advice was to pursue a policy of what he called "strategic offense—tactical defense"; that is, to manipulate the Union army into attacking the Confederate army where and when it was tactically advantageous to the Confederacy and when attacked to defend, inflicting great losses on the Federals. Longstreet pointed out that this approach had worked well at the two Bull Runs, at Antietam, and at Fredericksburg—all of which had resulted in costly repulses of the Federals (although Antietam ended as a very narrow Union victory).

Longstreet proposed a withdrawal to the south and a move against Meade from the rear.

Lee's impatience at this advice was uncharacteristic. No, he snapped. He would not *withdraw* his army after it had *won* a victory! To do so, he argued, would demoralize the men and, most likely, result in losing this opportunity to win a decisive victory.

The Fishhook

Practically everyone who has written about the opening of this second fateful day at Gettysburg has observed that the Union line was deployed in a giant, upside-down fishhook. Picture it. The hook's barb was just south of Culp's Hill, its turn was at Cemetery Hill, and the end of its shaft—its tie-end—at twin hills well to the south of town, known as Little Round Top and Big Round Top. Lee ordered Longstreet to attack the Union left, the shaft of the fishhook running along Cemetery Ridge and terminating at the Little and Big Round Tops. Lee himself would concentrate his forces northwest of the fishhook, where the curve met the shaft. Ewell to the north and northeast, above the curve of the fishhook, was to be prepared to swing down and smash the Union's right.

 SITES AND SIGHTS

Gettysburg National Military Park encompasses 3,850 acres, with 35 miles of park roads, 1,300 monuments, and some 400 cannon. A visitor's center at 97 Taneytown Road contains many exhibits. The Gettysburg National Cemetery is adjacent to the park. Contact the park at 717-334-1124.

Quick, Bold, Cheerful, and Hopeful

Despite the setback on July 1, George Gordon Meade was (as an aide described him) "quick, bold, cheerful, and hopeful" on the morning of July 2. These were not adjectives commonly associated with a commander who had a reputation for competent mediocrity. Yet when Lee's subordinates expressed relief that they were facing an enemy commander who lacked the boldness of "Fighting Joe" Hooker, Lee (who had served with Meade in the prewar army) pointed out that "Meade will commit no blunder on my front, and if I make one he will make haste to take advantage of it."

It is easy to understand why some of Lee's generals felt confident of victory. To look at the situation on a flat map would suggest to anyone that the Union was in grave trouble—surrounded on three sides. But both Lee and Meade had been trained at West Point as engineers, and neither looked at the world in just two dimensions. Both understood that battles are not fought on maps. Both Lee and Meade must have seen that the Federal position was actually quite strong, possessed of high ground that commanded clear fields of observation and clear fields of fire. Thanks to the absence of Jeb Stuart, what Lee did not know was that Meade now had almost 90,000 men at Gettysburg, opposing just 75,000 Confederates. This meant that the Union army's central position, surrounded by the rebels, actually leveraged a numerical superiority.

WAR NEWS

Confederate and Union troops fought fiercely at Gettysburg. But both were often terrified—so scared that many of them simply *forgot* to shoot. Some 27,500 muskets were recovered on the field after the battle. Of these, more than 12,000 contained 2 charges. They had been loaded, but not fired, and loaded again. Another 6,000 contained 3 to 10 charges and balls, and one musket was found stuffed with 23 rounds.

Temporary Insanity

Still, the Union army *was* partially surrounded. The stakes could not have been higher. If something went wrong, it could go very wrong.

Major General Daniel Sickles commanded the southernmost Union corps, the tie-end of the fishhook terminating at the Round Tops. A "political general," Sickles nevertheless had more military acumen than many other such commanders, having fought well at the Seven Days, Antietam, Fredericksburg, and Chancellorsville. Yet he also carried into battle a heavy freight of controversy.

Two years before the war, in Washington's Lafayette Park (just across Pennsylvania Avenue from the White House), Sickles shot and killed a man. The son of Francis Scott Key, author of "The Star-Spangled Banner," Philip Barton Key had been sleeping with Sickles's wife. Sickles was duly tried for a very public murder he certainly committed, but his lawyer (none other than the man who became Lincoln's secretary of war, Edwin M. Stanton) pleaded him not guilty by reason of "temporary insanity." It was the first time in legal history that this defense was used. Sickles's acquittal on this basis was scandalous enough, but he created even more of a scandal by taking his errant wife back.

Major General Daniel Sickles's impulsive and imprudent advance west of the Round Tops triggered a nearly disastrous attack by troops from Longstreet's corps. Hit in the leg during the battle, Sickles was carried from the field smoking a cigar. After his injured limb was amputated, he donated it to a medical museum; in later life he frequently paid visits to it.
(Library of Congress)

When Abraham Lincoln, a close friend, nominated Sickles as a brigadier general in September 1861, the Senate rejected the nomination. Only by twisting arms did Lincoln get a second nomination approved.

For many, it was at best disquieting to serve under a commander judged insane, temporarily or otherwise. And now, on this most critical of days, July 2, 1863, Sickles gave ample justification for that unease. Acting without orders from Meade, he advanced his III Corps about a half-mile from the rest of the Union line, where he stuck out, one combatant said, "like a sore thumb," exposing the Union's left flank to Longstreet's offensive.

Fortunately for the Union, Longstreet was as deliberate as Sickles was impulsive. It was four in the afternoon before the Confederate commander finally attacked. One of his subordinates, Major General John Bell Hood, hit Sickles in the Peach Orchard northwest of the Round Tops, pushing him back toward Little Round Top through a rocky area later dubbed the Devil's Den, on account of the ferocity of the fighting there.

The Professor

Battles are about planning and fighting of course, but they are also about seeing and understanding. Just before Hood launched his attack on Sickles, Brigadier General Gouverneur K. Warren, Meade's chief engineer, saw that Little Round Top was undefended, save for a few signalmen. He instantly understood that Hood's division would easily seize that high ground and thus be in position to turn the Union's flank, fighting right up the shaft of the Federal fishhook.

Warren sent his staff officers to round up a brigade under Colonel Strong Vincent to immediately occupy Little Round Top. Vincent soon fell in this action. At the same time, Brigadier General Stephen Weed advanced to Little Round Top with his brigade, at the extreme south end of which was the 20th Maine commanded by Colonel Joshua Lawrence Chamberlain. This battle-battered regiment, at less than half strength with just 500 men, made up the Federal flank.

Chamberlain was not a professional soldier. A professor of rhetoric at Bowdoin College, he took a sabbatical in 1862 intending to study in Europe, but joined the Union army instead. Now with just 500 men, including some mutinous soldiers who had been put under his guard, he held off attack after attack from a numerically superior force of Alabama troops. Finally, in one of the battle's greatest moments of extraordinary achievement, he defeated them. His ammunition was all but exhausted—a circumstance that should have compelled him to fall back. Instead, realizing the grave importance of holding his position and preventing the Confederates from turning the Union flank, he led a fierce downhill charge, scattering the rebels, exclusively using bayonets. The day, the battle, the Army of the Potomac, and perhaps the Union were saved.

WAR NEWS

Joshua Lawrence Chamberlain (1828–1914) was wounded at Gettysburg, and on three other occasions. He was given the honor of receiving the Confederate surrender at Appomattox Court House on April 9, 1865, and after the war, served several terms as governor of Maine. In 1893, he received the Medal of Honor for his actions at Little Round Top.

Devil's Den, Peach Orchard, and Wheatfield

Despite the failure of Hood's initial attack, the Confederates still held Devil's Den, below Little Round Top, and fired on the reinforced defenders of that hill from behind boulders. Action was hot, too, in the Peach Orchard and Wheatfield, to the northwest of Little Round Top. In the Wheatfield, no fewer than six Confederate attacks were met by six Union counterattacks, leaving casualties and corpses thicker than any wheat harvest.

Sickles's impulsive advance might have meant Union defeat, but Longstreet was never able to coordinate his attacks—devastating as they were—to decisive effect. Meade, as well as Major General Winfield Scott Hancock, now leading II and III Corps, repaired Sickles's error by skillfully redeploying forces as needed to check each major Confederate attempt at a breakthrough.

At sundown, the Confederates attacked Cemetery, East Cemetery, and Culp's Hills. The Federals held on to all their positions except at Culp's Hill, but then counterattacked there at 4:30 on the morning of July 3 and, after seven hours of fighting, turned back the Confederates.

Day Three: Massive Assault

As July 2 melted into July 3, the Union army continued to hold its high ground but, as Robert E. Lee saw it, tenuously. For Lee it was a tempting situation. He had done well on the 1st, and while he had failed to crush the Union army on the 2nd, he believed that he had worn it down sufficiently to defeat it decisively on the 3rd.

Longstreet Advises Again

As Lee saw it, he had been repulsed on July 2 repeatedly, but each time just barely. He now proposed an all-out attack. As usual, Longstreet protested the plan, but Lee insisted that too much blood had been invested to withdraw now.

Meade's forces had hardly been idle. During the night and early morning, in addition to retaking Culp's Hill, they greatly improved their defenses and positioned final reinforcements, bracing for the attack.

Both sides were tired, bone tired, as the warm morning of July 3 simmered into an oppressively sultry midday.

Pickett's Charge

The massive assault Lee had in mind was destined to be the single most celebrated operation of the war—though it was misnamed for the general Longstreet had assigned merely to form the brigades in preparation for the assault. Major General George Pickett was a courageous and high-spirited Virginian, but hardly the most skilled of Lee's commanders. He commanded just three of the nine brigades—a total of 12,500 men—who were massed for the attack. James Johnston Pettigrew and Isaac Ridgeway Trimble led the others.

By noon, they were arrayed: disciplined veteran soldiers perfectly aligned in battle ranks across a series of rolling hills, facing the Union soldiers dug in on Cemetery Ridge a mile away. In preparation for "Pickett's Charge," 150 Confederate cannon pounded the ridge, only to be answered by equally devastating fire from Union artillery.

At 1:45 in the afternoon, the 12,500 men, in closely formed ranks, advanced. The Union artillerists fired solid shot. Still, the gray-uniformed men—those who did not fall—advanced. When the advancing enemy was close enough, the Union gunners replaced their solid ammunition with canister shot, which consisted of iron balls packed into cans, which burst apart, spraying the field of fire with hundreds of deadly projectiles. The infantry, from cover and from the high ground, opened up with their muskets.

Major General George Pickett, CSA, forever regretted the desperate charge on July 3 that bears his name.
(Library of Congress)

"A Sob—a Gasp"

A Federal soldier described the rebel advance as "an overwhelming relentless tide of an ocean of armed men sweeping upon us! On they move, as with one soul in perfect order … magnificent, grim, irresistible."

But fated to fail and to die.

Two of Pickett's three brigadier generals were cut down in the charge, and the third was gravely wounded. All 15 regimental commanders engaged were killed or wounded. At a place called the Angle, 150 men led by Brigadier General Lewis Armistead did succeed in raising the Confederate colors above Cemetery Ridge, but all were quickly killed or captured.

Never Forget

Of the 12,500 men who charged Cemetery Ridge 5,000 lived to retreat to Seminary Ridge.

That night, Pickett wrote to his fiancée:

> My brave boys were so full of hope and confident of victory as I led them forth! Over on Cemetery Ridge the Federals beheld a scene which has never previously been enacted—an army forming in line of battle in full view, under their very eyes—charging across a space nearly a mile in length, pride and glory soon to be crushed by an overwhelming heartbreak.
>
> Well, it is all over now. The awful rain of shot and shell was a sob—a gasp.
>
> I can still hear them cheering as I gave the order, "Forward!" the thrill of their joyous voices as they called out, "We'll follow you, Marse George, we'll follow you!" On, how faithfully they followed me on—on—to their death, and I led them on—on—on—Oh God!
>
> I can't write you a love letter today, my Sally. But for you, my darling, I would rather, a million times rather, sleep in an unknown grave.

An ebullient, carefree man before July 3, 1862, George Pickett was forever sorrowful after that day. "That man," he said after the war, referring to Lee, "destroyed my division."

COUNT OFF!

The Union fielded 88,289 men at Gettysburg, of whom 3,155 were killed and another 14,529 were wounded, mortally wounded, or captured; 5,365 went missing. Of 75,000 Confederates engaged, 3,903 were killed; 18,735 were wounded, mortally wounded, or captured; and 5,425 were reported missing in action. Combined Union and Confederate casualties: 51,112.

But no one was harder on Robert E. Lee than Lee himself. Organizing the retreat from Gettysburg, he remarked, "It was all my fault; … let us do the best we can toward saving which is left us."

"My God, Is That All?"

Meade had won a great victory. To have lost at Gettysburg might have brought the defeat of Lincoln for reelection, perhaps an attack on Washington, and maybe a negotiated settlement with an independent Confederate States of America. Yet, in the aftermath, like McClellan after Antietam, Meade lacked the will to press his weary, battered army to pursue Lee's even wearier, more badly battered, and more severely reduced forces.

On July 4, 1863, the anniversary of American independence ("four score and seven years ago"), there was no more fighting at Gettysburg. "My God," Lincoln exclaimed when he heard that Meade had allowed Lee to retreat back across the Potomac and into Virginia. "My God, is that all?"

These Honored Dead

Yet Lincoln knew that, with the simultaneous collapse of Vicksburg in the West (see Chapter 13), Gettysburg was the irrevocable turning point of the war. On November 19, 1863, the president delivered an address at the dedication of the Soldiers' National Cemetery at Gettysburg, explaining that the "great civil war" tested whether a nation, conceived in Liberty, and dedicated to the proposition that all men are created equal "can long endure."

Gettysburg: Impact and Heritage

Lincoln's "Gettysburg Address," concluded in two minutes, is one of the most profound oratorical monuments ever erected to military achievement and human sacrifice. More than any other battle of the war, Gettysburg proved the limits of Confederate prowess of arms and the full extent of the Union's resolve and capacity to preserve the nation as a nation, indivisible.

The Least You Need to Know

- Robert E. Lee saw Gettysburg as his opportunity to crush the Army of the Potomac on Northern territory and thereby force the North to agree to a negotiated peace with an independent Confederate States of America.
- By seizing and holding the high ground around Gettysburg, Union forces obtained a decisive advantage against Lee's army.
- In a battle full of heroism, two of the most extraordinary actions were the defense of Little Round Top led by Colonel Joshua Lawrence Chamberlain of Maine on July 2 and "Pickett's Charge," a massive, gallant, and ultimately suicidal attack by the Confederates on July 3.
- By defeating Lee at Gettysburg, the Army of the Potomac turned the tide of war against the South; however, by allowing Lee's survivors to escape, Union General George Gordon Meade also prolonged the war.

"Not for Uncle Sambo"

In This Chapter

- The draft triggers a race riot in New York
- Attempts to create a rebellion in the North
- The role of African American soldiers in the war
- The 54th Massachusetts wins glory

As the second decade of the twenty-first century begins, our nation is deeply divided along political, cultural, economic, ethnic, and even racial lines. One hundred fifty years after the commencement of the Civil War, a few voices even speak of secession from the Union. Even so, for the great majority of Americans it remains difficult even to imagine a political and psychological scenario in which the country splits itself along a certain line and neighboring states suddenly become a foreign and hostile nation.

Yet the fact is that the nation was even *more* divided in the 1860s than neatly between North and South. Within the two regions, there were many sharp divisions as well, and none were sharper, more bitter, or more ugly than the division between blacks and whites. This chapter is about race, hate, treachery, and the glory that was born despite it all.

The Draft Riots

This book, like most other histories of the Civil War, tells you that the Union victories at Vicksburg and Gettysburg were turning points in the war. That these Union triumphs made the defeat of the Confederacy likely may be apparent in hindsight, but, in July 1863, the outcome was by no means clear to either North or South. War weariness gripped much of the North even as its armies approached the threshold of victory. In what should have been the triumphant afterglow of Vicksburg and Gettysburg, that despair, fanned by racial fear and hatred, burst into flames during one violent week in New York City.

Racial Rage

To most of the struggling immigrants who called New York City home, the prospect of a tidal wave of even more downtrodden immigrants, newly emancipated slaves coming up from the South following a Confederate defeat, was terrifying and enraging. In no immigrant group were such feelings stronger than among the 200,000 Irish New Yorkers, many of whom had fled the Great Potato Famine that had starved their native land in 1848. Most of the midcentury Irish immigrants endured discrimination and persecution, and earned their living mainly by supplying cheap common labor.

> **COUNT OFF!**
>
> Despite the draft, the Union army was a largely volunteer force. The number of draftees actually held to service during the war was a mere 52,068; 86,724 men paid the $300 commutation fee to receive exemption, and 42,581 men enlisted as substitutes for draftees.

Freed black slaves, they feared, would supply that labor for even less. A new famine was on the horizon, and worst of all, Lincoln's new draft law, the Conscription Act passed by Congress in March, would force the Irish to fight and die to free the very slaves who would take their jobs.

Aside, perhaps, from the beleaguered Irish and other disadvantaged groups, few Northerners objected to a draft. The Conscription Act even prompted a good many young men to enlist voluntarily; they felt it would be shameful to wait to fight until the law compelled them.

But it was nevertheless a grossly unfair law. Any conscript could avoid service by hiring a substitute or by paying a $300 "commutation fee." In 1863, only the well-to-do could afford such a sum. Immigrant laborers, who earned about a dollar a day, hadn't a prayer of scraping together a whole year's pay.

There were rumblings and violent demonstrations in Iowa, Illinois, Indiana, and Ohio, but the worst violence broke out in New York City.

A Ragged, Coatless Army

The draft commenced in the city on Saturday, July 11. On Monday the 13th, in the words of journalist Joel T. Headley,

> … a ragged, coatless, heterogeneously weaponed army heaved tumultuously along toward Third Avenue. Tearing down the telegraph poles as it crossed the Harlem & New Haven Railroad track, it surged angrily up around the building where the drafting was going on …. The mob seized the [draft-lottery] wheel in which were the names, and what books, papers, and lists were left, and tore them up.

When the rioters were unable to break open a safe, they set fire to the building. They overran and looted the Second Avenue armory, and pillaged jewelry and liquor stores as well.

Then they loosed their rage upon the race they scorned and feared. Knots of rioters ran down African Americans, beating some, hanging others from lampposts. On Tuesday, as the rioting and looting continued unabated, the Colored Orphan Asylum was set ablaze. The rioters cheered the flames.

By Wednesday, the rioters were tearing down the houses of African Americans by hand. But Wednesday evening, a detachment of General Meade's weary Gettysburg veterans marched into the city to restore order. "There was some terrific fighting," a witness recalled. "Streets were swept again and again by *grape[shot]*; houses were stormed at the point of the bayonet; rioters were picked off by sharpshooters as they fired on the troops from housetops; men were hurled, dying or dead, into the streets."

DEFINITION

Grape or **grapeshot** was a type of ammunition consisting of a cluster of small iron balls used mostly on ships as a cannon charge. Like canister ammunition, grapeshot was intended to spray out and kill personnel.

The New York Draft Riots (July 13 through 16, 1863) were racially motivated.
White rioters, mostly Irish immigrants, lynched blacks and burned the Colored
Orphan Asylum.
(Harper's Pictorial History of the Civil War, 1866)

Northern Rebellion?

Meade's men soon quelled the New York City Draft Riot, but sporadic violence
flared in nearby Brooklyn, Jamaica, Staten Island, Jersey City, Newark, and farther
afield in Albany and Troy, New York. Boston and Portsmouth, New Hampshire, as
well as Columbia and Bucks counties, Pennsylvania, all saw rioting, as did parts of
Kentucky. In Wisconsin, the governor called out the militia to put down disturbances
in Milwaukee and Ozaukee County.

COUNT OFF!

No accurate count was ever made of New York City's Draft Riot victims. At least
194 people died, including 75 African Americans, but contemporary estimates
range as high as a thousand killed on all sides.

A Pennsylvania newspaper headline summed up the "rebellion" in an ugly but accurate headline:

WILLING TO FIGHT FOR UNCLE SAM BUT NOT FOR UNCLE
SAMBO

Rebellion? The South hoped so. J. B. Jones, a clerk in the Confederate War Department, Richmond, noted gleefully in his diary for July 17: "… *awfully* good news from New York: an INSURRECTION, the loss of many lives, extensive pillage and burning."

> **DEFINITION**
>
> **Sambo** was one of the many demeaning names whites applied to African Americans during the nineteenth century. Some linguists have suggested that the term might be derived from the Fulani (Senegalese) word for uncle.

Copperheads: Snakes in the Grass?

If Southerners were thrilled by the prospect of riots growing into out-and-out rebellion in the North, many Northerners attributed the riots to a conspiracy of Confederate agents.

In truth, all the ingredients necessary to start a riot were amply present in the Conscription Act and what it meant to the Irish and other white workingmen. No outside agitators were required. Yet many saw the Draft Riots as evidence of disloyalty simmering in the Union states.

Knights and Castles: Secret Societies

The polite name for any Northerner who advocated restoration of the Union through a negotiated settlement with the South was *Peace Democrat*, but such people were more commonly called *Copperheads*. The term was first used by the *New York Tribune* on July 20, 1861, which compared the Peace Democrats to the venomous snake in the grass, which strikes without warning.

> **DEFINITION**
>
> A **Peace Democrat** was any Northerner who advocated a negotiated settlement of the war, with concessions to the South. **Copperhead** was the disparaging term applied to Peace Democrats, evoking the image of a venomous snake. Copperhead was a pejorative term, but many Peace Democrats embraced the title and even fashioned badges by cutting the goddess Liberty out of copper pennies. (Historians debate whether the badges came before or after the label was applied to Peace Democrats.)

The Copperheads opposed the Conscription Act as well as the Emancipation Proclamation, which, they argued, changed the Civil War from a struggle to preserve the Union to a "war for the Negro." They also opposed the *Radical Republican* view, as expressed by Pennsylvania Congressman Thaddeus Stevens, that following victory, the North should "treat those states outside of the Union as conquered provinces and settle them with new men."

Who would these "new men" be? Well, they would *not* be Democrats, which meant that Northern Democrats were being asked to fight a war that might restore the Union but would certainly destroy their party.

The most determined Copperheads organized secret societies either modeled on, or actual outgrowths of, so-called Southern Rights clubs, which had sprouted up during the Nullification Crisis of the 1830s (discussed in Chapter 2). In 1854, a physician of dubious medical credentials, George W. L. Bickley, founded the Knights of the Golden Circle. Headquartered in Cincinnati and full of elaborate rituals, the society—later called the Order of the American Knights and the Sons of Liberty—spawned satellite lodges ("castles," they were called) throughout Kentucky, Missouri, Iowa, Illinois, Indiana, and Ohio as well as in the South.

> **DEFINITION**
>
> **Radical Republicans** were Northerners who advocated continuation of the war to absolute, total victory, and they further proposed severe punishment for the South following its defeat.

A Man Named Vallandigham

If the Copperheads and Knights rallied around any one leader, it was Clement Vallandigham, a prodigy who knew the alphabet at age 2, spoke Greek and Latin at 12, became principal of Union Academy in Maryland at 19, and was editor of the

Western Empire, a radical Democratic newspaper, at 20. Vallandigham gained renown in Ohio as an unbeatable defense attorney.

Clement Vallandigham was the leading figure among Ohio Copperheads. He survived the Civil War, but in 1870, while practicing law in Ohio, he accidentally shot and killed himself when demonstrating a firearm that was an exhibit in a murder trial.

(Harper's Pictorial History of the Civil War, 1866)

After a term as lieutenant governor of Ohio, Vallandigham was elected to Congress as an anti-Abolitionist Democrat, but was defeated in 1862. His last speech before Congress, just after passage of the Conscription Act, urged his countrymen to stop fighting. Republicans called the speech treason; Copperheads heard it as a rallying cry.

The Great Northwest Conspiracy

Governor Oliver Morton of Indiana, fearing the spread of Copperhead influence in his state, appealed to Secretary of War Edwin Stanton to send Brigadier General

Henry B. Carrington to Indianapolis for the purpose of organizing a squad of under-cover agents to infiltrate Copperhead secret societies.

Although Carrington soon discovered widespread Copperhead activity, the administration in Washington dismissed groups such as the Knights of the Golden Circle as harmless fanatics. Carrington learned that certain Copperheads had graduated from preaching mere defeatism to actively aiding and abetting John Hunt Morgan, a Confederate guerrilla leader whose "Morgan's Raiders" were famed and feared in the Old Northwest and Kentucky.

John Hunt Morgan was a famed and much-feared Confederate guerrilla leader. His July 1863 raids into Indiana and Ohio were the farthest north any Confederate force penetrated during the Civil War. Morgan was killed by Union forces on September 4, 1864, in Greenville, Tennessee.
(Harper's Pictorial History of the Civil War, 1866)

Morgan Rides and Raids

On March 19, 1863, Carrington wired Lincoln that Morgan intended to "raise the standard of revolt in Indiana. Thousands believe this and his photograph is hung in many homes. In some counties his name is daily praised."

Morgan's Raid took place during July 2 to 26, 1863, and was the longest cavalry raid of the war: over 700 miles in 25 days of virtually continuous combat. Although his commanding officer, Braxton Bragg, had ordered him to stay south of the Ohio River, the impetuous Morgan believed that only by bringing the war into the North, and thereby winning Copperhead support, could action in the region be truly effective. However, Morgan did not attempt to distinguish between loyal Northerners and Copperheads. His men indiscriminately plundered homes and businesses, wrecked railroads and bridges, and generally looted whatever of value they found. His raid, though impressive, was of no strategic value because it did nothing to win support in the Ohio and Indiana region.

Half of Morgan's raiders were eventually run to ground, at Buffington Island on July 19, and Morgan himself was captured at Lisbon, Ohio, eight days later. Treated as common criminals, he and his men were sent to the Ohio State Penitentiary—from which they soon escaped.

Another Riot

On April 13, 1863, Major General Ambrose Burnside, who had been named Commander of the Department of the Ohio after his removal as commander of the Army of the Potomac following the disaster at Fredericksburg (see Chapter 12), issued an order authorizing the death penalty for couriers carrying secret mails, for enemy agents operating behind Union lines, and for "recruiting officers of secret societies."

During a May Day address to Democrats assembled at Mount Vernon, Ohio, Clement Vallandigham responded by spitting on a copy of the order. Burnside, in turn, ordered Vallandigham's arrest, which touched off riots in Dayton and elsewhere across the country. Even newspapers opposed to the radical Democratic Party line rose to defend Vallandigham's right of free speech, and the Ohio politician, whom few outside his own state and party took seriously, was now catapulted into national prominence.

With the North drawing as close to widespread insurrection as it ever would, Lincoln wisely intervened to defuse the crisis. Although Vallandigham was tried and sentenced to imprisonment for the duration of the war, the president commuted the sentence to banishment in the South.

Confederate authorities, however, informed Vallandigham that he could not remain in the South if he still considered himself loyal to the Union. Declaring himself loyal, he sailed for the West Indies and from there, made his way to Nova Scotia. Despite his banishment, the Ohio Democratic Party defiantly nominated him as its candidate for governor. On July 15, 1863, he opened his campaign—in exile—by directing an address to the people of Ohio from the Canadian side of Niagara Falls.

The Northern Revolt Sputters and Dies

Vallandigham was not elected and, with his removal, the Great Northwest Conspiracy—the South's poorly coordinated effort to collaborate with Northern Copperheads in order to bring about a revolution in Ohio, Indiana, Kentucky, and Illinois—sputtered and died.

Glory

Doubtless some Copperheads were moved by a sincere desire to see the end of bloodshed, but most were politically motivated by a desire to block the Radical Republican destruction of their party. Many also had an uglier motive. They did not want to fight and die to free the slaves.

In fact, a growing number of African Americans—freed slaves, runaway slaves, and Northern blacks who had never been slaves—did not want whites fighting and dying for them. More and more, African Americans petitioned for the privilege of fighting—and perhaps dying—to secure their own freedom. As early as August 1861, Frederick Douglass had spoken eloquently for the enrollment of black soldiers (see Chapter 5), but Northern resistance to the proposal was at first unyielding.

Many in the white military establishment believed that African Americans were inferior and untrainable. Others just didn't trust them with firearms. Still others flatly objected to putting blacks in the uniform of the United States.

There was another reason for the resistance. Military men feared that the presence of African American soldiers in the Union army would actually boost Confederate morale and incite Southern soldiers to renewed effort fueled by outrage. Lincoln worried that recruiting black soldiers would also turn the slaveholding border states against the Union.

Corps d'Afrique

In the spring of 1862, a group of free blacks who had formed a (never activated) Confederate regiment in 1861 offered their services to General Ben Butler after New Orleans fell to the Union. Butler declined the offer, until he was threatened with a Confederate attack in August, whereupon he recruited three black regiments as the Louisiana Native Guard, or Corps d'Afrique. The troops took to the field in November 1862, even though the War Department refused officially to muster them in.

In the meantime, also during the spring of 1862, on the Union-occupied Sea Islands of South Carolina, Major General David Hunter raised an African American regiment, which consisted of volunteers as well as men he drafted. The War Department refused to sanction the regiment, and Hunter disbanded all but a single company of troops by August.

Out west, in Kansas, James H. Lane, a major general of militia, raised two regiments of fugitive slaves and free blacks, which actually saw some action early in the war *before* they were officially recognized by the War Department in 1863.

WAR NEWS

In contrast to the U.S. Army, the U.S. Navy did employ African American sailors, even before the Civil War, albeit generally in menial capacities. During the Civil War, 15 percent of the U.S. Navy was African American.

Congress Acts

President Lincoln and the War Department vetoed the actions of Hunter and Butler, but as Union defeats weighed more and more heavily on public opinion, popular resistance to African American recruitment diminished. On August 25, 1862, the War Department authorized the military governor of the South Carolina Sea Islands to raise five regiments of African American troops on the island.

WAR NEWS

Although all black military units were commanded by white officers, a handful of African Americans (fewer than 100) *were* eventually commissioned as officers before the war ended. This included eight army surgeons commissioned as majors.

After the final Emancipation Proclamation was issued on January 1, 1863, President Lincoln personally called for four black regiments. By war's end, 178,985 African Americans were serving in 166 regiments. This represented about 10 percent of the Union army.

Civil War photographs of African American troops are extremely rare. This one shows the members of Company E, 4th U.S. Colored Troops, a unit formed in Baltimore during the summer of 1863.
(U.S. Army Military History Institute, Carlisle, Pennsylvania)

Muskets or Shovels?

The mass of white soldiers and officers did not greet the arrival of African American troops with open arms. The soldiers were wholly segregated in all-black regiments commanded by white officers. They were often subject to physical and verbal abuse. They were the very last in line to receive equipment and proper uniforms. For a time, they were paid less than white soldiers.

Most black regiments were initially assigned fatigue duty (common labor) and garrison duty (minding the fort). But eventually the need for soldiers at the front saw many blacks on the battlefield.

The 54th Massachusetts Regiment

Although many African American soldiers were relegated to laboring assignments, black units did fight in 449 engagements, including 39 major battles. The most celebrated black regiment was the 54th Massachusetts Infantry. It drew attention as the first African American regiment raised in the North (previous black units were all recruited from occupied Southern states), and it was led by the earnest, handsome, and dashing 25-year-old Colonel Robert Gould Shaw, son of a prominent Boston abolitionist family. But it was thrust into truly national prominence by its performance on July 18, 1863, in a desperate assault on Battery Wagner, a Confederate fort protecting the entrance to Charleston Harbor.

WAR NEWS

On May 1, 1863, the Confederate Congress authorized President Davis to "put to death or … otherwise [punish]" any black soldiers taken as prisoners of war. President Lincoln responded on July 30 with a warning that "for every soldier of the United States killed in violation of the laws of war, a Rebel soldier shall be executed; and for every one enslaved by the enemy or sold into Slavery, a Rebel soldier shall be placed at hard labor on public works."

Spearheading the attack by two brigades, the 54th took on a suicidal assignment—one soldier called it "the most fatal and fruitless campaign of the war"—but Gould and his men accepted it cheerfully. They failed to take the fort, losing 281 of the 600 men engaged including Shaw, whom the rebels sought to dishonor by throwing him into a common grave with the bodies of the black soldiers he had led. Hearing of this, the young hero's father spoke for his family: "We can imagine no holier place than in which he is."

COUNT OFF!

Approximately 37,300 African American soldiers died in the Civil War.

A 54th Massachusetts man, Sargeant William H. Carney, became the first African American to receive the Medal of Honor, for his service against Battery Wagner (16 other black soldiers and 4 sailors would also receive the medal during the war). President Lincoln, for so long reluctant to recruit black troops and then to commit them to battle, later called the "use of colored troops … the heaviest blow yet dealt to the rebellion."

Colonel Robert Gould Shaw was commander of the 54th Massachusetts Regiment,
the black unit depicted in the 1989 film Glory.
(Harper's Pictorial History of the Civil War, 1866)

The Least You Need to Know

- The Union's unfair Conscription Act, combined with the resentment some whites felt about fighting a war to free black slaves, touched off Draft Riots in New York City and elsewhere.

- Northern "Peace Democrats," popularly called Copperheads, agitated for a negotiated end to the war and concessions to the South.

- Some Copperhead secret societies collaborated with Confederate guerrillas to foment general insurrection in the North.

- Despite discrimination, persecution, and (often) relegation to menial labor, African American regiments performed with distinction.

From Mud to Mountain

In This Chapter

- Bloodless win at Chattanooga
- Counterattack at Chickamauga
- A costly Confederate victory
- Battles of Lookout Mountain and Missionary Ridge
- The Confederates lose the West

In the aftermath of the Union victories at Vicksburg and Gettysburg, the pace of the war slowed to an exhausted crawl. Confederate guerrilla John Hunt Morgan's 700-mile, 25-day cavalry raid across Ohio accomplished nothing of strategic value.

New York City, as we saw in Chapter 16, erupted into three days of draft and race riot but that, too, was quickly extinguished. And Lee, finding the Potomac flooded, entrenched his Gettysburg-battered soldiers at Williamsport, Maryland. Meade, exhausted as well, did not attack him despite the urging of a number of his officers, and by July 14, the Army of Northern Virginia had crossed the Potomac back into Virginia, with Major General Henry Heth successfully fighting a rearguard action against Union forces at Falling Waters, Maryland.

Slowly, the main battle action shifted from Mississippi and Pennsylvania to central Tennessee and northern Georgia.

By the Book

Ulysses S. Grant and his men might have been tired and worn after the fall of Vicksburg, but Grant was all for pushing on through southern Mississippi and

Alabama. He wanted to take Mobile, which would bring Confederate General Braxton Bragg running down from Chattanooga, leaving that key city along the Moccasin Bend of the Tennessee River firmly in Union hands. Grant wanted to push on because—well, who was there to stop him? Short on resources, the Confederates had no one to field against him.

But Henry Wager "Old Brains" Halleck, now the Union army's general-in-chief, *could* and *did* stop Grant. He was a by-the-book commander, and the book said that it was important for a victorious army to occupy the territory it took. Instead of concentrating Grant against the Confederate army, Halleck dispersed his forces to various places in Louisiana (for an invasion of Texas), to Missouri, to Arkansas, and to garrisons in occupied Tennessee and Mississippi.

"Old Rosy" Gets a Kick in the Pants

Union General William Starke Rosecrans, West Point Class of 1842, was at the head of the Army of the Cumberland in Tennessee. His opponent was Braxton Bragg, general in command of the Confederate Army of Tennessee.

"Old Rosy," as his troops called Rosecrans, had been sparring with Bragg since the end of October 1862, without taking the initiative. It is true that Rosecrans avoided disaster during the Battle of Stones River, Tennessee, during December 30, 1862 to January 3, 1863, but he had lost ground to Bragg. Tennessee, Lincoln was well aware, harbored many Union loyalists, and by seizing Chattanooga it would be possible to take Knoxville, and thereby gain control of the entire eastern portion of the state. Rosecrans was popular with his troops, but by spring 1863 Lincoln was making noises about relieving him.

Thus kicked, Old Rosy at last moved. After Grant crossed the Mississippi below Vicksburg on May 1, 1863, Union strategists realized that Bragg would most likely want to send reinforcements to the beleaguered river stronghold. Rosecrans's mission was to bottle up Bragg in Tennessee to prevent any troops from going to Vicksburg, but the Union general didn't get going until mid-June. Still his deliberation proved effective, for he maneuvered skillfully and in such a way, as to force Bragg to withdraw south of the Tennessee River.

Through a series of brilliant feints and deceptions—all carried out during 17 consecutive days of miserable, driving rain—Rosecrans moved his troops behind Bragg's right flank near Tullahoma. By July 4 (after another flanking movement) Rosecrans forced Bragg, outnumbered, to retreat from Tullahoma and withdraw to Chattanooga.

The city of Chattanooga during the war. Note the army tents in the foreground and Lookout Mountain in the background.
(National Archives and Records Administration)

At this point, Rosecrans begged for reinforcements in order to take Chattanooga. When none were forthcoming he decided to keep maneuvering, and he executed a surprise crossing of the Tennessee River 30 miles west of Chattanooga. Were Rosecrans a Burnside, he probably would have launched a desperate frontal assault on Bragg's defensive positions in Chattanooga. And like Burnside, he would have gotten his men slaughtered. Instead Rosecrans marched through a series of gaps in Lookout Mountain, the long ridge south-southwest of Chattanooga, and targeted the Western and Atlantic Railroad. This was Bragg's supply and communications line to Atlanta. With it severed, Bragg had no choice but to evacuate Chattanooga.

WAR NEWS

The Civil War was the first war that ran on rails. Of the 31,000 miles of railroad networking the nation in 1860, only 9,000 miles were in the South. Northern railroads tended to run east and west, Southern routes from inland terminals to seaports, mostly north and south. The result was poor rail interconnection that put the South at a decided disadvantage for moving large numbers of troops.

Counterattack at Chickamauga

Slow and deliberate, "Rosy" Rosecrans had pulled off one of the most brilliant and remarkable campaigns of the war. After two and one-half years of combat in which each small gain was paid for by a torrent of blood, he had taken the prize of Chattanooga almost without shedding any blood at all.

Inertia is the tendency of a body at rest to remain at rest, or—if in motion—to *stay* in motion. If one quality dominated the strategic thinking of William S. Rosecrans, it was inertia. He was slow to start his campaign, reluctant to accelerate his campaign, and, now that it was in full swing, he was not about to *stop* his campaign.

But he should have. Holding Chattanooga, his best move would have been to concentrate his forces there, rest them, resupply them, and then resume the offensive against Bragg. Instead, he kept going, and his three exhausted corps soon became separated from one another in the mountain passes.

Bragg in the meantime, halted at LaFayette, Georgia, 25 miles south of Chattanooga, where he was met by substantial reinforcements, including two divisions commanded by James Longstreet. Reinforced, Bragg moved in for a counterattack. The place was Chickamauga Creek, in Georgia, just 12 miles south of Chattanooga, Tennessee. The date was September 19.

> **SITES AND SIGHTS**
>
> The place where the fighting at Chickamauga started still stands. The recently restored Lee and Gordon's Mill, a half-mile south of the Chickamauga and Chattanooga National Military Park (profiled later in this chapter) can be reached by taking Exit 350 (Battlefield Parkway or Highway 2) off I-75 west to Three Notches Road. Turn left and drive 10 miles (the road becomes Burning Bush Road) to the mill. The mansion of mill owner James Gordon, The Gordon-Lee Mansion, briefly used by Rosecrans as his headquarters, is located in the town of Chickamauga. Today, it is a functioning inn. Contact: 706-375-4728.

In the Thick of It

The night before the battle, both sides shifted and moved troops, but in the dense woods, neither side knew the other's position. Worse, neither side was fully aware of the disposition of its *own* troops. With daybreak, Union General George Henry Thomas ordered a reconnaissance near Lee and Gordon's Mill, a local landmark on

Chickamauga Creek. These troops, led by Brigadier General John Brannan, encountered and drove back the dismounted cavalry of Nathan Bedford Forrest.

The Chickamauga battlefield on September 19, 1863. The solid rectangles represent Union troop positions, the open rectangles Confederate.
(Harper's Pictorial History of the Civil War, 1866)

Forrest called on nearby infantry units for help, and suddenly, an all-out battle exploded. Every division of the three Union corps was engaged, and of the Confederates, only two divisions were held in reserve.

The fighting—it lasted all day—was some of the bloodiest in this theater of the war. Yet for all the bloodshed, neither side had gained an advantage by day's end.

A "Gap" That Wasn't

Applied to the site of the contest at Chickamauga, the word "battlefield" was a misnomer. A *field* it was not—heavily forested, it was rugged terrain that had been churned into muddy soup by heavy rains. On the first night, both sides hastily tried to improve their positions, and Rosecrans's men dug in as best they could. That night, too, Bragg received reinforcements in the form of Longstreet's divisions.

At 9:00 on Sunday morning, September 20, the Confederates attacked, and for the next two hours, the Federals held them off.

Rosecrans was nothing if not a careful planner. But the terrain of Chickamauga could confuse any commander and confound any plan. He did not have an accurate picture of how his own units were deployed. By midmorning of this second day of battle, struggling to plug what he thought was a gap in his right flank, he ordered troops from what he thought was the left to shift to the right.

But there was no gap. There never had been. Worse, thinking he was moving troops from the left to the right, he actually moved them out of the right flank, thereby *creating* the very gap he had meant to fill. At 11:30, Longstreet attacked at precisely the gap Rosecrans had inadvertently made, hitting divisions commanded by Major General Philip Sheridan and by Brigadier General Jefferson Columbus Davis, shattering them, and driving the Union right into its own left.

Rock of Chickamauga

The Battle of Chickamauga was rapidly disintegrating into a military disaster as terrible as any that had ever befallen the Union army. Rosecrans and two of his corps commanders, Thomas Leonidas Crittenden and Alexander McDowell McCook, unable to rally their routed forces, believed that the entire army was being destroyed. They joined the chaotic retreat to Chattanooga.

WAR NEWS

Thomas Leonidas Crittenden was one of two sons of Kentucky Senator John Jordan Crittenden, whose Crittenden Compromise of 1860 was a last-ditch effort to avert civil war (see Chapter 4). Crittenden's other warrior son, George, became a *Confederate* general. For Alexander McDowell McCook, the Civil War was also a family affair. He was one of the 17 "Fighting McCooks of Ohio," who included six generals, an army surgeon, and a naval officer, in addition to other officers and enlisted men.

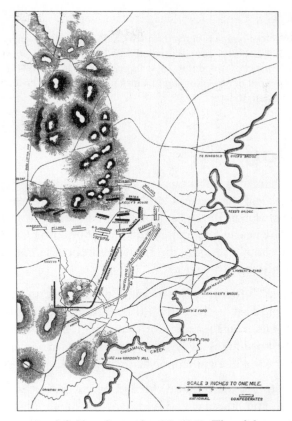

The Chickamauga battlefield on September 20, 1863. The solid rectangles represent Union troop positions, the open rectangles Confederate. The map shows how the Union lines were broken and pushed back against the thickly wooded hills. The Confederate line engulfed the Federal troops, leading Rosecrans to assume the Army of the Cumberland was done for.
(Harper's Pictorial History of the Civil War, 1866)

But Major General George Henry Thomas did not run. Instead, he rallied units under Brigadier General Thomas John Wood and Brigadier General John Brannan to block Longstreet on the south. Because Bragg had not held any men in reserve, he had nobody to send in to exploit Longstreet's initial breakthrough. In the meantime, Union General Gordon Granger deliberately violated his orders to remain in place to protect the army's flank and, instead, rushed to the aid of Thomas with two brigades. This action proved a splendid example of initiative on the field. Thomas—later hailed as the "Rock of Chickamauga"—was able to hold the field until nightfall and thereby save the Army of the Cumberland from destruction.

> **COUNT OFF!**
>
> The name Chickamauga is derived from a Cherokee word meaning "river of death." Of 58,222 Union troops engaged, 1,657 were killed, 9,756 wounded, and 4,757 went missing. Confederate losses were 2,312 killed, 14,674 wounded, and 1,468 missing out of 66,326 engaged. Chickamauga was the costliest battle of the war's western theater.

The Good Dog

The Battle of Chickamauga was a tactical victory for Braxton Bragg. He had driven Rosecrans from the field. However, Confederate losses were greater than those of the Union and, even worse, Bragg had coordinated the attack poorly. Even after Longstreet found the nearly fatal gap in the Union line, the Confederate assaults were piecemeal. Without a reserve, the Confederates could not exploit their gains to provide a strategically decisive victory.

"Bragg's a good dog," William S. Rosecrans had said after an earlier battle, "but Hold Fast's a better." "Hold Fast"—the name Rosecrans applied to himself—was swept away in the rout at Chickamauga and, for that, would be relieved of command. The reputations of his subordinates A. M. McCook, T. L. Crittenden, and Major General James Scott Negley would be ruined, or badly damaged.

As to Bragg, in frustration he relieved three of *his* subordinates, Leonidas Polk, Daniel Harvey Hill, and Thomas C. Hindman—all of whom were subsequently reinstated. The "good dog" himself would be relieved as commander of the Army of Tennessee at the end of December 1863.

Yankees Under Siege

But much more was at stake than the reputations of a handful of officers. The Union's Army of the Cumberland was holed up in Chattanooga, to which Bragg's Confederates were laying siege. Starvation and capture were the grim prospects staring the Union forces in their gaunt faces.

In one respect, the Army of the Cumberland's desperate situation was a boon to the Union cause. It suddenly riveted Washington's attention on what had been a neglected theater of the war. High command detached two entire army corps from Meade and sent them west under Joe Hooker. In the war's most dramatic demonstration of the strategic importance of rail transportation, they were transferred from the banks of eastern Virginia's Rappahannock River to Bridgeport, Alabama, in the space of eight days, arriving on October 2. In the meantime, William T. Sherman led part of the Union's Army of the Tennessee east from Memphis, and Ulysses S. Grant was given command of all military operations west of the Alleghenies (save Nathaniel Banks's hapless campaign along the Louisiana-Texas border).

Cracker Line

Grant took charge as only Grant could. Through a series of complex operations planned and executed with great vigor and precision, the new commander efficiently punched through a Confederate outpost on the Tennessee River west of Lookout Mountain and opened up a supply route to beleaguered Chattanooga. By this time, Major General Thomas had taken over command of the Army of the Cumberland from Rosecrans, and Thomas's miserable, hungry, lice-infested troops gratefully dubbed the new stream of supplies that flowed to them the "Cracker Line." The line, 60 miles long, was cobbled together with steamboats and scows (flat-bottomed boats), a pontoon bridge, and wagons.

A Battle Above the Clouds and a Soldier's Battle

Thanks to the Cracker Line, Braxton Bragg's plan to starve the Army of the Cumberland out failed. But Sherman did not reach the Union rallying point at Bridgeport, Alabama, until November 15, having been delayed by Major General Halleck's frustrating insistence that he pause to repair rail lines into Nashville.

On balance, it was perhaps just as well; for now the defenders of Chattanooga, fed by the Cracker Line, were refreshed and ready to fight. Grant, too, was in position, and after a delay imposed by heavy rains, Sherman was ready to attack as well. The fight was set for November 24.

Fighting Joe

November 24, 1863, dawned heavily overcast and foggy. Major General Joseph Hooker, a failure in command at Chancellorsville (see Chapter 14), was now subordinate to Grant. Ordered to take Lookout Mountain, the 1,100-foot prominence guarding the Tennessee River just outside Chattanooga, Hooker commenced what was literally an uphill battle at eight in the morning. It would continue until well after midnight. Then early on the morning of the 25th, soldiers from the 8th Kentucky Regiment scrambled up to the summit and planted the Stars and Stripes.

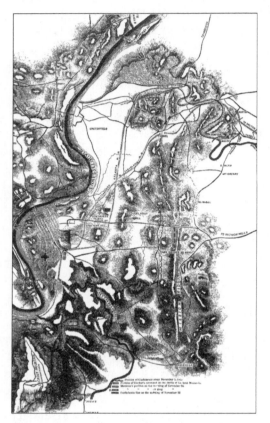

This map shows Chattanooga and the sites of the two most famous battles associated with its defense on November 24 and 25, 1863. The Tennessee River runs through the upper-left quadrant of the map; Chattanooga is halfway up the map at the left; Lookout Mountain is in the lower-left corner; and Missionary Ridge is in the lower-right quadrant.
(Harper's Pictorial History of the Civil War, 1866)

The sun had come out by then and the spectacularly dramatic effect was not lost on war correspondents, who dubbed the Battle of Lookout Mountain the "Battle Above the Clouds." And Joe Hooker? He was "Fighting Joe" again, a national hero.

Sherman

William Tecumseh Sherman did not fare as gloriously. He took his units upstream on the Tennessee and hit the Confederates' right wing, but made little headway against it. Finally, on the afternoon of November 25, Grant ordered Thomas to lead the men of the Army of the Cumberland forward to take the Confederate *rifle pits* at the base of Missionary Ridge, south of Chattanooga and just to the east of Lookout Mountain. Grant's object was to put enough pressure on Bragg to force him to recall troops from Sherman's front and possibly allow Sherman to break through.

> **DEFINITION**
>
> **Rifle pits** were the Civil War equivalent of World War II's foxholes: hastily dug shallow trenches that afforded riflemen a degree of protection.

"You Scaled the Mountain!"

The men of the Army of the Cumberland had been bottled up in Chattanooga for a long while. Clearly feeling that it had something to prove, the Army of the Cumberland advanced and took the rifle pits, thereby accomplishing the mission Grant had assigned them. Then, without orders from either Grant or Thomas, they kept right on going—partly because advancing was preferable to getting pinned down in the rifle pits—charging up the steep slope of Missionary Ridge and sweeping all before them. Incredibly, the Army of the Cumberland broke Bragg's line where it was the strongest, sending the Confederates into full retreat.

A Union war correspondent heard General Gordon Granger declare to the victorious men of his command: "You ought to be court-martialed, every man of you. I ordered you to take the rifle pits, and you scaled the mountain!" "His cheeks," according to the reporter, "were wet with tears as honest as the blood that reddened all the route."

Thus the Chattanooga Campaign came to a victorious conclusion for the Union. The assault on Missionary Ridge was a *soldier's battle*, an explosion of fury, frustration, and a desire to avenge defeat at Chickamauga, not because the "Rock of Chickamauga" or even U. S. Grant himself had given a command, but because it was what the soldiers *themselves* needed to do.

> **DEFINITION**
>
> The Army of the Cumberland's assault on Missionary Ridge was a classic **soldier's battle**—a battle in which the outcome is determined more by the action of the soldiers and the junior officers than by the leadership of principal commanders.

Sunset in the West

With the loss of the Chattanooga Campaign, the sun set on any hopes the Confederacy had in the West. For the Union however, this victory was the dawn of a new day. As Navy Secretary Gideon Welles wrote in his diary on December 31, 1863, "The year closes more satisfactorily than it commenced …. There have been errors and misfortunes … but the heart of the nation is sounder and its hopes brighter."

The Least You Need to Know

- Major General Rosecrans took Chattanooga in a campaign of brilliant maneuver with little cost, only to blunder into the Battle of Chickamauga and suffer a tactical defeat.
- Although tactically victorious at Chickamauga, Braxton Bragg failed to gain any strategic objectives and certainly failed to destroy the Army of the Cumberland.
- Relieving the Confederate siege of Chattanooga revealed Ulysses S. Grant at his most skillful, brilliant, and effective.
- The Union victory in the Chattanooga Campaign largely ended the Confederate threat west of the Allegheny Mountains.

The Last Full Measure

In this part, the principal commanders are Ulysses S. Grant, Robert E. Lee, and William Tecumseh Sherman. Grant, the new general-in-chief of all Union armies, personally leads the Army of the Potomac in its final thrust toward Richmond, but pays an unspeakably heavy price. Sherman decides to turn away from the enemy *army* and attack the enemy *people*, leaving a swath of destruction in his wake.

Grant finally breaks through at Petersburg, takes Richmond, and pursues Lee and his broken army to a place called Appomattox Court House. There, on April 9, 1865, Lee surrenders to Grant. Within days the other Confederate commanders also surrender, and the war is over.

Mr. Lincoln's General

In This Chapter

- Grant emerges as a Union leader
- "That devil Forrest"
- The Fort Pillow Massacre
- The fate of the Civil War prisoner of war

Military men, as well as historians, often speak of the "art of war," a phrase that might strike our ears as strange. Armies are about killing people and breaking things. What does war have to do with art?

Well, to look at a great commander's battle plan is to behold a work of art: a pattern of dynamic elegance. The word *art* also suggests a contrast with *science*. Whereas science deals in orderly fact, art embraces disorder, inventiveness, improvisation, brilliance of inspiration, and reliance on gut instinct.

Over and over again, in the American Civil War, this second connotation proved to be the chief feature of the art of war. Lincoln hired and fired one general after another to command the Eastern theater. Plan after plan, and man after man, failed in the disordered reality of war. Finally, on March 9, 1864, the president found Ulysses Simpson Grant. This chapter is about Grant's hard choices in a very hard war.

He Fights

Of all Lincoln's commanders, George B. McClellan certainly showed evidence of understanding the art of war. He built the Army of the Potomac into a well-organized and disciplined body—but it seemed he was forever ordering and organizing, rather than using the well-oiled machine he'd created. A good strategist, he was practically hopeless when it came to executing his strategy. Henry Wager "Old Brains" Halleck had written a book about war and had an academician's understanding of strategy and tactics. But the realities of combat showed this to be as much a liability as it was an asset. Ambrose Burnside was well liked and brave, but he proved sorely deficient in operational competence on a large scale. Joseph "Fighting Joe" Hooker was an able tactician, but Lee was abler.

Of all the men who had commanded the Army of the Potomac, George Meade was the least unsatisfactory. Almost immediately after assuming command from Hooker, he led the army to victory at Gettysburg, one of the great turning-point battles of the war. Yet he, too, fell short, allowing Lee and the Army of Northern Virginia to limp away from what might have been total, annihilating defeat.

Only after three full years of war did Ulysses S. Grant emerge as the most adept practitioner of its art. When the cost of Grant's victory at Shiloh (see Chapter 7) in April 1862—13,047 Union soldiers killed, wounded, or missing—was made public, calls came for Grant's dismissal. He was rumored to be a hard drinker, and rumors—now discredited—circulated that he was drunk during the battle. Lincoln, however, gave him his vote of confidence: "I can't spare this man," the president said. "He fights."

Grant's Will

It was a bold position for the president to take. Of all his generals, Grant seemed one of the least likely to succeed in independent command. His West Point record was unpromising (he graduated 21st out of a class of 39 in 1843). After he resigned his commission in 1854, he failed as a farmer, a real estate speculator, and a merchant, which compelled him to take a job as clerk in the small-town tannery owned by his father and brother. Most of the army's other generals either enjoyed military careers of uninterrupted success or were captains of industry, like McClellan, who had been president of the Illinois Central Railroad. Grant entered the Civil War not as a regular army officer, nor even as a politician important enough to merit a patronage commission, but as the drillmaster of the patriotic but provincial volunteer militia from his hometown of Galena, Illinois.

If war proceeded by orderly plan, Grant might have remained an obscure commander. But war, especially *this* war, killed plans as prodigiously as it killed men. As it exposed the inadequacy of one commander after another, war brought out in Ulysses Grant a genius for combat on a scale unprecedented on the American continent.

By the time Lincoln tapped him for top command, Grant firmly grasped the terrible common denominator at the root of this war. The South had fewer men, less money, and fewer resources than the North. The South could not afford to lose what little it had. The North *could* afford to lose more of what it had because it had so much more. It was the terrible calculus of attrition, written in flesh and blood. Grant understood this equation and, even more important, had the will to accept it.

Grant's Strategy

Summoned to Washington on March 9, 1864, to receive his commission as lieutenant general and supreme commander of all the Union armies, Grant was also prepared with a strategy as deadly simple as the equation that drove this war.

Henry Wager "Old Brains" Halleck, until now Grant's commanding officer, was a conventional man who understood the art of war in conventional terms. He believed an army should hold and occupy the "strategic points," the cities and towns, of the territory it captured. The result of this thinking was the repeated dispersal and dilution of forces west of the Alleghenies.

Now Grant would do things differently. Not with the occupation of land and the subjugation of cities would victory come, but only with the death of the Confederate armies. The only reason to attack a city, Grant reasoned, was to force the enemy army to fight so that the army could be destroyed. As for the city itself, it was nearly an irrelevant objective.

Two main armies needed to be destroyed: Robert E. Lee's Army of Northern Virginia and the Army of Tennessee, now under the command of Joseph E. Johnston, who had replaced Bragg after the loss of Chattanooga.

To be sure, other Confederate forces were fighting west of the Mississippi River. But Grant, unlike Halleck, understood that his own victories in that region had severed those forces from the rest of the Confederacy. Isolated, they hardly mattered now. The only crucial fight was against Lee and Johnston.

Grant's New Right Hand

With good judgment, Grant turned over command of the western theater to a general who had earned his most profound respect, William Tecumseh Sherman.

Like Grant, Sherman did not possess a distinguished record of achievement, military or otherwise. He had been stationed in California as an administrative officer during the Mexican War, and so missed the fighting and the glory. When he resigned his commission in 1853, he started a banking and building firm, which went belly up four years later. He practiced law briefly in Leavenworth, Kansas, and then became superintendent of a Louisiana military academy.

Sherman's early record in the Civil War was disappointing (see Chapter 7), but, like Grant, he had an unflinching vision of the realities of this war. When he spoke frankly about what he saw as the conflict's likely cost in lives, he was branded insane by the press, and his career was nearly ended. Subsequent bloody months would prove Sherman all too sane (and, conversely, perhaps the rest of America mad).

Sherman performed brilliantly at Shiloh and in all subsequent operations under Grant, and, like Grant, he learned from his past mistakes. In charge of action in the West as the new commander of the Military Division of the Mississippi, Sherman was to move down the route of the Western and Atlantic Railroad, advancing inexorably against Atlanta—and, more to the point, doing battle with the Army of Tennessee.

"I was to go for Joe Johnston," Sherman laconically observed of the role Grant had assigned him.

A New Strategy of Coordination

While Grant had overall command of the forces "going for" Robert E. Lee, he asked General Meade to remain in command of the Army of the Potomac, although Grant himself exercised much personal control of that army. He saw the Army of the Potomac for what it was: a remarkable fighting force that had been poorly and inconsistently led, its tremendous exertions and sacrifices having therefore yielded disappointing results.

Grant brought one more officer into top command in the Army of the Potomac. Philip Sheridan—Little Phil, his men affectionately called him—was a scrappy, no-nonsense fighter and a resourceful, courageous infantry commander, whom Grant now tapped to lead the cavalry.

 WAR NEWS

Sheridan was as blunt-spoken as Sherman. After the Civil War, Sheridan was named military commander of Louisiana and Texas, but he was so harsh in administering the stringent and punitive Reconstruction measures that President Andrew Johnson soon removed him. "If I owned both Hell and Texas," Sheridan reportedly declared, "I'd rent out Texas and live in Hell."

As Sherman would advance on Atlanta, forcing Johnston to fight him in order to defend the city, so would Grant advance on Richmond, less with the objective of taking the Confederate capital than with the purpose of killing the Army of Northern

Virginia—which would rush to the capital's defense. In addition to the main body of the Army of the Potomac, Grant aimed two other armies at Richmond: the Army of the James, 33,000 men under Ben Butler, and a force in the Shenandoah Valley, led by Franz Sigel. For the very first time in this three-year-old war, the Union army would make a truly coordinated movement: one army against Atlanta and three against Richmond. The grand operation began on May 4, 1864.

Short, scrappy Philip Sheridan was trained as an infantry commander, but Grant put him in charge of the Army of the Potomac's cavalry. He performed brilliantly.
(Harper's Pictorial History of the Civil War, 1866)

"And Fightin' Means Killin'"

Who were the great antagonists of the Civil War? "Grant and Lee" is a good answer, although they became adversaries only during the climactic months of the war. Although it is true that Grant was *the* great Union general, and Lee was *the* great Confederate general, perhaps Grant's truer opposite number was not Robert E. Lee, but Nathan Bedford Forrest.

A Tale of Two Generals

We first met Forrest in Chapter 7, when he indignantly refused to join generals Simon Bolivar Buckner and Gideon Pillow in surrendering Fort Donelson. He deftly escaped the fort, saving his own command, and hundreds of additional volunteers, from surrendering.

That was only one of the many remarkable things this officer did. He had been raised in poverty in Tennessee with almost no formal education, but nevertheless made a fortune as a slave trader. He enlisted in the Confederate army as a private one month before his fortieth birthday in 1861; then, in October of that year, raised a battalion at his own expense and was commissioned a lieutenant colonel to command it. Forrest fought a brilliant rearguard action at Shiloh, thereby preserving the battered Confederate army after that costly battle. Severely wounded in that action, he narrowly escaped paralysis from a bullet lodged near his spine.

Nathan Bedford Forrest was deemed by Union General Sherman the most dangerous commander of the war. His philosophy: "War means fightin', and fightin' means killin'." His strategy: "Get there first with the most men."
(Harper's Pictorial History of the Civil War, 1866)

Promoted to brigadier general, Forrest conducted raids in 1864 throughout Mississippi, Tennessee, and Alabama so brilliant and destructive that Sherman, calling him "that devil Forrest," declared that he must be "hunted down and killed if it costs ten thousand lives and bankrupts the Federal treasury." Sherman continued: "There will never be peace in Tennessee till Forrest is dead."

After the war, both Sherman and Confederate General Joe Johnston named Forrest the most remarkable soldier of the entire conflict. Johnston declared that, if Forrest "had had the advantages of a thorough military education and training, [he] would have been the great central figure of the Civil War." Forrest himself summed up his theory of battle in a single sentence: "Get there first with the most men," a maxim popularly misquoted as "Git thar fustest with the mostest."

The Fort Pillow Massacre

Forrest had another saying. "War," he said, "means fightin', and fightin' means killin'." Like Grant, Forrest had no patience with romantic concepts of chivalry and "civilized" rules of engagement.

Grant and Forrest, had they ever met, would have understood one another, and yet, for all his willingness to kill and to suffer casualties in order to kill, Grant remained a soldier. Forrest, apparently, crossed the line and became something else.

It happened on April 12, 1864. Forrest sent a Confederate division under Brigadier General James R. Chalmers to Fort Pillow, an earthwork fort and trading post on a high bluff overlooking the Mississippi, originally built by Confederate General Gideon Pillow it was now occupied by a Union garrison. Its mission was to defend Union supply lines.

Forrest's mission was to disrupt Union supply lines. Taking Fort Pillow would allow him to do just that. The fort was garrisoned by 557 soldiers, 262 of whom were African American—many of them Tennesseans loyal to the Union. After Chalmers had driven in the fort's pickets and surrounded the garrison, Forrest arrived to take personal command. He made a surrender demand, which was refused. Then the Confederates swarmed into the fort.

At this point, Southern and Northern accounts differ. What is certain is that some 231 members of the garrison were killed and another 100 grievously wounded; in addition, 168 white soldiers and 58 black soldiers were captured. Southern losses were disproportionately slight: 14 killed, 86 wounded. Southerners explained that the Federal losses were the result of resistance to surrender, whereas Northern sources claimed that the garrison surrendered as soon as the fort had been breached. The rebels (Northern survivors said) shouted, "No quarter! No quarter! Kill the damned niggers; shoot them down!"

And, over it all presided Nathan Bedford Forrest.

A Congressional Committee on the Conduct of the War concluded that Forrest and his troops were guilty of atrocities: murdering most of the garrison *after* it had surrendered, burying some African American troops alive, and putting to the torch tents sheltering the Federal wounded. Most historians believe that atrocities were committed.

After the war, Nathan Bedford Forrest rebuilt his fortune, and served as the Grand Wizard of the Ku Klux Klan, though he stepped down when he believed it had become too lawlessly violent.

Prisoners of War

Civil War atrocity came in many forms. Among the most shocking and heartbreaking were the war crimes committed against prisoners of war (POWs).

Exchange and Parole

By the nineteenth century, most Western nations had made some attempt to treat POWs humanely. The most humane way to handle POWs was simply to exchange them. In nineteenth-century Europe, there were no large POW camps; instead, prisoners were exchanged on a regular, one-for-one basis. But President Lincoln declined to set up a formal exchange system because he did not want to make any treaty with the Confederacy, arguing that to do so would be implicitly recognizing the Confederate States of America as a sovereign nation, rather than an illegal collection of rebellious citizens.

Nevertheless, he allowed his generals to make informal exchanges under flags of truce. By 1862, this casual arrangement was formalized by an agreement, the Dix-Hill Cartel of July 22, whereby prisoners were to be exchanged within 10 days of capture.

When the exchange system soon broke down, military leaders decided to try parole. From the very beginning of the war, civilians suspected of disloyalty—or caught out-and-out spying for the enemy—were not imprisoned or executed (that form of punishment came later in the war), but were merely "paroled." A man caught spying in the North was sent to the South in return for his pledge (his *parole*) not to come North again. When the Dix-Hill Cartel faltered, POWs awaiting exchange were not housed in prison camps, but were sent back to their lines in exchange for their pledge that they would not return to duty until they had been formally exchanged for another prisoner.

> **DEFINITION**
>
> **Parole** comes from the French word for *word* or *promise* and, during the Civil War, meant the act of releasing a POW to his own lines on the condition that he give his word of honor not to fight until he was officially exchanged for a prisoner held by the enemy.

A Grim Decision

Taking prisoners was a good thing because it removed enemy soldiers from action. Holding prisoners, however, was also a burden on the manpower and supplies of the victor. After his triumph at Vicksburg (see Chapter 13), Grant captured more than 31,000 rebel POWs. Faced with the prospect of transporting and guarding them, he decided to parole them instead.

Then, during the Chattanooga campaign (see Chapter 17), Grant discovered that an alarmingly high proportion of the prisoners he now took were the very men he had paroled back at Vicksburg. After Grant was given overall command of the Union armies, he called a halt to all prisoner exchanges on April 17, 1864.

Grant enforced President Lincoln's directive refusing to exchange prisoners unless black POWs were treated on the same basis as whites. But Grant was also frustrated by the Confederacy's refusal to exchange African American POWs and white officers of black regiments. Even more important, he understood that prisoner exchange was of far more benefit to the manpower-poor Confederacy than it was to the relatively manpower-rich Union. The South desperately needed its prisoners returned; the North could afford to lose some prisoners. Moreover, Northern prisoners in Southern POW camps put an added burden on a government so strained that, as Grant and anyone else could see, it was hard pressed to clothe and feed its own army properly.

It was a grim decision. Both Lincoln and Grant knew that conditions in Confederate POW camps were unspeakably filthy and cruel, that starvation rations and rampant disease were the norm, and that a refusal to exchange prisoners was, for many of his soldiers, a death warrant as well as a guarantee that conditions would only worsen.

But both the president and his general also knew that, however hard the consequences were on his own side, they were far harder on the other. It was one more equation of war.

Andersonville and Other Horrors

Early in the war, prison camps were fairly civilized places governed by a sense of "Christian charity." But as the war ground on, life, it seemed, grew cheaper, bitterness sharper, supplies scarcer, and the desire for revenge ever more powerful. In Richmond, the warehouse of Libby & Sons Ship Chandlers and Grocers was converted into a prison for Union officers. The floor plan of the three-story building measured only 100 by 150 feet, but into it were jammed 1,200 men. Ostensibly to prevent escapes—and there were escapes—jailer Dick Turner gave his guards leave to shoot anyone who ventured to a window, say, to catch the sound of birdsong, a glimpse of sunlight, or even a breath of fresh air.

These Confederate prisoners (captured at Gettysburg) strike casually defiant poses for a Union photographer.
(Library of Congress)

As bad as conditions were in Richmond-area prisons, they were far worse at the place officially called Camp Sumter, but better known by the name of the adjacent town: Andersonville.

Set in the sweltering heart of Georgia, the Andersonville stockade was built to accommodate 10,000 POWs. Tents provided the only shelter, medical care was nonexistent, food was next to nil, and water came from Stockade Creek, which also served as the prison latrine and sewer. At the height of its operation, prisoners poured in at the rate of 400 a day. By August 1864, Andersonville harbored 33,000 POWs.

SITES AND SIGHTS

The Andersonville National Historic Site, along State Route 49, 10 miles northeast of Americus, Georgia, includes, in addition to the prison site, the National Prisoner of War Museum and a National Cemetery. Contact: 229-924-0343.

In March 1864, Swiss-born Captain Henry Wirz took command of the prison. He soon earned a reputation for extravagant cruelty and took pride in the knowledge that (as one prisoner heard him declare) he "was killing more damned Yankees with his treatment than they were with powder and lead in the army."

COUNT OFF!

Of 45,000 prisoners confined at Andersonville during 1864 and 1865, 13,000 died and were buried in proper graves; the actual death toll was probably significantly higher. Nevertheless, at minimum, mortality at Andersonville ran to 29 percent. Only one Confederate prison, the much smaller 10,000-man camp at Salisbury, North Carolina, had a higher mortality rate: 34 percent.

After the war, Henry Wirz was tried by a Union tribunal, which found him guilty of unjustly causing at least 10,000 deaths, mostly from neglect and starvation. He was executed on November 10, 1865.

Andersonville might have been the worst and most notorious of Civil War prison camps, but it wasn't the only scene of inhumane prisoner treatment. The North (which, unlike the South, had plenty of food and other supplies to go around) also treated its POWs abominably. At the POW camp in Elmira, New York, for example, the death rate among some 12,000 prisoners ran to 25 percent—the result of poor rations, disease, and perhaps most of all, exposure to the upstate winter. (Some recent historians have suggested that much of the abuse, on both sides, was more the result of inexperience and ignorance than deliberate neglect.) Prison camps like Andersonville and "Hellmira" (as rebel POWs called the Elmira facility) lifted the veil, exposing this war for what all war finally is: a business of death.

The Least You Need to Know

- Ulysses S. Grant emerged as the man to command the Union armies only after three years of war.
- Grant was a fine strategist and tactician who was willing to invest lives in ending the war.
- Grant's victory strategy emphasized destroying the enemy army over taking cities and occupying territory.
- After prisoner exchange was halted in the spring of 1864, POWs on both sides suffered great inhumanities; many died of disease, starvation, abuse, and neglect.

"The Butcher"

In This Chapter

- Why Lee kept fighting
- Battle of the Wilderness
- South to Spotsylvania
- Jeb Stuart dies at Yellow Tavern
- Grant's ill-fated assault on Cold Harbor
- Missed opportunity at Petersburg

Chewing on a cigar, his short, dark beard rough rather than gentlemanly, his uniform somehow always rumpled, Ulysses S. Grant bore the name of an epic hero, but didn't much look the part. Nevertheless, Lincoln and the nation embraced him eagerly as he ascended to overall command of the Union forces. On March 9, 1864, the day he was promoted to lieutenant general, they had faith in him and placed their hopes in him. But, soon, many would call Grant "the Butcher."

Down in the Confederate states, faith and hope were as scarce as food and clothing by March 1864. Manpower dwindled daily, through death, disability, and desertion. Conscription was extended to include boys (age 17) and middle-age men (age 50). In the cities many talked surrender, but in the armies, despite epidemic desertion, officers were still able to lead, and many men were willing to follow. As hopes brightened in the North and dimmed in the South, the war in its final 12 months grew more violent than ever.

Lee's Hope

Abraham Lincoln was up for reelection in November 1864 and was opposed by others, chiefly George B. McClellan, who, although he personally wanted victory in the war, had powerful supporters who wanted an immediate armistice and negotiated peace. As Robert E. Lee saw it, if he could make the battles costly enough for the North, perhaps Lincoln would lose, and the North would agree to peace on terms acceptable to the South. The great thing was to stay in the fight.

Lost in the Wilderness

On May 4, 1864, Grant led the 118,000-man Army of the Potomac across the Rapidan River to fight what he knew to be Lee's badly outnumbered Army of Northern Virginia in the open country south of the Rapidan.

Grant was right about Lee's being outnumbered—he could field no more than 66,000 men—but he was wrong in assuming that Lee would fight where he wanted him to. With a boldness apparently untempered by defeat at Gettysburg, Lee attacked the Federal columns as they passed through the tangled and densely forested area known as the Wilderness—the same Wilderness that had brought such disastrous confusion to "Fighting Joe" Hooker at Chancellorsville almost a year to the day earlier (see Chapter 14).

Two Days and 17,666 Men

By the conventional standards of warfare, the overgrown Wilderness was what commanders called "bad ground"—no place to fight a battle. The only thing more difficult than moving your army was *seeing* the opposing army, and that was just the way Lee wanted it. Outnumbered almost two to one, he used the difficult terrain as an ally. Lee knew that, without open ground, Grant could not readily move his superior numbers to meet his attacks. Also, the lack of clear fields of fire rendered Grant's formidable artillery all but totally useless.

The fighting began on May 5 and went on through the 6th. The intense gunfire touched off innumerable brush fires, and soon the Wilderness was ablaze. Although both sides periodically called off the fight to retrieve the wounded, at least 200 men would suffocate or burn to death.

COUNT OFF!

Federal losses were 17,666 (of which 2,246 were killed, 12,073 wounded, and the rest missing) out of 101,895 engaged in the battle. Two Union generals were killed, two wounded, and two captured. Confederate records are sketchy, but estimates are that, of 61,025 engaged, losses amounted to 11,125 killed, wounded, or missing. Three generals were killed and four more were wounded but recovered, including James Longstreet, accidentally shot by his own men on almost the same spot where Stonewall Jackson was fatally wounded by friendly fire a year earlier.

The fighting on the 5th was bloody, but indecisive. On the 6th, however, the arrival of Confederate General James Longstreet turned the tide, and with nightfall, the Union's II Corps, under Major General Winfield Scott Hancock, began to withdraw.

Spotsylvania

The Wilderness was a tactical defeat for the Union, but a strategic defeat for Lee. Grant kept uppermost in his mind the grim calculus he knew would determine the outcome of the war. *He* could afford to lose men. *Lee* could not. Instead of doing what a defeated army is supposed to do, retreat, Grant advanced, south to Spotsylvania Court House, at a crossroads on the way to Richmond.

Grant would force Lee to fight and fight again. Lee might win the next battle and even the next, but he would lose men with each fight, even if victorious, and because of this, Grant knew that Robert E. Lee would ultimately lose the war.

The trouble was that Lee didn't yield to the logic of the equation. With his customary genius for reacting quickly to his opponent's moves, Lee beat Grant to the crossroads. A skirmish developed on May 8, and then blossomed like some monstrous, fatal flower into combat lasting through the 19th.

Every day for 11 days there was some of the most desperate fighting of the war. As the armies clashed, Grant kept shifting his troops to the left, always probing for Lee's flank. And each time Lee succeeded in covering his flank, his troops fiercely defending their positions from hastily dug rifle pits, the Civil War equivalent of the World War II foxhole. With each shift, Lee saved his army but lost more men. During the course of the Overland campaign, the Army of Northern Virginia suffered at least 33,508 casualties.

SITES AND SIGHTS

The Fredericksburg and Spotsylvania County Battlefields Memorial National Military Park (540-373-6122) encompasses the battles of the Wilderness and Spotsylvania. The Wilderness portion is at the junction of routes 3 and 20, where part of the Wilderness Tavern chimney stands. Reach the Spotsylvania section via Grant Drive, and Spotsylvania Court House (junction of routes 608 and 208) features the Old Berea Christian Church, a landmark during the battle, now a museum (540-582-7167). Contact Spotsylvania County Tourist Center, 4704 Southpoint Parkway, Fredericksburg, VA 22407 (1-877-515-6197).

This rare photograph shows a strongly built Confederate rifle pit on the Spotsylvania battlefield.
(U.S. Army Military Institute)

Yellow Tavern

With the opposing forces quite literally *locked* in combat, Phil Sheridan, commander of the Army of the Potomac's 10,000-man cavalry, proposed a mounted raid toward

Richmond, which would draw Jeb Stuart and the Confederate cavalry (about 4,500 troopers) into a fight. Sheridan confidently boasted that he would "whip Stuart out of his boots."

Sheridan could hardly conceal the massed movement of 10,000 troopers, whose line, even riding four abreast, stretched for 13 miles. Seeing the advance, Stuart placed his 4,500 cavalrymen squarely between the Union column and Richmond, at an abandoned wayside inn called Yellow Tavern, only six miles north of the city.

On May 11, the two cavalry forces dueled. Stuart had secured a formidable defensive position, and his soldiers, defending their capital, were determined to stop the Union advance. After three hours, Sheridan withdrew, but not before one of his troopers spied an ostentatiously uniformed rebel officer some 30 feet off and shot him.

It was none other than Stuart, who died the following day. For Lee, it was a blow second only to the loss of Stonewall Jackson at Chancellorsville (see Chapter 14).

The Mule Shoe

Having probed for a weak spot since the fighting began, Grant, on May 11, ordered Major General Winfield Scott Hancock to lead his 20,000 men against Confederate General Richard Ewell's corps. Because Ewell had deployed his forces in entrenchments shaped like an inverted "U," the *salient* (the most advanced part of the defenses) was called the Mule Shoe. After a day of hand-to-hand combat here, the "Mule Shoe" became known as the "Bloody Angle."

DEFINITION

A **salient** is any part of a defensive work that projects outward.

Hancock, one of the central heroes of Gettysburg, was a superb and determined field commander. He unleashed the attack at 4:30 on the morning of May 12, and within a quarter hour, his men were pouring through gaps they had punched in the Confederate lines. During the next 45 minutes, they captured at least 2,000 prisoners (some sources say 4,000), including 2 generals, and 20 artillery pieces.

But then the Union advance was stopped, and for the rest of the day and into the night, combat was at close quarters, hand to hand, and unremitting, as a rainfall that had begun on the 11th became increasingly heavy.

Mule Shoe/Bloody Angle was the last heavy fighting at Spotsylvania, as Grant again moved the Army of the Potomac south, always toward Richmond. Each day there was a skirmish or minor battle, such as those at the North Anna River (May 24), where Lee's defensive positions proved too strong to overrun, and, farther south, at Totopotomoy Creek (May 26–30). None of these exchanges was decisive. Grant achieved no breakthrough, but each engagement cost the Southern army blood it could ill afford to shed, and each engagement was fought closer to the Confederate capital.

Sigel Struggles, Butler Beaten

During this time, other elements of the Union army were flailing and wallowing elsewhere in Virginia. Major General Franz Sigel, a German immigrant who had served in the German military and then fled to the United States after participating in the ill-fated revolution of 1848, performed a great service to the Union by rallying fellow Germans to the Union cause. ("I fights mit Sigel" was their battle slogan.) His political weight brought Sigel promotion, but as a commander he was inept, as evidenced by his defeat on May 15 at New Market, in the Shenandoah Valley, at the hands of Major General John C. Breckinridge, who was gallantly assisted by 247 youths from the Virginia Military Institute. (Ten VMI boys died, and 47 were wounded.) Sigel was soon relieved of command.

Benjamin Butler's Army of the James advanced up the river for which it was named, only to be defeated at Bermuda Hundred late in May. Like Sigel, Butler was "a political general"—a powerful Democrat who, unlike many other leaders of his party, supported the war. Butler foolishly made camp on the Bermuda Hundred peninsula, thereby putting his forces in a cul de sac. The Confederates built a line of fortified *earthworks* across the base of the little peninsula, efficiently corking Butler and his army in a bottle. With these forces out of action, Lee could draw badly needed reinforcements from that front to use against Grant.

DEFINITION

Earthworks are entrenchments or mounded earth parapets used as defensive positions.

"To Fight It Out on This Line"

In a May 11 telegram to the War Department in Washington, Grant reported his losses at Spotsylvania as heavy, but "I think the loss of the enemy must be greater." He concluded, "I propose to fight it out on this line, if it takes all summer."

And so Grant fought on, not from victory to victory, but from heartbreak to heartbreak. When repulsed, he did not retreat, but sidestepped and advanced even farther south.

Cold Harbor

On the night of June 1, Grant and Lee both raced toward a crossroads called Cold Harbor, a half-dozen miles northeast of Richmond. Lee got there first and dug in. During June 1 and 2, Grant lost perhaps as many as 3,000 men knocking against the entrenched Confederate positions. Determined as ever, Grant mounted a massed assault. His buglers blew the charge at 4:30 A.M. on June 3. Sixty thousand Federal soldiers moved against an army that was all but invisible within its entrenchments. Confederate artillery roared into action, and men were buried in eruptions of earth, rock, and metal.

During the month of nonstop fighting that had begun at the Wilderness and culminated now at Cold Harbor, the new commander of the Union armies, Ulysses S. Grant, lost more than 50,000 men, killed or wounded. Perhaps as many as 3,500 of these were lost in the "grand charge" at Cold Harbor.

"I have always regretted that the last assault at Cold Harbor was ever made," Grant wrote in his *Personal Memoirs* years later.

For three days and nights after Grant's final assault, both armies sat in position, stunned and exhausted. Not until June 7 was a truce called to pick up the wounded and bury the dead. Some five acres were heaped with the dead, and those unlucky enough to still be dying.

Among the crowds who had cheered Grant's promotion to lieutenant general and his elevation to command of the Union armies back in March were now some who decried him as "Butcher Grant."

Abraham Lincoln was not one of these. Lincoln understood that whereas 50,000 Union casualties represented a staggering 41 percent of Grant's original strength, the 33,508 casualties incurred by Lee amounted to more than half of the original strength of his forces. Lincoln knew, too, that the Union's losses would be replaced in a matter of weeks, whereas the South could never restore the manpower it had lost.

Petersburg

Grant did not lick his wounds for long. He slipped his army out of Cold Harbor under cover of darkness and crossed the Chickahominy. Lee naturally assumed that he was heading toward Richmond and hurriedly dispatched most of his troops to the outskirts of the city. But Grant's objective was Petersburg, a rail junction vital to the supply of Richmond. Take and control this, and Richmond—starved, cut off from the rest of the Confederacy—would fall as surely as Vicksburg had fallen.

Lee had missed his guess, and, when the first 16,000 Federals arrived at Petersburg on June 15, only 3,000 Confederates, commanded by P. G. T. Beauregard, were there to defend it.

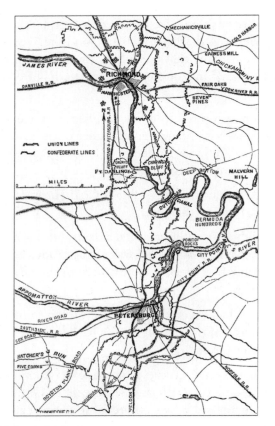

Map of the Petersburg area.
(Harper's Pictorial History of the Civil War, 1866)

But Petersburg would prove yet another missed Union opportunity. The Federal troops under Major General William Farrar "Baldy" Smith were battle worn and slow to attack. In truth, so was Smith. His assault against Petersburg on June 15 was bungled, and Beauregard gained time to reinforce his position. Smith was relieved of field command, and Grant assumed responsibility for two more assaults, on the 16th and 18th, which failed. As at Vicksburg, Grant settled in for a long siege.

The Crater Catastrophe

One of Grant's subordinates besieging Petersburg was Ambrose Burnside. To him came Colonel Henry Pleasants, a mining engineer now in command of a Pennsylvania regiment made up almost entirely of coal miners. Pleasants proposed to smash through the rebel fortifications defending Petersburg by digging a tunnel under them and blowing them up. Persuaded, Burnside approved the plan, and the miners commenced digging on June 25. By July 27, the tunnel was completed, and the miners transported four tons of black powder to its end, under the Confederate entrenchments.

COUNT OFF!

The Petersburg mine tunnel was 510.8 feet, ending behind the Confederate lines and directly under a Confederate strong point. The longest military tunnel ever excavated, it was dug by the hand labor of 400 men at the rate of 40 to 50 feet a day. They moved some 18,000 cubic feet of earth. The tunnel was packed with 320 kegs of black powder explosive.

In the wee hours of the morning of July 30, Burnside prepared his assault force, which would rush through the gap blown in the fortifications. Once again, however, Union commanders managed to snatch defeat from the jaws of victory. Burnside had planned to use an African American division to make the initial attack through the gap. Beginning on July 18, these soldiers specially trained for the mission; they were ready and eager to serve. But on the day before the planned assault, Major General George Meade had second thoughts. He told Burnside that using "colored" troops for such an unconventional and hazardous mission was unacceptable. If they suffered severe losses, the army would be criticized for sacrificing black soldiers as if they were of inferior value to those of white soldiers. Now at the eleventh hour, Meade ordered Burnside to find a white division to lead the assault.

The exhausted Burnside refused to make a command decision and instead had his division commanders draw straws for the dangerous work. The short straw was drawn by a unit under one James H. Ledlie—by the consensus of contemporaries and historians alike among the very worst of Union generals.

The mine was detonated with devastating effect: 175 feet of Confederate entrenchments exploded spectacularly, sending men and debris hundreds of feet into the air, destroying an artillery battery then burying virtually an entire regiment. But the ill-prepared, ill-led, last-minute replacement lead division bungled the attack. They charged into the blast hole—175 feet across, 34 feet deep—rather than around it. They hadn't even thought to bring ladders. Ultimately they, and the others who followed, were trapped in the crater and the ruined entrenchments near it. Union casualties in the assault topped 4,000 killed and wounded.

"It was," Grant later remarked, "the saddest affair I have witnessed in the war."

The Petersburg mine blast: stage one of the disastrous assault on "The Crater,"
which Grant called "the saddest affair I have witnessed in the war."
(Harper's Pictorial History of the Civil War, 1866)

Another New Kind of War

The Civil War had brought a host of innovations to combat: rail transportation for troops and supplies, ironclad warships with revolving gun turrets, the submarine, new forms of artillery and artillery projectiles, improved breech-loading rifles for rapid fire, and so on. In some places, it also introduced a new landscape to warfare.

For the next eight months, while Petersburg lay under siege, the countryside was net-worked with trenches. Christened Fort Sedgwick, these siege lines—filthy, miserable ditches shored up with lumber and *gabions*—anticipated the trenches that would scar the face of Europe in World War I.

DEFINITION

Gabions were woven basketlike containers filled with earth and used as anti-blast reinforcements to strengthen the walls of entrenchments.

The entrenchments of the Petersburg siege.
(Library of Congress)

The Least You Need to Know

- Robert E. Lee's objective was to make the war so costly to the North that President Lincoln would lose his bid for reelection and a Democratic president would sue for a negotiated peace favorable to the South.

- Union losses at the Wilderness, Spotsylvania, and Cold Harbor surpassed Confederate losses; nevertheless, the Confederates lost a greater proportion of their forces, and, unlike the North, could not draw on a large pool of manpower to replace their dead, wounded, and captured.

- In his Overland campaign, Grant repeatedly exchanged tactical defeat (with heavy casualties) for strategic victory as he advanced on Richmond and Petersburg, forcing Lee to spend precious manpower.

- Through the bungling of a subordinate commander (W. F. "Baldy" Smith) and the failure of the so-called Battle of the Crater, Grant missed an opportunity to break through at Petersburg, the principal rail junction supplying Richmond; he was forced to settle into a long and costly siege.

Damn the Torpedoes

Chapter 20

In This Chapter

- Rebel commerce raiders
- Career of the CSS *Alabama*
- Farragut's victory at Mobile Bay
- The submarine *Hunley*
- Lincoln reelected

President Abraham Lincoln understood and approved of what Grant was doing in his advance on Richmond, bloody though it was. But would the nation continue to accept the formula by which Grant proposed to redeem the Union, outspending the Confederacy in human life?

Lincoln often doubted the Union's willingness to accept that terrible calculus. As the elections of 1864 drew nearer, he expected to lose to a candidate whose party promised to negotiate an immediate end to the war. This chapter shows how a Union admiral and a Union general helped Lincoln retain the White House and continue the fight.

Pirate Navy

As the strength of the U.S. Navy grew from 42 vessels in 1861—of which only 3 were steam-powered)—to 641 modern ships by 1865, the Anaconda blockade of Southern imports and exports became increasingly effective, cutting Southern imports and exports by as much as 95 percent.

Confederate naval strategy was not limited to running the blockade. The Jefferson Davis government knew it could never match the Union navy ship-for-ship, but under Davis's naval secretary, Stephen R. Mallory, the tiny Confederate States Navy pitted its few vessels (many skippered by civilians) not against U.S. Navy warships, but against Union vessels of commerce: privately owned ships carrying goods.

When a government employs pirates it is called *privateering*, and by the 1860s it had many precedents, stretching back to the exploits of Sir Francis Drake (1540–1596) in the service of England's Queen Elizabeth I.

DEFINITION

A **privateer** is a privately owned, armed vessel commissioned by a warring state to attack enemy vessels of commerce. The word can also be applied to the captain of the privateer vessel. Captains and crews were generally not paid by the government, but were entitled to claim captured ships as prizes for their own profit.

From *Enrica* to *Alabama*

While Confederate privateers preyed on Union shipping, the single most famous Confederate raiding vessel was a Confederate States Navy craft.

The CSS *Alabama* had been clandestinely ordered in 1861 by the Confederate agent in charge of procuring European arms, James D. Bulloch, from the Laird Shipyards of Birkenhead, UK. Despite the protests of the U.S. minister (equivalent to ambassador) to England, Charles Francis Adams, the ship was launched (as the *Enrica*) on May 15, 1862. The British government might have been officially neutral, but plenty of members of Parliament favored the Confederate cause and were willing to turn a blind eye toward profitable trade in arms.

Although frustrated, Adams knew that, before it could set out on the high seas, the ship had to be fitted with masts and engines at a *graving dock* in Liverpool. Adams hired famed barrister Robert R. Collier, who presented British foreign secretary Lord Russell with a legal opinion that, if the *Enrica* were allowed to sail, the United States would have a valid claim against Great Britain for any and all damages she might cause to American shipping.

DEFINITION

A **graving dock** is a dry dock where major work is done on ships.

While Russell consulted an attorney on this matter, Bulloch saw to it that *Enrica* was rushed to completion and launched for what he announced as "sea trials" on July 29.

She never returned to Liverpool, heading instead for the Welsh coast, where Bulloch planned to board her, steal out of English waters, sail beyond the influence of U.S. diplomatic pressure, and then, after fitting her guns in the Azores, take command of her as the CSS *Alabama*.

WAR NEWS

British authorities sought to preserve the fiction of their neutrality by pretending that vessels such as the *Alabama* were being built for commerce, not war; therefore, no ships commissioned by the Confederates were actually *armed* in British docks. The ships were built in England, and so were the guns, but they were *installed* in some remote, non-British location, such as the Spanish-controlled Azores.

But Confederate Secretary of the Navy Mallory had a different commander in mind. *Enrica* evaded a Federal sloop and braved a bad storm in the Irish Sea to rendezvous with the *Agrippina*, from which Captain Raphael Semmes, a 53-year-old Maryland-born Alabamian, boarded her and took command.

Raphael Semmes was the justly legendary captain of the CSS Alabama, *which captured or sank 69 vessels before it was sunk by the USS* Kearsarge.
(Library of Congress)

Adventures of the *Alabama*

On February 15, 1861, Semmes resigned his commission as a commander in the U.S. Navy and joined the Confederate service. In command of the CSS *Sumter*, he sliced through the Anaconda blockade, sailed out of New Orleans, and raided the high seas for six months, taking 18 *prizes*. Abandoning CSS *Sumter* in Gibraltar, he boarded *Agrippina*, and took command of the *Alabama*.

From September 1862 until June 1864, Semmes was the terror of the high seas. He preyed upon the commercial shipping lanes, capturing or destroying 69 vessels and, in the process, monopolized the resources of a significant portion of the Union navy in vain pursuit of him.

> **DEFINITION**
>
> In naval jargon, a **prize** is a captured vessel and all cargo it carries.

Duel at Sea

On Sunday, June 12, 1864, the USS *Kearsarge*, an 8-gun, 1,083-ton sloop with a crew of 162, was lying at anchor off the Dutch coast when Captain John A. Winslow received word that the CSS *Alabama* (which he had been chasing fruitlessly for the better part of a year) had steamed into the French port of Cherbourg to discharge prisoners and take on coal. Winslow reached Cherbourg in two days. Bowing to international law, he assumed a position in the English Channel, just beyond the three-mile territorial waters limit. And he waited.

Semmes was determined to fight his way out even though the *Kearsarge* outgunned his vessel. By the time he sailed, at 9:45 on Sunday morning, June 19, crowds of French onlookers were on hand to watch the battle.

Winslow was reading the Sabbath service to his crew when the watchman announced: "She's coming out and she's headed straight for us!"

With that, the captain hastily concluded services and headed for more open waters, so that the *Alabama*, if crippled, could not find easy refuge. Winslow wanted a fight to the finish.

At 10:57, with the two vessels a mile apart, *Alabama* opened fire with a 100-pounder. Semmes fired again and again, but Winslow was closing so fast that *Alabama*'s shots were all too high; the gunners could not adjust their trajectories quickly enough. Only after he had closed to half a mile did Winslow return fire.

The two commanders and crews were a study in contrast. Semmes and his gunners fired rapidly and wildly, whereas Winslow and his men were methodical in pacing and aiming their shots. Winslow fired about 173 volleys—half what the *Alabama* got off—in the course of little over an hour, but far more of them found their mark.

As noon approached, the *Alabama* began to sink. Seeing Semmes and his crew beginning to abandon ship, Winslow launched his only two lifeboats that had not been smashed by Confederate shells. Realizing that these could not hold all survivors, Winslow called out to a British yacht that had sailed out to watch the battle: "For God's sake, do what you can to save them!"

Outgunned by the USS Kearsarge, *CSS* Alabama *sinks near Cherbourg, France.*
(Harper's Pictorial History of the Civil War, 1866)

At 12:24, CSS *Alabama* disappeared under the waves. USS *Kearsarge* took aboard 70 men, French boats picked up a dozen more, and the British yacht *Deerhound* saved 42, including Semmes, who thereby evaded capture. About 20 men lost their lives. After a gentlemanly tour of the Continent, Semmes returned to the Confederacy as commander of the James River squadron.

The *Alabama* Claims

The sinking of the *Alabama* was not quite the end of its story. After the Civil War, relations between the United States and Great Britain deteriorated, in part because the United States held England responsible for the destruction caused by the *Alabama*. A joint high commission was set up to adjudicate the matter, and, on May 8, 1871, the Treaty of Washington established a system of arbitration to settle the "*Alabama* Claims" and other disputes. On September 14, 1872, the tribunal found Britain legally liable for direct losses caused by the *Alabama* and other ships and awarded the United States damages of $15,500,000 in gold.

> **COUNT OFF!**
>
> The United States had demanded payment of $19,021,000 from Great Britain for damage done by 11 Confederate craft (including the CSS *Alabama*) built in England. Pursuant to the 1871 Treaty of Washington, a high commission of five representatives—one each from the United States, England, Italy, Switzerland, and Brazil—awarded the United States $15,500,000, which was duly paid in 1873.

Impatient Admiral

Having been the prime force in the capture of New Orleans in 1862 (see Chapter 8), Rear Admiral David Glasgow Farragut was running out of patience as commander of the squadron blockading the Gulf coast. With New Orleans in Union hands, the Confederates' principal Gulf port became Mobile, Alabama, and, despite the Anaconda, plenty of shipping still made it in and out of that harbor.

The only way to bottle up Mobile Bay was to capture it. But the 30-mile-long bay was defended by three forts, three gunboats, and a mighty *ram* named the *Tennessee*. Moreover, the channel that gave passage into the harbor was mined with mines known as *torpedoes*. The entire network of Confederate defenses was commanded by Franklin Buchanan, skipper of the CSS *Virginia* (the former USS *Merrimack*) and a man who had, before the war, served with Farragut. They knew one another well.

> **DEFINITION**
>
> A **ram** is a vessel expressly built, with a specially reinforced iron prow (or "beak"), for deliberate collision with other ships. A ram sinks enemy vessels by punching through the enemy's hull at or below the water line. At the time of the Civil War, a **torpedo** was not a projectile, but a stationary mine, often a beer barrel made watertight and packed with explosive black powder. The torpedo would explode when struck by a vessel.

Mobile Bay, August 5, 1864: 6:00 A.M.

Though the odds were against him, Farragut decided to run the Confederate gauntlet with a flotilla of 4 ironclad monitors and 14 conventional wooden vessels. The latter he lashed together in pairs so that they could better endure the pounding they would get from the forts. At six in the morning on August 5, he led the flotilla from the deck of his flagship, USS *Hartford*. When the firing became intense and visibility was reduced to a minimum, the 63-year-old admiral climbed the rigging and ordered a sailor to lash him to the mast, so he wouldn't fall if wounded. After the smoke of battle grew too thick for him to see at all, he untied himself, climbed higher, then lashed himself to the rigging again.

Tecumseh Sinks

The do-or-die moment came when one of the Union's monitors, the *Tecumseh*, struck a torpedo and sank. This gave the other captains pause, and the advance through the bay slowed, even as the rebel bombardment continued.

That's when Farragut shouted down to his flag captain, Percival Drayton, a phrase that has echoed through history to become a permanent part of the English language: "Damn the torpedoes! Full speed ahead, Drayton!"

With that, *Hartford* poured it on, and the rest of the flotilla followed. One of the Confederate gunboats was captured, and two more were damaged beyond use. Only the CSS *Tennessee*, with Franklin Buchanan commanding, remained in the fight.

Tennessee Strikes Her Colors

Buchanan built up a head of steam and aimed his ram directly for the *Hartford*. The collision proved anticlimactic however, causing little damage, and now the Union vessels *Monongahela*, *Lackawanna*, and *Hartford* exacted their vengeance, ramming the *Tennessee* repeatedly, by turns, at five-minute intervals. Although the *Tennessee* endured pounding from the wooden ships, it could not live long under fire from the ironclads. By 10:00 A.M., the vessel was out of control, Buchanan was badly wounded, and *Tennessee's* skipper, J. D. Johnston, struck her colors (surrendered).

Within the next two days, two of the Mobile Bay forts fell to the Union, and the last fort, Fort Morgan, surrendered on August 23.

The *Hunley* Saga

Born in Sumner County, Tennessee, in 1823, Horace L. Hunley served in the Louisiana State Legislature and practiced law in New Orleans. In 1861, after the outbreak of war, he joined James R. McClintok and Baxter Watson in building an innovative submarine for the Confederacy with the express purpose of providing a means of overcoming the Anaconda blockade. The *Pioneer*, however, had to be scuttled in 1862 to prevent its capture. The three partners later financed construction of the *American Diver*, which was soon lost in Mobile Bay; and another vessel, launched in July 1863, known by various names including *Fish Boat*, but ultimately called the *H. L. Hunley*.

Anatomy of a Submarine

Just under 40 feet long, the *Hunley* resembled a large steam boiler. Its hull was constructed of wrought-iron plates onto which were affixed two conning towers, sets of dive planes for maneuverability underwater, and, on top of the hull, five sets of portholes. A bellows was connected to a snorkel to draw fresh air into the vessel, but the system never worked well, and the boat could remain underwater only as long as the available air held out. For the eight or nine crewmen, that meant two more or less suffocating hours—at most.

A crankshaft ran the length of the submarine. Seven or eight seated crewmen turned the shaft, which drove a single screw (propeller). The commander steered, using rods and cables connected to a rudder, and controlled depth with a lever attached to the dive planes and by pumping ballast water in or out using a hand-powered pump.

CSS *Hunley* was fitted with a single weapon: a "torpedo," packed with 90 pounds of black powder and affixed to a long spar that projected from the bow. The planned method of attack was to aim for the broadside of the target vessel, crank like mad, and then ram the vessel with sufficient force to penetrate the hull with the spar and its torpedo. This accomplished, the crew would crank—again, fiercely—in reverse, leaving the torpedo in the target vessel's hull. At a safe distance from the enemy ship—about 200 feet—a crewman would tug at a lanyard attached to the torpedo, which would detonate, destroying the enemy.

Brave Men, Doomed Men

The *Hunley* was transported to Charleston, South Carolina, by rail, and tests were begun. The boat submerged beautifully, but getting her back up proved problematic. Once on the surface, she was barely seaworthy. During one test, while riding with her hatches open, a steamer passed by, flooding the *Hunley* with her wake water. The submarine sank with the loss of six crewmen—two men and the skipper were able to jump overboard before she went under.

The *Hunley* was refloated, and Horace Hunley personally took command of his namesake for some practice dives. On October 15, 1863, she dived in a burst of air bubbles and did not resurface. A hatch had sprung a leak, and all hands, including Hunley, drowned.

She was again refloated, and sailors opened her hatch to reveal the doomed crew. General Beauregard, commanding officer at Charleston, a soldier accustomed to battlefield deaths, was wholly unprepared for the sight of what he described as men "contorted into all sorts of horrible attitudes, some clutching candles … others lying in the bottom tightly grappled together."

Death of the *Housatonic*

Appalled, Beauregard forbade further tests, but *Hunley* skipper Lieutenant George Dixon persuaded him to allow an attack. The general reluctantly agreed, provided that the boat submerge only partially.

On February 17, 1864, at 8:45 P.M., the *Hunley* rammed the nine-gun Federal sloop USS *Housatonic* in Charleston Harbor. Pierced through to her powder magazine, *Housatonic* was rocked by an explosion, heeled to port, and sank stern first. Five crewmen were drowned, but the water in this part of the harbor was so shallow that most of the crew saved themselves simply by clinging to the masts and rigging, which remained above the surface as the shattered vessel hit bottom.

According to eyewitnesses on the *Housatonic*, the *Hunley* pulled back. But the *Hunley* was not seen again and was generally assumed to have been lost with its victim.

Yet there is a U.S. Navy record of a report of light signals exchanged, after the attack, between the shore and "some object" at sea. In August 1994, preservationists exploring under the auspices of the privately funded National Underwater and Marine Agency detected a metal object roughly matching the dimensions of the *Hunley* about 1,000 feet southeast of the boiler of the *Housatonic*, which still rested at the bottom of Charleston Harbor, near Sullivan's Island. A diving expedition confirmed the discovery of the *Hunley* in May 1995, and on August 8, 2000, a massive salvage operation raised and recovered the boat.

 SITES AND SIGHTS

As of 2010, the *Hunley* is under a costly and time-consuming restoration at the Warren Lasch Conservation Center in Charleston, South Carolina. A team of forensic archaeologists from the Smithsonian Institution studied the remains of the crew, who were then buried with military honors at Magnolia Cemetery in Charleston, on April 17, 2004. Visitors can visit the Hunley Submarine Museum at 1250 Supply Street, Charleston, SC; call 1-877-448-6539 for information and tickets. The most complete source of current information on the *Hunley* and conservation efforts may be obtained from the Friends of the *Hunley* website at www.hunley.org.

Why had the *Hunley* sunk, apparently after the successful completion of its mission? Perhaps the blast had damaged the vessel. Assuming that the *Hunley* did send a light signal, perhaps an excited crewman had failed to secure the porthole from which he had signaled. The Smithsonian Institution forensic archaeologists who studied the remains of the vessel's crew have suggested the possibility that the skipper may have prematurely opened the main hatch, perhaps because the damaged submarine was in distress.

Welcome Victory

While the development of the submarine would have a profound effect on twentieth-century naval warfare, the single, fatal mission of the *Hunley* had negligible effect on the course of the Civil War. Far more consequential was David Farragut's great victory in Mobile Bay, which cut off a major source of supply to the Confederacy. But of even greater consequence is what Farragut's triumph did to improve Abraham Lincoln's prospects for reelection.

Lincoln versus McClellan

Although some radical Republicans pressed for the nomination of uncompromising abolitionist Major General John C. Frémont (who had been relieved of command on June 28, 1862, and had been "awaiting orders" in New York ever since), the nod went to Lincoln, albeit with a new running mate, governor of Tennessee Andrew Johnson, replacing Vice President Hannibal Hamlin.

In August, as the victory at Mobile Bay unfolded, the Democratic Party convention in Chicago nominated George B. McClellan. The party's platform included a pledge that "efforts be made for a cessation of hostilities"—in other words, a negotiated peace as opposed to unconditional surrender. Many expected McClellan to run on this platform, but he soon repudiated it. Nevertheless, Lincoln ensured that McClellan was tarred with the defeatist Democrat brush, and he campaigned for reelection by drawing a simple contrast between "the Democrats" and himself: *They* would throw away the great sacrifices that had been made, while *he*, Abraham Lincoln, would honor those sacrifices by fighting through to nothing short of total victory.

Sherman Enters Georgia

With the fall of Mobile Bay, Lincoln's political prospects brightened. On May 6, 1864, while Grant fought his costly series of battles against Lee on the way to Richmond, William Tecumseh Sherman began his advance on Atlanta, fighting Joe Johnston's Army of Tennessee. As we shall see in the first part of the next chapter, it would be a four-month fight through Georgia. But when Sherman finally marched into Atlanta on September 2, 1864, the sun shone fully on the president, and his reelection on November 8, 1864, was assured.

The Least You Need to Know

- The diminutive Confederate navy did not attempt to fight the Union navy ship-for-ship, but relied on a strategy of commerce raiding to disrupt Union shipping.
- The most famous—and destructive—Confederate raider was CSS *Alabama*, which captured or sank 69 vessels before being sunk itself by USS *Kearsarge*.
- The Confederate *H. L. Hunley* was the first submarine actually used in combat.
- Admiral Farragut's daring victory at Mobile Bay not only tightened the stranglehold around the throat of the Confederacy, but also helped propel Abraham Lincoln to a second term.

"I Almost Tremble"

In This Chapter

- Sherman and the concept of "total war"
- Evacuation, occupation, and destruction of Atlanta
- Sherman's "March to the Sea"
- Capture of Savannah, Charleston, and Fort Sumter

On June 19, 1879, William Tecumseh Sherman, now filling Grant's place as commanding general of the army, addressed the graduating class of the Michigan Military Academy. "War," he said, "is at best barbarism …. Its glory is all moonshine. It is only those who have neither fired a shot, nor heard the shrieks and groans of wounded who cry aloud for blood, more vengeance, more desolation. War is hell."

This was not the opinion of a pacifist. With Grant, Sherman was probably the nation's fiercest warrior. It was the conclusion of a realist, and what is more important, a realist willing to *embrace* the reality he saw—and the reality he created. War is hell? Yes, and for the citizens of Georgia and South Carolina, General Sherman was the very devil.

This chapter explains what Sherman did to bring the war home to the people he believed had made the war in the first place.

The Atlanta Campaign

On the surface, Grant's orders to Sherman were simple: "To move against Johnston's army, to break it up, and to get into the interior of the enemy's country as far as you can, inflicting all the damage you can against their war resources."

The first part of the mission required little analysis, but the second part left vast latitude for interpretation. Just what constitutes "war resources"?

Most important towns and cities develop near great rivers or other bodies of water, but not landlocked Atlanta. It owed its existence to the railroads. Situated at the southern end of the Appalachian Mountains, Atlanta developed as the gateway through which overland traffic passed from the Southern coast to the West. In 1837, the Atlanta downtown neighborhood now called Five Points was chosen for the southern terminus of a railroad to be built north to Chattanooga. By the Civil War years, several other key Southern rail lines converged on Atlanta, clearly making the city a nexus of "war resources."

But Grant believed that all Southern resources were war resources in this *civil* war, and Sherman understood that he was to bring the battle to the civilian population and their property. He would, he said, "make Georgia howl."

William Tecumseh Sherman (1820–1891) carried out Grant's directive to target all of the South's resources for war.

Sherman at Dalton

General Sherman began his advance from Chattanooga into Georgia on May 7, 1864. Confederate General Joe Johnston had assumed command of the Army of Tennessee from Braxton Bragg at Dalton, Georgia, a few miles below the Tennessee state line. Johnston, unlike Bragg, was popular with his soldiers.

Although Sherman commanded 100,000 men against Johnston's 62,000, he realized that the Confederate defensive position at Dalton was too strong to attack head on. A fierce warrior as well as a canny tactician, Sherman was not about to repeat the errors of Ambrose Burnside at Fredericksburg (see Chapter 12) and Joe Hooker at Chancellorsville (see Chapter 14). Instead, he sent a division under James Birdseye McPherson, preceded by a cavalry division under Judson Kilpatrick, to force Johnston to turn his vulnerable flank as Major General George Henry Thomas ("The Rock of Chickamauga") proceeded frontally and John M. Schofield menaced the Confederate right.

Except for a protracted skirmish at Rocky Face Ridge (May 5–9), Johnston skillfully maneuvered to avoid major battle. He fell back on Resaca, about 10 miles down the railroad.

Here, once again, Sherman maneuvered to envelop Johnston from the west, and, once again, Johnston wriggled out of a major engagement, although the armies skirmished from May 13 through 16. Johnston retreated farther south down the railroad, about 25 miles, to Cassville.

Counterattack at Cassville

At Cassville, Johnston concentrated to counterattack Sherman's widely separated corps. He planned to send generals William J. Hardee and Joseph Wheeler against McPherson and Thomas, and John Bell Hood against Schofield. The battle-scarred Hood was a singularly courageous and daring commander, but he was not a sophisticated tactician. Deceived by the positioning of Federal cavalry, he mounted his attack from the wrong direction, creating a delay that fouled the timing of Johnston's intricate plan of coordinated attack. Johnston had to scrap his plan and pull back to Allatoona Pass, about 12 miles south of Cassville.

Once again, Sherman realized that the Confederates had withdrawn to a point too strong for him to attack frontally. After resting his army, fatigued from so much pursuit, he executed a series of maneuvers and skirmishing actions that pushed Johnston to Kennesaw Mountain.

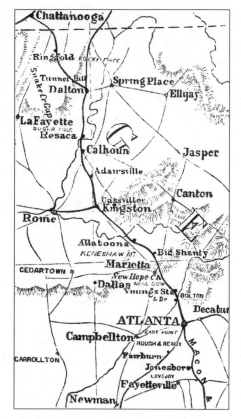

Atlanta and vicinity during the Atlanta campaign. The railroad line down which Sherman progressed runs south from Chattanooga to a junction at Dalton, Georgia. All the battle and skirmish sites lie along the rail line. This 1866 map misspells Kennesaw as "Keneshaw" and erroneously calls the town of Newnan (at the bottom of the map) "Newman."

(Harper's Pictorial History of the Civil War, 1866)

Assault at Kennesaw Mountain

The twin peaks of Big and Little Kennesaw are landmarks just north of Atlanta—uncomfortably *close* landmarks, as far as the citizens of the city were concerned—but in withdrawing to Kennesaw, Johnston had found another strong position. Using towropes, he hauled up his artillery, which thereby commanded the railroad below and much of the level area between Kennesaw, Pine, and Lost mountains.

On June 19, Sherman ordered his forces into a position from which he hoped to flank Johnston. Critical to his plan was getting troops south of the Confederate left and in secure possession of the road leading to Marietta. Johnston, however, grasped the situation as well as Sherman did and ordered Hood to defend the road at the farm of the widow of Valentine Kolb. On June 22, Union forces found themselves checked by Hood at this position.

Then Hood did what he was all too apt to do: he acted rashly and with blind aggression. Instead of holding his strong defensive position as ordered, he attacked. The result was heavy Confederate casualties in a totally unnecessary action. The result, too, was friction within the Confederate as well as Union armies. Johnston reprimanded Hood, who chafed under his commander's apparent reluctance to offer battle as the Yankees drew closer and closer to Atlanta. And Sherman scolded Hooker, who, he said, had grossly overestimated the enemy at Kolb's Farm, thereby relinquishing the initiative to the rebels.

COUNT OFF!

Of 16,225 Federals engaged at Kennesaw, 1,999 were killed or wounded, and 52 went missing. Of the 17,333 Confederates engaged, 270 were killed or wounded, and 172 missing.

Sherman was in ill humor. Even as Johnston was being criticized in the Southern press for failing to make a stand and stop Sherman, so the Northern press began printing its doubts about Sherman as a "fighting general." Frustrated and pressured, Sherman overrode his own better judgment to risk a frontal assault on Kennesaw Mountain.

Attacking uphill is a long shot under the best of circumstances. Eight o'clock on the morning of June 27 offered anything but the best circumstances. The weather was miserable, and the mountain slope was tangled with underbrush. Not surprisingly, Sherman's attack failed with very heavy losses.

Although Sherman gained nothing at Kennesaw, Johnston did pull back closer to Atlanta, taking up a position on the Chattahoochee River at the outskirts of the city. With each withdrawal Johnston picked up reinforcements, but he also admitted Sherman to the very threshold of Atlanta.

SITES AND SIGHTS

Kennesaw Mountain National Battlefield Park, in Kennesaw, Georgia, was the site of Sherman's only serious setback during the Atlanta campaign. Sherman's men never reached their objective, Pigeon Hill, which is stop two on the battlefield tour. The site is beautiful ("too beautiful to be disturbed by the horrors of war," Sherman remarked), with ample hiking opportunities. From I-75 take exit 269, Barrett Parkway, and follow signs to the park. Contact: 770-427-4686.

Hood Succeeds Johnston

Why did Joe Johnston relinquish so much ground to Sherman? Having taken the measure of Sherman, Johnston concluded that he was no McClellan, Burnside, or Hooker. He did not believe he could defeat Sherman, but, in tune with Robert E. Lee's overall war strategy, he did believe he could keep his own army intact and delay the taking of Atlanta long enough to cost Lincoln reelection. With a Democratic administration in office, the Confederacy had a chance of negotiating a favorable peace.

But the government of Jefferson Davis did not see it this way. It saw only a Yankee army on Atlanta's doorstep. On July 17, 1864, Davis summarily replaced Joseph E. Johnston with John Bell Hood and ordered his new commanding general to drive Sherman off.

"War Is Cruelty"

Elaborately ringed with fortified earthworks, Atlanta was a formidable objective. Instead of assaulting these, Sherman set out to cut the four rail lines into the city, which would force the Confederates to come out for a fight or to retreat and relinquish the city. In executing this plan, however, Sherman left a gap. McPherson's Army of the Tennessee and Schofield's Army of the Ohio made contact with one another, but they were separated from Thomas's Army of the Cumberland. While Schofield and McPherson approached the city from the east, Thomas was crossing Peachtree Creek, north of the city. It was at the gap that Hood chose to attack and, on July 20, the savage Battle of Peachtree Creek was fought.

Fortunately for Sherman, Thomas repulsed the attack, which might otherwise have defeated his army before he could join it to those of McPherson and Schofield.

Confederate defensive works outside of Atlanta. Look carefully at the two houses in the middle ground. They have been stripped to their frames for the wood needed to construct obstacles and defenses.
(Library of Congress)

Then on the 22nd, Hood attacked McPherson's Army of the Tennessee, nearly flanking it by swinging around it to the east. This was the beginning of the Battle of Atlanta, and it was one of the hardest fought of the war. McPherson died in the struggle, as his army was attacked simultaneously from the front and the rear, but the Union rallied and, with superior numbers, forced Hood back into his defensive works.

Having succeeded in cutting the rail line north and east, Sherman brought his army down around to the southwest of Atlanta to seize the Macon and Western Railroad. On July 28, Hood emerged again and attacked the Army of the Tennessee, now commanded by O. O. Howard, at Ezra Church, west of the city. In a hard fight, Howard repulsed Hood, inflicting heavy losses. In all, Hood's ill-considered offensives cost him about half his available forces.

SITES AND SIGHTS

Atlanta's city seal bears the Latin word *resurgens*—meaning, rising—above the image of a phoenix emerging from the flames. The modern city bears no trace of the conflict, except for many historical markers placed by the Georgia Historical Commission and the remains of fortifications at Fort Walker in Grant Park. (The park is *not* named for the Union's general-in-chief!) A building in the park houses the second-largest painting in America, created during 1885 and 1886 by German artists, it's an intricately detailed cyclorama depicting the Battle of Atlanta; a three-dimensional diorama accompanies the painting. A Civil War museum is also part of the exhibition, located at 800 Cherokee Avenue, SE, Atlanta, GA 30315. Contact: 404-658-7625.

Sherman had Atlanta within his grasp. Yet he also knew that, in a sense, he had failed. Johnston's (now Hood's) army was reduced but still very much intact. Worse, Sherman realized if Hood could keep him out of Atlanta sufficiently long, the Union rear would be vulnerable to Nathan Bedford Forrest (who, on July 15, had forced Union Major General A. J. Smith to withdraw from Tupelo, Mississippi).

Sherman's next step was as bold as it was unexpected. On August 25, he called off bombardment of Hood's entrenchments. The next day, most of his army disappeared. Hood concluded that Sherman had retreated. It was wishful thinking.

What Sherman *had* done was to swing far to the south, cutting the Macon and Western Railroad, the last rail connection into the city. Forrest, far to the northwest, had indeed performed brilliantly, but even in defeat, the Union force there kept him occupied, and he was unable to march to Hood's aid.

It was September 1 before Hood realized what Sherman had done. To avoid being trapped in Atlanta, the Confederate commander evacuated the city. On September 2, the Yankees marched in.

Sherman ordered the city evacuated of noncombatants, and when Atlanta's mayor and two city councilmen protested, he wrote them a letter: "War is cruelty …. You might as well appeal against the thunderstorm as against the terrible hardships of war."

Ordered by Sherman to evacuate, these refugees set out from Atlanta.
(National Archives and Records Administration)

Fiery March to the Sea

In the end, only about half of Atlanta's population had heeded his evacuation order when Sherman began transforming the Southern city into a Northern fortress. His victory accomplished three things—only two of which had been envisioned by Sherman and Grant. Number one, the South was deprived of a major rail hub and industrial city, and number two, Lincoln was assured of reelection.

These outcomes had been expected, but now Sherman found himself unexpectedly rethinking basic strategy. He had concurred with Grant that war would likely continue as long as the South had armies to fight it. Destroy those armies, and the war would end. Having taken Atlanta, however, Sherman understood that the Confederacy was not merely weak. It was hollow. He therefore proposed to Grant that, instead of pursuing Hood with the bulk of his army, he detach only a part of it to march west and instead lead most of his men away from Hood in a "March to the Sea." His object was to destroy war resources, to demoralize the Southern populace, and ultimately to position his army to come at Lee's Army of Northern Virginia from the south, even as Grant continued to bear down on it from the north—a classic *pincer movement* which would attack the enemy from opposite directions.

> **DEFINITION**
>
> A **pincer movement** is a strategy of attacking an enemy army from opposite directions, effectively squeezing it between the jaws of a pincer.

The March to the Sea would accomplish another, even more important, but less immediate, military objective. Sherman intended for the Union soldiers to live off the land, wrecking or burning whatever they didn't need to live on, thereby adding to the Confederacy's economic ruin and to its psychological destruction. As for the forces of Hood and Forrest, well, they wouldn't be totally ignored, but as Sherman pointed out, they could accomplish little; whereas Sherman could demonstrate to the people of the North, as well as the South, that the Confederate army was powerless to defend their lives, homes, and property. After considerable soul-searching, Grant approved Sherman's revised strategy.

Hood's Gamble

Leaving a corps in Atlanta to hold the city, Sherman did pursue Hood early in October as the Confederate general tried to disrupt the Federals' greatly extended lines of supply. But by the middle of November, Sherman began executing the strategy he proposed to Grant. Turning away from Hood, he began his march from Atlanta to the sea in Savannah.

Hood's Move

As Sherman turned away from Hood, Hood turned away from Sherman and commenced a long march toward Nashville, Tennessee. His new plan was to coordinate with Nathan Bedford Forrest in an operation designed to overwhelm the 30,000 men under Major General George Thomas, who had been sent to clear the Confederates out of Tennessee.

By menacing Thomas, Hood reasoned, Sherman would be forced out of Atlanta to come to Thomas's aid. At the very least, Hood believed the operation would halt Sherman's raid of the Deep South and, in the best case, might even recover Tennessee for the Confederacy. This would give Hood a base of operations in Nashville, from which he could launch an invasion of Kentucky and knock at the door of Cincinnati.

He might even be able to attack Grant's army from the rear, thereby relieving Lee and Richmond.

It was an ambitious plan. Had Hood and Forrest sufficient men to execute it, it might even have been considered a visionary plan. But the Southern military was so greatly reduced that, in reality, the plan was both desperate and doomed.

Who Burned Atlanta?

Anyone who's seen the 1939 movie *Gone with the Wind* (or read the Margaret Mitchell novel on which it is based) knows that Atlanta was put to the torch. The question is, who really did it?

Southerners are quick to answer that the city was burned by Sherman's order, but at least some Northerners will counter that the rebels themselves set the city ablaze.

In fact, both answers are true. After the evacuation of Atlanta, Hood dispatched men to blow up the Confederate ammunition train to keep it from falling into Union hands. Embers from the blast touched off a large fire in the early morning hours of September 1, 1864. But this was only the first burning of Atlanta. On November 11, Sherman ordered everything of military significance in Atlanta to be destroyed. Interpreting this liberally, Union troops set fire to just about everything that hadn't been destroyed in September. By the time Sherman marched out of the city on November 16, Atlanta was a smoldering ruin.

Franklin and Nashville

In Nashville, during early November, Major General George Thomas augmented his forces to some 50,000 men. He was braced for an attack by Hood and Forrest. Hood had been advancing against Union General John M. Schofield, maneuvering him into a vulnerable position at Spring Hill, Tennessee, on November 29 that could have cut off his retreat from Columbia, Tennessee, to Franklin, just south of Nashville. But Hood's plans of envelopment failed in their execution, and Schofield's army continued its withdrawal.

At Franklin, on November 30, a frustrated Hood recklessly ordered a frontal assault on Schofield's well-defended position. Of the 18,000 men he fielded in this attack, more than 6,000 were killed or wounded. Schofield continued his withdrawal to Nashville, where he combined with Thomas's force. Hood had fewer men than Thomas to begin with. Now he was outnumbered two to one.

No one could doubt the courage of George Thomas, the "Rock of Chickamauga," but, in contrast to John Bell Hood, Thomas did not confuse rash action with courageous action. Confident that he was in control of the situation around Nashville, he took his time organizing an attack. However when it was delayed by a bad ice storm, Grant, back in Virginia, was seized with doubt. Fearing that Thomas was allowing Hood to slip away, Grant cut an order relieving him of command. Just before Grant transmitted the order, Thomas attacked, and during December 15 and 16, he decisively defeated Hood. Brilliant rearguard action by Forrest prevented the outright destruction of the Army of Tennessee, but it was nevertheless driven from the field and washed up as an effective fighting force.

A Gift for His President

During this period, Sherman marched southeast from Atlanta, toward Savannah, Georgia, cutting a broad, burned swath of destruction and misery as he went. Judson Kilpatrick's cavalry left many barns and homes in ruins, and the notorious army foragers, called *bummers*, were especially ruthless.

 DEFINITION

Bummers were soldiers of Sherman's army who were ordered to forage aggressively.

On December 22, 1864, Sherman's forces reached the Georgia port city of Savannah. The town surrendered without a fight and, that evening, the general sent a telegram to Abraham Lincoln: "I beg to present you as a Christmas gift the city of Savannah, with one hundred and fifty heavy guns and plenty of ammunition; also about twenty-five thousand bales of cotton."

Shortly before Sherman's forces left Savannah to invade South Carolina, a fire broke out—apparently set by accident—and spread to a Confederate arsenal. It exploded, touching off a blaze that engulfed much of the city despite the efforts of citizens, freed slaves, and Union troops to put the fires out.

Columbia Burns

Sherman argued that the swath of destruction his troops wrought was a "military necessity," but many subsequent historians have called the "March to the Sea" nothing less than a war crime. Sherman thought the war itself was a crime—committed by Southern traitors and, having made Georgia howl, he pledged next to "punish South Carolina as she deserves."

That state was where the Civil War had begun, Sherman noted. "The whole army is burning with an insatiable desire to wreck vengeance upon South Carolina. I almost tremble for her fate."

On February 16, 1865, his army reached the South Carolina capital of Columbia. The mayor surrendered the city on the next day, whereupon fires broke out, razing half the town. Confederate General Wade Hampton, in a letter read before the U.S. Senate in 1866, accused Sherman of burning Columbia "to the ground, deliberately, systematically, and atrociously." Sherman responded that the fires had been started by Confederates in an attempt to destroy valuable cotton bales in order to keep them out of Federal hands.

The Stars and Stripes over Sumter

On February 18, the day after Columbia was occupied, the Confederates abandoned Fort Sumter as Union troops closed on Charleston. This city had stoutly resisted all Union attempts to capture it, but now, with the interior of South Carolina a hollow shell, there was no point in making a stand. Charleston surrendered, and the Stars and Stripes were raised above Fort Sumter for the first time since April 13, 1861. Just now, there was no time for ceremony—Sherman needed to continue his drive northward toward the rear of Robert E. Lee's army—but on April 14, 1865 (a matter of hours before John Wilkes Booth would murder Abraham Lincoln), Major General Robert Anderson, who had valiantly, if reluctantly, defended Sumter in the early spring of 1861, returned to raise over the fort the same flag he had taken down four years earlier.

The Least You Need to Know

- In the process of taking Atlanta and then marching "to the sea," General Sherman targeted a broad array of "war resources" including factories, farms, and livestock in order to destroy both the South's will and resources to continue to fight.

- Confederate General John Bell Hood sought in vain to draw Sherman away from his massive raid of Georgia and South Carolina by attacking Union forces in Tennessee. But Major General George Thomas effectively neutralized Hood's Army of Tennessee at the Battle of Nashville.

- The capture of Atlanta helped to ensure the reelection of Abraham Lincoln even as it deprived the South of a key railroad hub and manufacturing center.
- The Confederate withdrawal from Fort Sumter was a dramatically symbolic moment for the North.

On to Richmond!

In This Chapter

- Jubal Early menaces Washington
- Sheridan wages "total war" in the Shenandoah Valley
- Confederate terrorism
- Grant breaks through at Petersburg
- Davis and his cabinet evacuate Richmond

Although Atlanta was a prime military, transportation, and industrial prize, the most coveted psychological objective remained the Confederate capital of Richmond. Yet even as Sherman advanced through Georgia, took Atlanta, invaded South Carolina, and began his roll through North Carolina, Grant was still dug in outside Richmond's backdoor with Meade's Army of the Potomac, who was continuing its interminable siege of Petersburg, which had begun in June 1864.

While the armies pounded one another from the Petersburg entrenchments, Confederate General Jubal Early dared to menace Washington with his small army of 10,000 to 12,000 infantrymen and 4,000 cavalry troopers. And a far smaller band of Confederates was operating, out of uniform and undercover, to bring the war home to Northern civilians, just as Sherman was bringing it home to their wives, mothers, and children in the South.

Such was the substance of the penultimate act of the long national tragedy.

Menace in the Shenandoah Valley

Gray-bearded Jubal Early was six feet tall, but he was stooped by arthritis contracted in the 1840s, during the U.S.–Mexican War. He had never favored secession, but his loyalty to the South was beyond question, and many thought his skill as a commander was second only to that of Stonewall Jackson or Robert E. Lee, who, in affectionate reference to his infamous public disavowal of religion, called him "My Bad Old Man."

Early's Raid

On June 27, 1864, Early set off from Staunton, chief town of the Shenandoah Valley in Virginia, to invade Maryland. Not until July 5 did Henry Wager Halleck or Ulysses S. Grant take Early's offensive seriously and begin scrambling to reinforce Washington's defenses. On July 9, Early attacked Federal troops under Major General Lew Wallace at Monocacy, Maryland, 40 miles northwest of Washington. The Confederates sustained heavy losses, but at the end of the day the Federals were soundly beaten, and Early claimed the only reason he did not pursue them was to avoid burdening his small force with Union POWs. Despite his defeat, Wallace had bought time for the reinforcement of the capital's defenses. In so doing, Grant later said, Wallace accomplished more in defeat than many generals achieve by victory.

COUNT OFF!

Of 6,050 Federal troops engaged at Monocacy, 1,880 were wounded, killed, or missing. Early suffered about 900 casualties, almost all killed or wounded, out of the 14,000 troops he had in action.

After Monocacy, Early menaced Baltimore with a brigade of cavalry as he marched with the main body of his army on Washington. Grant sent men from the Army of the Potomac to defend the capital, which also called on local administrative troops and civilians to pitch in.

On July 11, Early reached the forts defending Washington itself. As the Confederates approached, the War Department cobbled together all available forces, including old soldiers from the Soldiers' Home and disabled veterans from the Invalid Corps. On the verge of ordering a general attack, Early was apparently dismayed by the sudden appearance of the Union's VI Corps, a veteran unit, and withdrew after a brief fight outside the lines of the forts. Early began a general withdrawal during the night of July 12 into early July 13, backtracking into the Shenandoah Valley.

On July 11 and 12, President and Mrs. Lincoln, accompanied by political dignitaries, visited Fort Stevens (located in northwest Washington). There was a sharp exchange with rebel sharpshooters, and Lincoln mounted a firing step to peer over the parapet for a view of the action, thereby exposing his head and chest to the enemy fire. A surgeon standing beside Lincoln was wounded, and a young officer shouted to the president, whom he did not recognize: "Get down, you damn fool!" That officer was Captain Oliver Wendell Holmes, Jr., who would later become the most eloquent and celebrated associate justice ever to sit on the U.S. Supreme Court.

Sheridan the Ruthless

Through the first week of August, Early harried Union units in the Shenandoah until Grant finally dispatched Phil Sheridan with about 48,000 men to defeat Early and take the Valley out of the war once and for all. The region was important for two reasons: first, it loomed always as an avenue of invasion, a backdoor to Washington, Baltimore, and Philadelphia; second, it was the breadbasket of the Confederate armies.

Grant ordered Sheridan to raze the Shenandoah croplands so that "a crow flying across the Valley would have to carry its own rations." Accordingly, he chased Early up the Shenandoah Valley while burning barns, burning crops, and destroying cattle. In turn, Sheridan's columns were harassed by guerrillas, the most famous of which was Colonel John Singleton Mosby, the "Gray Ghost of the Confederacy," at the head of his "Partisan Rangers."

Although Sheridan's forces greatly outnumbered those of Early, and guerrilla leaders like Mosby, combat was nevertheless sharp. Sheridan won a major victory at Winchester on September 19 and another at Fisher's Hill on September 22. But Early was far from finished. At dawn on October 19, he surprised the Federal position at Cedar Creek, Virginia, sending troops into disordered retreat. Sheridan, who was at Winchester following a visit to Washington, heard the distant thunder of artillery, galloped to the scene, and personally got the troops back into order and into the fight. By 4:00 that afternoon, he staged a furious counterattack, turning a Federal rout into a victory that essentially brought to a successful conclusion Sheridan's Shenandoah Valley campaign.

"Kilcavalry" Raids Richmond

Union Brigadier General Judson Kilpatrick was a twenty-eight-year-old West Pointer with unbounded dreams of glory. Short, slight, sporting ginger-colored, mutton-chop whiskers, he wore a rakish hat, a specially tailored cutaway uniform coat, and buff-colored cavalry trousers tucked into high boots. None of this impressed his men, one of whom remarked that it was "hard to look at him without laughing." Worse, Kilpatrick didn't care how many of his troops died in pursuit of his dreams. This earned Kilpatrick the nickname of "Kilcavalry." William Tecumseh Sherman simply called him "a hell of a damned fool."

Early in 1864, hearing that the Confederates had left Richmond very thinly defended, Kilpatrick persuaded his superiors to let him stage a lightning cavalry raid against the rebel capital with the purpose of harassing Confederate lines of supply and communication, disrupting government, and liberating the 5,000 Union prisoners languishing in two POW camps, Libby Prison and Belle Isle. When Ulric Dahlgren heard about the raid, he rushed to volunteer as second in command, despite having lost a leg at Gettysburg. At twenty-one, Dahlgren was the youngest colonel in the Union army. He was the son of Rear Admiral John A. Dahlgren, inventor of the famous Dahlgren gun used on most Union warships.

The raiders, 3,585 troopers, set off at 11 P.M. on February 28, 1864. At Spotsylvania, Dahlgren was detached with 500 men to proceed along the James River, upstream from Richmond, while Kilpatrick and the main force approached Richmond directly from the north. As Dahlgren approached from the southwest, Kilpatrick was to enter from the north, forcing the defenders to divide their already scant forces.

That was the plan. But Dahlgren never materialized, and Kilpatrick encountered much stiffer resistance than he had anticipated. Just outside of Richmond, Kilpatrick withdrew, stumbling into the 260 survivors of Dahlgren's detachment at a place called Tunstall's Station, near the Pamunkey River. Dahlgren, they told him, was dead, and almost half his command had been killed or captured.

The Kilpatrick-Dahlgren raid might be remembered as simply a failed military venture were it not for a handwritten speech on Third Division stationery the Confederates found in Dahlgren's pocket:

> You have been selected from brigades and regiments as a picked command to attempt a desperate undertaking ....

> We hope to release the prisoners from Belle Island first, and, having seen them fairly started, we will cross the James river into Richmond, destroying the bridges after us, and exhorting the released prisoners to destroy and burn the hateful city, and do not allow the Rebel leader, Davis, and his traitorous crew to escape. ... Jeff Davis and Cabinet [are to be] killed ....

The document was conveyed to President Davis, who had it published in the Richmond newspapers as evidence of Northern treachery. The dogs were resorting to assassination!

In response to the newspaper stories and official protests from the Confederacy, Dahlgren's and Kilpatrick's superiors disavowed any knowledge of an assassination plot. No Federal conspiracy to assassinate Davis has ever been proved, but neither has it been disproved. The ultimate objective of the Kilpatrick-Dahlgren Raid remains a mystery of the Civil War.

Of Terror and Greek Fire

In the late spring and early summer of 1864, with the Confederacy crumbling, some residents of coastal Maine reported seeing artists sketching along the shore. These "artists" were, in fact, 50 Confederate topographers making maps of secluded coves and inlets that could harbor two armed steamers, the *Tallahassee* and the *Florida*, during a planned terrorist assault along the Northern coast. But word of the operation leaked to the American consul in St. Johns, Quebec, who notified the War Department, which alerted the local Home Guard. When the raiders, seeking to fund their operations, hit the Calais (Maine) National Bank late in July, guardsmen, police, and the Portland marshal were ready for them. The ringleaders were captured, and one of them, Francis Jones, revealed the scope of the entire scheme. Jones's revelations led to the arrest of Confederate operatives in Maine, Massachusetts, New York, Pennsylvania, Maryland, Illinois, Missouri, Kentucky, Tennessee, and Ohio.

The St. Albans Raid

While most covert Confederate operations during 1864 proved abortive, an October 19 raid by about 20 men against 3 banks in the border town of St. Albans, Vermont netted the Confederacy nearly $250,000 of badly needed funds. One citizen was killed and another wounded; a number of the town's principal buildings were burned to the ground by hurled bottles of an incendiary fluid known as *Greek fire.*

> **DEFINITION**
>
> **Greek fire** was a highly flammable fluid consisting of sulfur, charcoal, saltpeter, and possibly quicklime, which burst into flame when suddenly exposed to air. Typically, it was poured into a glass jar, which was then tightly sealed. If suddenly broken, the contents would ignite explosively.

Following the operation, the raiders fled to Canada, which was a headquarters and staging area for Confederate covert operations during the late phases of the war. A posse gave chase, crossed the border, and apprehended eight of the raiders, but had to remand the men to Canadian custody. A team of slick lawyers fought the raiders extradition to the United States, and all eight escaped prosecution.

The Fires of New York

Some Confederate agents wanted to do far more than rob banks. An uprising was set for November 8, 1864, election day in the Union, and targeted Chicago, Cincinnati, towns throughout Missouri and Iowa, and, in particular, New York City.

The Chicago operation was aborted as Union counterintelligence rooted out the scheme and, with the failure of the Chicago uprising, the planned revolts elsewhere likewise came to naught. But three die-hard agents—Colonel Robert Martin and Lieutenant John W. Headley (both former subordinates of famed raider John Hunt Morgan), plus a shadowy figure known only as Captain Longuemare from Missouri—resolved to act on their own. Their plan was to organize other operatives to check into New York City's 19 most prominent hotels. Each man would go up to his room, set it on fire, and calmly walk out. Longuemare ordered 144 four-ounce bottles of Greek fire from a compliant chemist in Greenwich Village. Headley lugged this heavy and highly combustible load in a carpetbag valise several blocks, boarded a crowded, uptown-bound horsecar, sat behind the conductor, and tucked the valise between his legs. His destination was a Confederate safe house near Central Park (which, in 1864, was still under development).

WAR NEWS

In addition to the hotels, the arsonists hit the famed Barnum's Museum on lower Broadway, creating a blaze made even more terrifying by the roar of lions and tigers, and the trumpeting of elephants trapped in their cages. The flames drove Barnum's seven-foot-tall giantess into a frenzy, requiring five strong firemen and a physician's sedative to bring her under control.

As the car jostled along the tracks, Headley detected the rotten-egg stench of hydrogen sulfide. He looked down at the valise between his legs, expecting to see a telltale puddle of Greek fire.

But, no.

Then a woman, sniffing, called out: "Something smells dead here! Conductor, something smells dead in that man's valise!"

But nobody did anything. Headley got off the horsecar, walked to the safe house, and distributed the bottles. He and the other agents then left and, beginning about 7:00 in the evening, registered at the hotels. Each signed in, received his key, walked up to his room, and closed the door. Headley later related what he had done at the Astor House: "I hung the bedclothes loosely on the headboard and piled the chairs, drawers of the bureau, and washstand on the bed, then stuffed some newspapers about among the mass and poured a bottle of turpentine over it all." Instead of hurling the bottle of Greek fire against the wall, which would have exploded, attracting immediate attention, he just spilled it on a "pile of rubbish. It blazed up instantly and the whole bed seemed to be in flames before I could get out. I locked the door and … left the key at the office as usual." Walking through the lobby with calm deliberation, he went off to register at the City Hotel, his next target.

After igniting other hotel rooms, Headley strolled along the West Side wharves and hurled Greek fire at a number of vessels tied up there.

For once, a rebel conspiracy seemed to work. Panicked rumors of an invasion buzzed through the streets—and, yet no general conflagration developed. Two floors of the Belmont Hotel and the Metropolitan were destroyed, and the St. Nicholas was a complete loss. A dry goods firm was gutted, and a few ships damaged. But that was about all. Perhaps the Greenwich Village chemist had prepared a weak batch of Greek fire, or perhaps the fires in the hotel rooms burned out too quickly because none of the arsonists had thought to open a window to fan the flames; the fires were oxygen starved.

The disappointed conspirators fled back to Canada and, as the fires died in New York, so, too, the last of the Confederate conspiracies passed into oblivion.

"With Malice Toward None"

No one—not Robert E. Lee, not Joseph E. Johnston, not John Bell Hood, and not a band of determined terrorists—was able to prevent the reelection of Abraham Lincoln, a president committed to fighting the war to total victory. Yet, on inauguration day, March 4, 1865, Lincoln made it clear that total victory did not mean wreaking vengeance on the Southland. His brief inaugural address concluded:

> With malice toward none, with charity for all, with firmness in the right as God gives us to see the right, let us strive to finish the work we are in, to bind up the nation's wounds, to care for him who shall have borne the battle and for his widow and his orphan, to do all which may achieve and cherish a just and a lasting peace among ourselves and with all nations.

From the leader of a country on the painful threshold of victory in a war far more costly than either side had ever remotely envisioned, these were remarkable words of justice, compassion, and forgiveness. Yet they must nevertheless have rung hollow in the ears of Southerners whose property was stolen or burned, and whose lives were in countless ways shattered.

The war went on.

Breakout from Petersburg

For nine months Petersburg lay under siege. The Army of the Potomac entrenched here numbered about 125,000 men against an Army of Northern Virginia of perhaps half that number. Lee's men were hungrier than ever before (and they had often been hungry before), and their commander knew they were trapped. Jefferson Davis had insisted they stay put to defend the capital at all costs. In extremity, Lee finally persuaded Davis that the only chance of averting total defeat and unconditional surrender lay in escape from siege. Lee proposed a breakout from Petersburg and a retreat southeast so that he could unite his forces with the ragged remnants of the Army of Tennessee—since February 22 once again under the command of Joe Johnston—now fighting Sherman in North Carolina.

These Federal soldiers in the Petersburg siege lines await Grant's spring offensive.
Union troops here were numerous and well equipped.
(National Archives and Records Administration)

Johnston's army of just 30,000 men was comprised of veteran survivors and home guardsmen, overage and poorly equipped. Nevertheless Lee hoped that, by uniting his forces with Johnston's, they might still compel a negotiated peace, even if Richmond fell. To be sure, the odds against such an outcome were astronomical, but starving in the trenches of Petersburg offered no odds at all.

Diplomacy and Politics

The Richmond government made its own attempts to force negotiation. Confederate Secretary of State Judah P. Benjamin appealed to France and England for recognition as a sovereign nation on condition that the CSA abolish slavery. It was too late for such a proposal, since very little of the Confederacy was left to recognize. We cannot know whether the irony of the proposal was apparent to the Richmond government. To avoid surrender, the Confederacy proposed to give up the very institution it had fought to preserve.

In January, Jefferson Davis put out very tentative peace feelers, meeting in Richmond with Francis P. Blair, Sr. (father of Lincoln's former postmaster general, Montgomery Blair, and of Francis P. Blair, Jr., one of Sherman's corps commanders). Blair's visit, while approved by Lincoln, was entirely unofficial, but Davis nevertheless seized the opportunity to propose a reunion of the states and then, both bizarrely and irrelevantly, to propose that the reconstituted nation invade Mexico in order to eject the French-supported regime of Emperor Maximilian.

A semiofficial peace conference convened on February 3 aboard a Federal steamer in Hampton Roads, Virginia, came to absolutely nothing.

> **WAR NEWS**
>
> Many people could not accept that nothing came of the peace conference at Hampton Roads, and a popular myth circulated that Lincoln took a fresh sheet of paper, inscribed the heading "REUNION" at the top, handed it to Stephens, and told him to fill in the rest.
>
> No such thing ever happened.
>
> Lincoln would *accept* no terms and would *offer* only two: the South must lay down its arms and must recognize the absolute authority of the United States government.

"Wake Up. We Are Coming"

On the Petersburg front, Lee assigned Major General John Brown Gordon to attack with 12,000 men a hardened Union position called Fort Stedman, a mere 150 yards from the Confederate lines. The idea was to force Grant to contract his lines, thereby opening a route through which Lee could push a portion of his army and begin the march into North Carolina.

In the wee hours of March 25, the Confederates sent *sappers* with axes to cut down obstructions in front of the fort. An alert Union picket heard the noise and called out, "Who goes there?"

"Never mind, Yank. We are just gathering a little corn," one of the rebels replied.

"All right, Johnny," the Union picket called back. "I'll not shoot at you while you are drawing rations."

At 4:00 A.M., Gordon ordered the quick-thinking soldier to fire a shot to signal the commencement of the assault. When he hesitated, the Confederate general repeated the order. The soldier looked at his general, and then at the Yankee lines.

"Hello, Yank!" he shouted. "Wake up. We are coming."

His conscience thus salved, he fired the shot, and the attack began.

DEFINITION

In the nineteenth-century military, **sappers** were soldiers (sometimes also called "pioneers") sent in advance of a column, or in preparation for an attack. Armed with axes, their mission was to clear debris, undergrowth, and other obstacles to marching or attacking.

Fort Stedman Taken ...

Not only did Fort Stedman quickly fall—with the capture of a thousand Union soldiers and one very surprised Union general—but so did a number of surrounding positions.

Next, Gordon was supposed to capture smaller forts behind Fort Stedman. But two things went wrong. First, Confederate reinforcements were delayed. Second, Gordon was uncertain in which direction to continue his attack—all around him were well-fortified Yankee entrenchments.

... And Given Back

Without reinforcements and unable to decide which way to go, Gordon's men were stranded. By 7:30 A.M., Union reinforcements poured in, forcing the Confederates back into Fort Stedman. At 8:00, Lee, watching from his lines, ordered a retreat, but by this time the Federals were also raking the Confederate line of retreat with artillery fire. Many rebels surrendered where they stood rather than retreat into certain death. Of 12,000 men engaged, the Confederates lost 4,000, killed, wounded, or captured. And Lee, of course, remained pinned at Petersburg.

Five Forks

Although the siege at Petersburg had consumed nine months, it was not stalemated. Grant had been steadily extending his lines westward in order to force Lee to stretch his much thinner lines to the breaking point. After the exchange at Fort Stedman, it was clear to Grant that Lee's lines had now stretched *beyond* the breaking point. He accordingly attempted a drive around Lee's right, but was repulsed. Then General Sheridan returned from the Shenandoah Valley with 12,000 cavalry troopers and, on March 31, headed for Five Forks, a junction not only crucial to the Confederates' contemplated move into North Carolina but vital to their army's line of supply. Take it, and Lee not only would be cut off from Johnston, but he would soon be forced to evacuate Petersburg as well as Richmond.

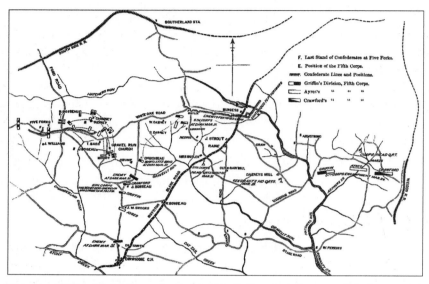

This map of Five Forks shows the South Side Railroad at the upper left. Lee needed this rail line for supplies and to get him to Johnston's army in North Carolina.
(Harper's Pictorial History of the Civil War, 1866)

Lee sent 19,000 (some estimates put this figure at a mere 10,000) men under George Pickett to hold Five Forks, but Sheridan was reinforced by an infantry corps. Outnumbered, Pickett was also outgeneraled. His forces were flanked and routed by Sheridan, some 5,000 men were taken prisoner, and the rest, those not killed or wounded, "skedaddled" (fled).

The disaster at Five Forks has been called "the Waterloo of the Confederacy."

Evacuation

After a nine-month gestation, the birth of victory at Petersburg came suddenly. Grant broke through Lee's lines on April 2 in a quick assault that resulted in the death of Confederate General Ambrose Powell (A. P.) Hill. Lee fell back on Petersburg and evacuated it, retreating west toward Amelia Court House.

At 11:00 on this Sunday morning, April 2, Jefferson Davis was seated in his pew at St. Paul's Church in Richmond. A War Department messenger approached and handed him a telegram from Robert E. Lee. It advised that "all preparation be made for leaving Richmond tonight."

Those seated near the Confederate president remarked that a "gray pallor" suddenly crept "over his face" as he read the message. He rose, walked out of church, went to the War Office, and gave orders for evacuation. He and his cabinet would meet that evening and board a train bound for Danville, a Virginia town just north of the North Carolina state line, which would become the new Confederate capital. Davis ordered that all the Confederacy's ready funds from the Treasury—a mere $528,000 in gold and silver coins and ingots—be boxed for shipment to Danville. Davis packed his wife and children off to Charlotte, North Carolina, a location relatively remote from the war.

The Nightmare Gone

The war, which had been measured in agonizing months and years, was now becoming a matter of days. The Confederate government evacuated Richmond on April 2, and Federal troops under Major General Godfrey Weitzel were the first to enter the city the next day, trooping into a place that, like so many other Southern cities and towns, was now ablaze. The night before, Confederate authorities blew up the ironclads docked along the James River in order to keep them out of Union hands. The explosions touched off fires in wharf-side tobacco warehouses, and those fires spread to large sections of the city before they burned out on the evening of the 3rd.

On this day, Grant entered Petersburg and was met there by Abraham Lincoln, who strode up to the general, and (as an aide to the general recalled) shook his hand "for some time … pouring out his thanks and congratulations."

When he set off for Richmond on the morning of April 4 in David Porter's flagship, Lincoln remarked to the admiral: "Thank God I have lived to see this. It seems to me that I have been dreaming a horrid dream for four years, and now the nightmare is gone."

The ruins of Richmond appear in ghostly silhouette in this period photograph. The fires were touched off when Confederates, evacuating the city, blew up ironclads docked on the James River in order to keep them from being captured.
(National Archives and Records Administration)

The Least You Need to Know

- After Confederate General Jubal Early attacked the outskirts of Washington, General Grant ordered Philip Sheridan to defeat and, in the process, to lay waste to the Shenandoah Valley.

- Confederate acts of terrorism against the North were conceived on a grand scale, but rarely amounted to much. The most famous raid against the North was the attack on three banks in St. Albans, Vermont, on October 19, 1864.

- The Battle of Five Forks, in which Union Commander Philip Sheridan defeated Confederate General George Pickett, has been called the "Waterloo of the Confederacy."

- After Grant's breakthrough at Petersburg, Davis and his government fled Richmond, which instantly fell to the Union. It was the beginning of the war's final act.

- President Lincoln was quick to visit the fallen Confederate capital; his object was to underscore the defeat of the rebel government.

Appomattox Ending

Chapter 23

In This Chapter

- The pursuit of Lee to Appomattox Court House
- The decision to surrender
- Lee surrenders the Army of Northern Virginia
- The war ends

As the first Union general officer to enter Richmond, Godfrey Weitzel laid claim to the choicest headquarters, setting himself up in the abandoned Governor's Mansion—for four years the Confederate White House. After walking two miles through the streets of the fallen capital, Abraham Lincoln was tired. Weitzel admitted him into Jefferson Davis's study.

Perhaps it was war weariness, or simply the long walk—or something deeper—that prompted Lincoln to slump into Jefferson Davis's chair. He made no speech, no profound pronouncement, just a request: "I wonder if I could get a glass of water?"

During these moments, there was neither rest nor refreshment for Grant, Lee, and their armies. This chapter describes the final pursuit of the Army of Northern Virginia and the last days of the war.

Pursuit

No one knew better than Robert E. Lee that Union victory was now inevitable.

At this point, he was not motivated by questions of victory or defeat, but by duty. He felt it was his duty to continue to fight, while he still could, in order to preserve as much of a chance as possible to negotiate surrender terms that were, at least, something more than abject and unconditional. By today's standards we might argue that, by prolonging combat, Lee acted without humanity. By the standards of 1865, however, the loss of honor was perceived as inhumane.

Lee took what was left of his army, slightly fewer than 50,000 men, and marched west. To be sure, he was being chased, but he was not so much fleeing as trying to reach Amelia Court House, where he expected to find supplies and gain access to the Danville and Richmond Railroad, which would take his army to that of Johnston.

Namozine Church

After Five Forks (see Chapter 22), a brigade of George Armstrong Custer's cavalry pursued a brigade of Confederate cavalry, commanded by Robert E. Lee's nephew Fitzhugh Lee, and fought first at Willicomack Creek, and then at Namozine Church. Here Custer repulsed a desperate Confederate counterpunch. Following this the Confederates split up, Fitzhugh Lee making for Amelia Court House, while his subordinate, William Henry Fitzhugh Lee—called Rooney—headed toward Bevill's Bridge. Rooney was Robert E. Lee's second-eldest son.

> **WAR NEWS**
>
> George Armstrong Custer was only 23 when he was promoted to brigadier general. Lacking academic skills and self-discipline, he had almost failed to graduate from West Point, but showed such courage and initiative on the battlefield—he was especially celebrated for his reckless cavalry charges—that his star rapidly rose. After the war, he earned fame as an Indian fighter in the West commanding the Seventh Cavalry. That fame culminated at the Battle of the Little Big Horn in June 1876. Custer attacked the village of Sitting Bull and Crazy Horse, whose warriors responded by wiping out Custer and more than 200 of his men.

Amelia Springs

By April 5, the bulk of Lee's army was concentrated at Amelia Court House, about 30 miles west of Petersburg. Sheridan, and others, blocked the Confederates from making a break down the Richmond and Danville Railroad. Worse, in the confusion of Richmond's fall, no one had dispatched the promised rations—a fact that hit the half-starved army particularly hard. Sheridan sent a brigade to reconnoiter in the direction of Lee's retreat, and, at Amelia Springs, it attacked a wagon train attached to Lee's army. The Federals took 320 white military prisoners and about as many civilian black teamsters, then set fire to 200 of Lee's wagons, probably destroying all the general's headquarters records in the process.

This map shows Lee's route of retreat from Petersburg west to Appomattox Court House. Jetersville (misspelled on this map as "Jettersville") is the site of the Amelia Springs battle and is midway between Petersburg and Appomattox Court House (which is also misspelled, as "Appomatox").
(Harper's Pictorial History of the Civil War, 1866)

Sayler's Creek

Having failed to connect with rations and supplies at Amelia Court House, and unable to make a rail connection there, Lee turned to the southwest toward a place called Rice Station, where he could get supplies by rail and then push on south to link up with Johnston. However Grant ordered attacks, and pursuing Federal forces hit the Confederate wagon train.

At Little Sayler's Creek, Confederate General Richard S. Ewell counterpunched, driving back the Union center, but the arrival of more Federals soon checked this penetration. As Federal strength continued to build, Union forces counterattacked, effecting a *double envelopment* of Ewell's badly outnumbered command.

> **DEFINITION**
>
> In a **double envelopment,** the enemy army is completely surrounded by having been outflanked on both the left and the right.

Three Confederate commanders—Richard H. Anderson, Bushrod Johnson, and George Pickett—escaped, but Ewell remained behind in an effort to lead his troops out of the trap. There was fierce hand-to-hand fighting, but it was hopeless. Ewell's men were engulfed and he was captured, along with five other Confederate commanders, including George Washington Custis Lee, Robert E. Lee's eldest son.

As for Robert E. Lee himself, the commander in chief witnessed the rout from high ground in the rear. He turned to a subordinate and observed, "General, that half of our army is destroyed."

In truth, Lee had lost a third of his entire forces—which was certainly bad enough.

High Bridge and Farmville

Confederate General John Brown Gordon suffered heavy losses at Sayler's Creek, as did the other rebel commanders; but, unlike them, Gordon successfully rallied his troops and led them farther west to High Bridge, a structure built on 60-foot piers across the Appomattox River at Farmville. There he joined Longstreet in retreating across the bridge, leaving Fitzhugh Lee to fight a rearguard action.

William "Little Billy" Mahone, commanding a division that was covering Gordon's withdrawal, should have ordered High Bridge put to the torch once all the units had crossed it. But before the war Mahone had been a railroad construction engineer, and then president of the Southside Railroad—the owner of this particular structure. He did not burn it (skirmishers later tried, without success) and, in consequence, the Federals quickly closed on the rear of Lee's army. Nevertheless Union forces failed to stop Lee's westward progress here, and the Confederate army even had the opportunity to draw rations at Farmville.

At 10:00 that night, Lee received a message from Ulysses Simpson Grant. It requested the surrender of the Army of Northern Virginia.

Wordlessly Lee passed the note to James Longstreet, who had been the voice of realism when Lee proposed to invade Maryland and, later again, when he resolved to invade Pennsylvania. Now Longstreet read the note, looked at his commander, and said: "Not yet."

Appomattox Station and Appomattox Court House

What must Lee have been feeling on April 8, when he concentrated the remnant of his ragged, hungry army between Appomattox Station, on the rail line, and Appomattox Court House, a few miles to the northeast? How much farther could he lead these men who had put their lives in his hands?

General Custer's division moved rapidly against Appomattox Station, drove off two Confederate divisions, and captured their supply train as well as 30 pieces of artillery. Custer then pressed on toward Appomattox Court House, where he discovered the Confederate defenses just to the southwest of the town. Sheridan, with the main body of troops, caught up with Custer and prepared to launch an attack the next day.

In fact at 5:00 on the morning of April 9, 1865, it was Lee's generals, John Brown Gordon and Fitzhugh Lee, who attacked first, assaulting hastily constructed Federal breastworks. This proved effective, though the success was short lived. Union cavalry and infantry pressed from the northeast, from Appomattox Court House, and, having gotten across Lee's line of march, also closed in from the southwest, from Appomattox Station. At this point, Lee was down to perhaps 30,000 soldiers, of whom only little more than half were still armed.

"I Had Rather Die a Thousand Deaths"

Lee saw that his broken army lay within the jaws of a vise. It could not go forward. Nor could it retreat. It was time to end it. "There is nothing left me but to go and see General Grant, and I had rather die a thousand deaths."

Like a Wraith of Morning Mist

On April 9, General Joshua Laurence Chamberlain, the former Bowdoin professor of rhetoric who had held Little Round Top and saved the Union army at Gettysburg, was poised for attack with his regiment. He watched the Confederate lines apprehensively, until (as he later wrote) …

> Suddenly rose to sight another form, close in our own front—a soldierly young figure, a Confederate staff officer undoubtedly. Now I see the white flag earnestly borne, and its possible purport sweeps before my inner vision like a wraith of morning mist ….

> The messenger draws near, dismounts; with graceful salutation and hardly suppressed emotion delivers his message: "Sir, I am from General Gordon. General Lee desires a cessation of hostilities until he can hear from General Grant as to the proposed surrender."

> … "Sir," I answer, "that matter exceeds my authority. I will send to my superior. General Lee is right. He can do no more."

The grim fact is that Lee *could* have done more. A man of lesser moral integrity might have bitterly directed his army to disband, to take to the hills, to fight as partisans and guerrillas, and, in this way, year after year, decade after decade, kill every Yankee they encountered south of the Mason-Dixon Line.

But instead, Lee directed Colonel Charles Marshall "to go forward and find a house where he could meet General Grant." Marshall recalled that the first person he met was a "man named [Wilmer] McLean who used to live on the first battle field of Manassas, at a house about a mile from Manassas Junction. He didn't like the war, and having seen the first battle of Manassas, he thought he would get away where there wouldn't be any more fighting, so he moved to Appomattox Court House."

Marshall asked McLean to show him a house where the generals could meet. McLean took him to a dilapidated shell devoid of furniture. Marshall said it was unsuitable.

"Then [McLean] said, 'Maybe my house will do!'"

Grant accepted Lee's surrender in the McLean house at Appomattox Court House. This was McLean's second house. His first stood on what became the Bull Run battlefield—he had moved to a place he thought would never see combat.
(Library of Congress)

In the McLean House

No account of the surrender at Appomattox is clearer, simpler, or more moving than what Ulysses S. Grant wrote in his *Personal Memoirs*, published in 1885:

> … When I went into the house I found General Lee. We greeted each other, and after shaking hands took our seats …
>
> What General Lee's feelings were I do not know. As he was a man of much dignity, with an impassable face, it was impossible to say whether he felt inwardly glad that the end had finally come, or felt sad over the result, and was too manly to show it. Whatever his feelings, they were entirely concealed from my observation; but my own feelings, which had been quite jubilant on the receipt of his letter [offering surrender], were sad and depressed. I felt like anything rather than rejoicing at the downfall of a foe who had fought so long and valiantly, and had suffered so much for a cause, though that cause was, I believe, one of the worst for which a people ever fought …
>
> General Lee was dressed in a full uniform which was entirely new, and was wearing a sword of considerable value, very likely the sword which had been presented by the State of Virginia; at all events, it was an entirely different sword from the one that would ordinarily be worn in the field. In my rough traveling suit, the uniform of a private with the straps of a lieutenant-general, I must have contrasted very strangely with a man so handsomely dressed, six feet high and of faultless form ….
>
> We soon fell into a conversation about old army times …. Our conversation grew so pleasant that I almost forgot the object of our meeting. After the conversation had run on in this style for some time, General Lee called my attention to the object of our meeting, and said that he had asked for this interview for the purpose of getting from me the terms I proposed to give his army. I said that I meant merely that his army should lay down their arms, not to take them up again during the continuance of the war unless duly and properly exchanged. He said that he had so understood my letter …

The terms Grant wrote were generous. He would take no prisoners, but simply secure the paroles of officers and men not to take up arms "until properly exchanged"; for although the principal Confederate army had been vanquished, the war was not yet over. Confederate troops under other commanders remained in the field. Officers were permitted to retain their sidearms, and officers and men could keep their horses and their personal effects. Everyone would be "allowed to return to their homes, not to be disturbed by United States authority so long as they observe their paroles …"

> … General Lee, after all was completed and before taking his leave, remarked that his army was in a very bad condition for want of food, and that they were without forage; that his men had been living for some days on parched corn exclusively, and that he would have to ask me for rations and forage. I told him "certainly" …

SITES AND SIGHTS

The Appomattox Court House National Historical Park, a 1,325-acre facility centered on the town of Appomattox Court House, includes the fully restored McLean House, furnished as it is supposed to have looked on April 9, 1865, when Lee surrendered the Army of Northern Virginia to Grant. Contact: 434-352-8987, ext. 26.

Coda

Robert E. Lee surrendered an army, not a nation. But the event historian Bruce Catton called the "stillness at Appomattox" did, for all practical purposes, end the Civil War. Except for the desperate, deluded performance of a Southern-sympathizing matinee idol in Washington's Ford's Theatre on the evening of April 14 (see Chapter 24), the rest of the tragedy's last act was an anticlimax.

WAR NEWS

The tradition of the vanquished commander surrendering his sword is so appealing that rumors soon circulated that Lee surrendered his to Grant, and Grant graciously handed it back. In his *Personal Memoirs*, Grant observed that "the much talked of surrendering of Lee's sword and my handing it back, this and much more that has been said about it is the purest romance." It didn't happen.

Montgomery, Alabama, fell to James H. Wilson's Union cavalry on April 12, and Federal troops entered Mobile (long blockaded, but never captured) the same day. On the 13th Sherman occupied Raleigh, North Carolina, where, during the 17th and 18th, he sat with Joseph E. Johnston and hammered out a broad armistice that was, in effect, a peace treaty. It traded a blanket amnesty, civil as well as military, for total and absolute military surrender. Unlike Grant, who never asked Lee for his sword, Sherman accepted Johnston's weapon as a symbol of the surrender.

Sherman accepted Johnston's surrender at the house of James Bennett in Raleigh, North Carolina.
(Harper's Pictorial History of the Civil War, 1866)

Sherman's veterans pass in grand review down Washington's Pennsylvania Avenue.
(Harper's Pictorial History of the Civil War, 1866)

On April 21, the new president of the United States, Andrew Johnson, and his cabinet rejected and angrily repudiated the Sherman-Johnston document. It was, after all, the generals' province to make war, but the politicians' prerogative to make peace. On the 26th, Johnston accepted a narrower armistice, identical to what Grant had offered Lee, and on the same day, the Confederate cabinet held its last meeting, in Charlotte, North Carolina, after which it dissolved.

With the rejection of the Sherman-Johnston armistice, Davis and his ministers were not protected by any amnesty and, in fact, had been branded criminals and fugitives by President Johnson.

Jefferson Davis was captured by Federal troops at dawn on May 10, 1865, near Irwinville, Georgia. He was imprisoned and remained under lock and key for two years. In May 1867, he was released on bail and lived in Canada, awaiting trial for treason. Davis was eager for a trial, which he intended to use as a forum in which to argue that states had a constitutional right to secede. Perhaps to avoid just such an argument, the government refused to prosecute Davis, and charges were formally dropped on December 25, 1868.

 SITES AND SIGHTS

Called Beauvoir House, Jefferson Davis's final home is located at 2244 Beach Boulevard, Biloxi, Mississippi 39531, a site that now includes the house, the Jefferson Davis Presidential Library, a Confederate Museum, a historic cemetery, the Tomb of the Unknown Confederate Soldier, and a gift shop. It is open to the public for an admission fee. Contact: 228-388-4400.

Davis eventually became president of a Memphis-based insurance company; then, in 1877, retired to a small estate near Biloxi, Mississippi, which an admirer provided for him. He died, unrepentant, in 1889.

After the war, in September 1865, Robert E. Lee accepted the presidency of Washington College (after his death, renamed Washington and Lee College in his honor) in Lexington, Virginia. Prematurely aged and plagued by heart disease, he died five years later, on October 12, 1870. His U.S. citizenship was not officially restored until 1975, by act of Congress.

In May, the very last of the fighting ended. Confederate Lieutenant General Richard Taylor, son of Zachary Taylor, twelfth president of the United States, was in command of the Department of East Louisiana, Mississippi, and Alabama. On May 4, he surrendered to Union General E. R. S. Canby at Citronelle, Alabama.

WAR NEWS

Stand Watie (1806–1871), son of a full-blooded Cherokee father and half-blooded Cherokee mother, was a Confederate brigadier general from Indian Territory—present-day Oklahoma. His unit fought in more battles west of the Mississippi than any other Confederate force, and he was the very last Confederate general officer to surrender, doing so on June 23, 1865, at Doakville, in the Choctaw Nation of the Indian Territory. His Cherokee name, *Degataga*, means "stand firm."

On May 10, President Andrew Johnson declared that armed resistance was "virtually at an end," but three days later, at Palmito Ranch, near Brownsville, Texas, Confederate troops under Edmund Kirby Smith skirmished with Federals. This small engagement was the last fighting of the war. Ironically, it resulted in the repulse and retreat of the Union troops—a Confederate victory. Kirby Smith surrendered to Canby on May 26.

The Least You Need to Know

- After the fall of Petersburg and Richmond, Robert E. Lee hoped to join his forces with those of Joseph E. Johnston in North Carolina in order to prolong the war and give the Confederacy some leverage in peace negotiations.

- The surrender of the Army of Northern Virginia, the Confederate's principal army, did not officially end the war, but did, in practical terms, end it.

- In surrender, Lee sought—and Grant provided—honorable terms and humane treatment for his army.

- The last fighting unit to surrender was that of Edmund Kirby Smith in Texas, on May 26, 1865; and the last general officer to surrender was the Cherokee Confederate Brigadier General Stand Watie, on June 23, 1865.

Taps and Reveille

Secure in the knowledge that the Union was saved, but knowing, too, that he now faced the daunting task of "binding the nation's wounds," Abraham Lincoln sought solace in an evening of comedy at Ford's Theatre.

The president's assassination on April 14, 1865, robbed the nation of perhaps the only man capable of guiding it through the process of healing. Lincoln's successor, Andrew Johnson, was beaten into submission by a Congress eager to bring righteous vengeance on the South. The result was a long, bitter period known as Reconstruction, in which the South suffered politically, economically, and emotionally, and in which the newly freed slaves found that their former masters were still powerful and capable of new cruelties, perhaps even more humiliating and terrifying than those of slavery itself.

The book concludes with a consideration of the unfinished business of the Civil War, a nation never wholly reunited, and with the role the Civil War continues to play in our national political life and our collective national memory.

Malice Toward One

In This Chapter

- Lincoln is assassinated
- Andrew Johnson becomes president
- Johnson battles Congress over Reconstruction
- Reconstruction legislation and abuses

On April 14, 1865, the day General Robert Anderson ceremonially raised over Fort Sumter the very flag he had taken down four years earlier, President and Mrs. Lincoln invited General Grant and his wife to spend the evening with them in Washington. Jealous of Grant's popularity, which she saw as somehow damaging to her husband, Mary Todd was never very pleasant to Julia Grant, and the couple politely declined the invitation to attend, with the Lincolns, a performance of the popular comedy *Our American Cousin* at Ford's Theatre.

Lincoln had much to be grateful for on April 14, but he knew that, at the outset now of his second term, he continued to face the gravest of responsibilities. He had only to look south of the nation's border, to Central and South America, to see examples of peoples for whom virtually uninterrupted civil war was a way of life, a chronic, bitter guerrilla struggle that never formally began and never formally ended. To ensure that such a bloody twilight would never descend on the reunified United States, Lincoln knew he had to make good on the promises of his Second Inaugural Address: to "bind up the nation's wounds" and to act with "malice toward none and charity for all." Happily, the American people had given him four more years to set this healing work afoot.

An Evening at Ford's Theatre

On Tuesday evening, April 11, 1865, Abraham Lincoln revealed a nightmare to Mrs. Lincoln, his close friend Ward Hill Lamon, Iowa Senator James Harlan, and a handful of others gathered in the Red Room of the Executive Mansion.

There was, he said, "a deathlike stillness about me. Then I heard subdued sobs, as if a number of people were weeping. … the mourners were invisible. I went from room to room. No living person was in sight … where were all the people who were grieving as if their hearts would break?"

At last, the dreaming Lincoln entered the East Room.

"Before me was a catafalque, on which rested a corpse in funeral vestments. Around it were stationed soldiers who were acting as guards: and there was a throng of people, some gazing mournfully upon the corpse, whose face was covered, others weeping pitifully.

"'Who is dead in the White House?' I demanded of one of the soldiers.

"'The President,' was his answer. 'He was killed by an assassin.'"

Matinee Idol

John Wilkes Booth was born in 1838 near Bel Air, Maryland, the ninth of ten children of the celebrated American actor Junius Brutus Booth. Young Booth debuted to little acclaim in Baltimore in 1856 and played minor roles through 1859, when he joined a Shakespearean company in Richmond. Southern audiences loved him, and Southern belles in particular loved his energetic performance and dark good looks.

Southerners also appreciated Booth's outspoken advocacy of the Confederate cause (he had served as a volunteer in the Richmond militia that hanged John Brown in 1859) and his equally outspoken hatred of Abraham Lincoln.

Late in 1864, he resolved to transform his words into deed and gathered about him a small group of conspirators, one of whom, John Surratt, was a courier who regularly worked for the Confederate "secret service." They met in the Washington boarding house of Surratt's mother, Mary, where Booth laid out a bold plan to kidnap Lincoln and hold him hostage. The ransom price? Liberation of all Confederate prisoners of war.

John Wilkes Booth, photographed when he was a successful actor in Richmond.
(National Archives and Records Administration)

Like so many other undercover Confederate plots, the plan came to nothing. But Booth hatched a second scheme, this time to abduct the president at Ford's Theatre on January 18, 1865. But Lincoln didn't attend the theater that evening, and this scheme also evaporated.

Still Waters Run Deep

The next month, a new conspirator joined Booth's band, which now included the courier Surratt, Michael O'Laughlin and Sam Arnold (boyhood friends of Booth), George A. Atzerodt (a Maryland carriage maker), and David Herold (a drugstore clerk, age 23, but who seemed almost childlike in his insatiable desire to please). The newcomer was a powerfully built former Confederate soldier who called himself Lewis Paine, but whose real name was Louis Thornton Powell. By the middle of the next month, Booth had a new plot for them all.

President and Mrs. Lincoln were scheduled to attend a matinee performance of *Still Waters Run Deep* to be given at Campbell Hospital, just north of the city. John Surratt called at the tavern in Surrattsville that his father had once owned and that his widowed mother subsequently leased to a dipsomaniac innkeeper named John M. Lloyd. Against Lloyd's wishes, Surratt secreted in the tavern two army carbines, some rope, and a monkey wrench. The plan was to waylay the president's carriage as it passed out of the city, kidnap Lincoln, and ransom him for the Confederate POWs.

Herold, Surratt, Paine, Atzerodt, Arnold, and O'Laughlin waited for word from Booth, who ascertained that the president's visit had been cancelled.

Booth fell into a black mood. He had been supporting his band and was now running out of money. The curtain was ringing down on the great drama of the Civil War, and John Wilkes Booth had yet to play a part.

But what part was there left to play? Kidnapping Lincoln was to have forced the release of Confederate prisoners. The war was about to end, there was no more army, and the prisoners would go home. What could John Wilkes Booth do to Abraham Lincoln now?

He could kill him.

SITES AND SIGHTS

Located at 511 and 516 Tenth Street, NW, Washington, D.C., Ford's Theatre National Historic Site encompasses both the theater and the Petersen House across the street, where Lincoln was taken after he was shot. Ford's Theatre is still a working playhouse and is closed to tours during rehearsals and performances. Otherwise, the theater and Petersen House are open for touring from 9:00 to 5:00 every day but Thanksgiving and Christmas. Contact 202-347-4833 for the theater, 202-426-6924 for general information, or log on to www.fordstheatre.org.

"Sic Semper Tyrannis!"

On Good Friday, April 14, Booth assigned Atzerodt to kill Vice President Andrew Johnson, and Paine and Herold were tasked with assassinating Secretary of State William H. Seward—an easy mark, since the old man was convalescing from serious injuries sustained in a carriage accident. Booth himself would shoot the president.

Things went wrong from the beginning. Atzerodt backed out and never tried to kill Johnson. As to Paine, while Herold waited outside holding his horse, he entered Seward's house bearing a package of "medicine." Seward's son Frederick told Paine that his father was sleeping and could not take medicine at this time. When Paine insisted, Seward ordered him to leave, whereupon Paine pulled a pistol, placed it to young Seward's head, and pulled the trigger. When it misfired, he repeatedly brought the butt down on Frederick Seward's head, cracking his skull.

Paine entered the secretary's darkened bedroom, where he found Seward's young daughter, Fanny, and a male military nurse, George T. Robinson. Robinson rushed Paine—described as a giant of a man—who slashed him across the forehead with a knife and knocked him to the floor before striking Fanny Seward and knocking her unconscious.

Paine stabbed the bedridden Seward again and again, tearing a gaping hole in his cheek. Seward rolled off and under the bed, at which moment Robinson came to and attacked Paine, who stabbed him. Another of Seward's sons, Major Augustus Seward, then burst into the room. Paine slashed his forehead and hand, then bounded out of the room and down the stairs—in time to encounter a State Department messenger. Slashing him, he ran out the front door screaming, "I am mad! I am mad!"

Incredibly, all of those Paine assaulted recovered; and, in 1867, as secretary of state in the cabinet of Andrew Johnson, Seward would go on to negotiate the controversial purchase of Alaska from the czar of Russia.

As for Booth, he calmly entered the president's box at Ford's Theatre at about 10:20 P.M. The lock on the door of the box had been broken a few days earlier, but nobody bothered to report it, let alone fix it. Nor had Booth, a familiar face at Ford's, met with any challenge.

Booth entered the box, quietly leveled his *derringer* between Lincoln's left ear and spine, and squeezed the trigger.

> **DEFINITION**
>
> A **derringer** is a pocket-size handgun with a short barrel and large bore. It is named for gunsmith Henry Deringer (whose name is spelled with one *r*).

Few in the audience heard the report of the diminutive weapon. Even Mrs. Lincoln, seated next to her husband, and Major Henry Rathbone, seated in the presidential box with his fiancée, Clara Harris, were not much startled by the dull pop. Booth knew the script of *Our American Cousin* well, and he had timed his shot to coincide with the play's biggest laugh—just after actor Harry Hawk, playing Mr. Trenchard, drawls, "Wal, I guess I know enough to turn you inside out, you sockdologizing old mantrap."

After tangling with Rathbone, whom he stabbed in the arm, Booth leaped down from the box to the stage, catching his right foot either in the Treasury Regiment flag or the American flag that festooned the box. His left leg took the full impact of his fall, and the bone snapped just above the instep. Turning to the audience, Booth shouted "Sic semper tyrannis!"—*Thus ever to tyrants*, the state motto of Virginia. The actor-assassin limped into the wings, fell, recovered, and lurched offstage. Stunned by the spectacle, no one gave chase.

Death Watch

A 23-year-old surgeon, Dr. Charles Augustus Leale, was in the theater and came to Lincoln's aid. He was quickly joined by another physician, Dr. Charles Sabin Taft, and the two attempted to revive the president. At length, Leale, in tears, said to Taft: "I can't save him. His wound is mortal. It is impossible for him to recover."

Lincoln was borne out of the theater and across the street to a house owned by a German tailor named William Petersen. At over six-foot-four, Lincoln was too tall for the bed on which he was placed, so the doctors positioned him diagonally across it.

April 15, 1865, 7:22 A.M.

Among those who watched the president's life ebb during the night of the 14th and the early morning of the 15th was Secretary of War Edwin Stanton. At 7:22 A.M., the doctors pronounced Lincoln dead, and Stanton raised his hand with great solemnity, put his hat on his head, and then, majestically, removed it. Turning to Lincoln's clergyman, he said, "Doctor, lead us in prayer." After this, as the officials present began to file out, Stanton went about the room, closing curtains on the windows.

"Now he belongs to the ages," said the secretary of war.

"Useless, Useless"

For 11 days, John Wilkes Booth eluded the army of troopers, policemen, and detectives sent in pursuit of him. At last, after midnight, on April 26, a detachment of

Federal cavalry ran him to ground at a tobacco farm near Port Royal, Virginia. Booth and Herold were in a tobacco barn. Herold surrendered, but Booth resolved to shoot it out, whereupon the troopers set fire to the structure.

They all saw the assassin's silhouette against the flames, a man leaning on a crutch and carrying a carbine. With his revolver, Sargeant Boston Corbett fired a shot that passed through the actor's neck.

Booth was dragged out of the blazing barn and was set down on the porch of the Garrett house. The actor was paralyzed, the bullet having severed his spinal cord.

"Tell Mother I die for my country," he managed to gasp out.

He asked that someone lift his lifeless hands so that he might look at them. This was done. He gazed at his hands.

"Useless, useless."

These were Booth's last words, uttered at sunup on the same day General Kirby Smith surrendered to General E. R. S. Canby the last significant Confederate field army.

WAR NEWS

John Wilkes Booth is buried in Green Mount Cemetery in Baltimore. His grave is unmarked.

Accomplices All

With the exception of John Surratt, all of Booth's co-conspirators were rounded up. Paine, Herold, Atzerodt, and Mary Surratt (John's mother and the owner of the boarding house in which the conspirators met) were all sentenced to hang and were executed together on July 7, 1865.

Michael O'Laughlin and Sam Arnold were sentenced to life imprisonment, as was Samuel Mudd, a Maryland physician and member of the Confederate underground who had patched up Booth's broken leg when the actor stopped by his Charles County farmhouse in the wee hours of the morning after the assassination. (Mudd was pardoned by Andrew Johnson in 1868 after he saved many lives during a prison epidemic.) Edman (or Edmund) Spangler, a Ford's Theatre carpenter convicted on dubious evidence of having assisted Booth, was sentenced to six years. (Arnold and Spangler were paroled the following month. O'Laughlin died in prison.)

After the assassination, John Surratt fled to Canada, thence to England, and then to Italy, where he joined the Papal Zouaves, Swiss mercenary troops who guarded the Pope. A fellow Zouave turned him in, and he was arrested on November 8, 1866, but escaped and fled to Egypt. He was apprehended there and was returned to the United States on June 10, 1867. Tried, his case was dismissed after a hung jury failed to convict him. The government attempted to try him under the District of Columbia treason law, but gave up due to the expiration of the statute of limitations.

The fate of Major Henry Rathbone, who was unable to stop Booth, was more cruel. He married Clara Harris, with whom he had sat in the presidential box, but in 1894 he murdered her because, he said, he was jealous of her love for their children. Confined to an asylum for the criminally insane, he died in 1911. His last words were: "The man with the knife! I can't stop him! I can't stop him!"

Those found guilty of conspiracy in the assassination of Abraham Lincoln were executed on July 7, 1865. Among them was Mary Surratt, mother of Booth associate John Surratt and owner of the Washington boarding house in which the conspirators met.

(National Archives and Records Administration)

Reconstruction Without Lincoln

John Wilkes Booth killed perhaps the only man in America capable of beginning to heal the nation. At the time, Northerners felt the tragedy of his loss keenly and personally but, in the end, it would be the South that would suffer most as a result of the president's assassination.

The New President: A Tailor by Trade

Although Abraham Lincoln had been willing to fight the war without compromise and to absolute victory, he was a moderate in comparison with the radical faction of his Republican party. These "Radical Republicans" wanted the South punished and those who led the rebellion arrested and tried for treason. Lincoln favored amnesty and, in general, an effort to heal.

In choosing a running mate for Lincoln in 1864, the party had purposely avoided pairing him with a Radical Republican. They did not want to scare off moderate voters. In a gesture of unity and healing, a *Democrat* was chosen as the vice presidential candidate and the pair ran as members of what was called the "National Union Party."

It all seemed safe enough—a mere gesture. In the nineteenth century, vice presidents had little authority. At 55, Lincoln was relatively young, and before 1865, presidential assassination was almost unknown (although in 1835 an attempt was made on Andrew Jackson).

Born in North Carolina in 1808, Johnson spent his youth in Tennessee. Lacking formal education, he was a tailor by vocation and a politician by avocation, becoming mayor of his town before he was 21, a state legislator for 8 years (1835–1843), a congressman for 10 (1843–1853), then governor of Tennessee (1853–1857). He was elected to the U.S. Senate in 1856 and cleaved to the conventional Democratic Party line until 1860, when he came out against Southern secession. When Tennessee seceded in June 1861, Johnson was the only Southern senator who remained in the Senate and refused to join the Confederacy. In acknowledgment of his loyalty to the Union, Lincoln appointed Johnson military governor of federally occupied Tennessee in May 1862.

Thrust so unexpectedly into office, Johnson was determined to carry out what he saw as Lincoln's mild program of reconciliation. As the war wound down, Lincoln had drawn up plans to create loyal governments in the Southern states quickly. Even before Lincoln's murder, new governments had been set up in Louisiana, Tennessee, and Arkansas, and Johnson was eager to see this work proceed.

Andrew Johnson, 17th president of the United States, battled Congress, impotently and bitterly, over Reconstruction policy.
(Harper's Pictorial History of the Civil War, 1866)

But Johnson was no Lincoln. Whereas the martyred president radiated an endearingly homespun wisdom and soft-spoken intelligence, Johnson was loud, boorish, abrasive, sour, and ineloquent. If Lincoln was a man difficult not to like, Johnson invited contempt.

Wade-Davis Plan

Congress had refused to recognize the new governments set up for Louisiana, Tennessee, and Arkansas, and instead passed the Wade-Davis Bill, sponsored by Radical Republican senators Benjamin F. Wade and Henry W. Davis, which provided for the appointment of provisional military governors in the seceded states. Only after a majority of a state's white citizens swore allegiance to the Union could a constitutional convention be called. Each state constitution would be required to abolish slavery, repudiate secession, and bar all former Confederate officials from holding office or even voting. Moreover, to qualify for the vote, each and every citizen would be required to swear an oath that he had never voluntarily given aid to the Confederacy; this, of course, would exclude former Confederate soldiers and, in truth, anyone who had actively supported the government of Jefferson Davis.

President Lincoln exercised a *pocket veto* of the bill and, after he assumed office, President Johnson modified the Wade-Davis plan by issuing an outright amnesty to anyone who took an oath to be loyal to the Union *from now on*; moreover, the creation of state governments would not be made contingent on a majority's taking these oaths. Johnson did require that states ratify the new Thirteenth Amendment, which abolished slavery and required states to forbid slavery in their own constitutions, repudiate debts incurred during the rebellion (so that the federal government would not be responsible for them), and explicitly declare secession null and void. By the end of 1865, all the former Confederate states had complied, except Texas, which at last fell into line the following year.

DEFINITION

If a bill is presented for presidential signature within 10 days of congressional adjournment, the president may indirectly veto it by holding it, unsigned, until after Congress adjourns. This is a **pocket veto.**

Congress Acts

Abraham Lincoln would have faced a difficult struggle in opposing Wade-Davis. For Johnson, the battle was hopeless. Congress not only feared and resented restoring power to the very individuals who had brought about the rebellion, it was loath to allow the Democratic Party to revive. There was also great outrage over the way in which the former Confederate states, while ostensibly freeing the slaves, kept them in subservience, effectively denying them the vote and other rights.

Freedmen's Bureau and Civil Rights

In 1866, Congress passed the Freedmen's Bureau Act and the Civil Rights Act. The *Freedmen's Bureau* was designed to assist African Americans in their transition from slave life to freedom, and the Civil Rights Act defined African Americans as citizens of the United States, declaring specifically that states could not restrict their rights to testify in court or to own property. President Johnson vetoed both measures, but Congress easily overrode the vetoes.

Fourteenth Amendment

When Congress overrode the presidential veto on April 9, 1866, it effectively seized control of *Reconstruction* from the executive branch. All hope for compromise and moderation evaporated as the Radical Republicans self-righteously seized the helm.

To be sure, much of Reconstruction was motivated by the noblest of purposes: to ensure that slavery would never again become an issue in American society and government (hence the Thirteenth Amendment), and to aid African Americans in the formidable transition from slavery to freedom (with the Freedmen's Bureau and the Civil Rights Act).

> **DEFINITION**
>
> The **Freedmen's Bureau** was the popular name for the United States Bureau of Refugees, Freedmen, and Abandoned Lands, which was established by Congress to provide practical aid to newly freed African Americans in their transition from slavery to freedom. **Reconstruction** is the general term for the transition of the former Confederate states from Federal control to restoration of statehood. The period of Reconstruction spanned 1865 to 1877.

Another act of Reconstruction, the Fourteenth Amendment, explicitly defined citizenship to extend to everyone "born or naturalized in the United States," forbade states from enacting laws "which shall abridge the privileges or immunities of citizens of the United States," and guaranteed the voting rights of all citizens. Section 2 of the amendment stipulated that if any state prohibited any part of the adult male population from voting, that state's representation in Congress would be proportionately decreased.

Yet like Reconstruction itself, the Fourteenth Amendment was a mixture of noble purpose and naked vengeance. Section 3 of the amendment barred former Confederates from holding federal—*or state*—offices unless individually pardoned by a two-thirds vote of Congress, and Section 4 repudiated debts incurred by the former Confederate government and also repudiated compensation for "the loss or emancipation of any slave." By law, slaves *had* been property, and now (as many in the South saw it), with neither compensation nor due process of law, this property had been seized.

Military Government

The only former Confederate state to ratify the Fourteenth Amendment was Tennessee; the others refused. Congress responded with a harsh series of

Reconstruction Acts. The first, passed on March 2, 1867, put all of the South, save Tennessee, under military government, with a major general serving as chief executive of each state. The only escape from under military rule was to draft and ratify a state constitution providing for enfranchisement of African Americans and disenfranchisement of ex-Confederates; moreover, Congress would withhold approval of a state's constitution pending that state's ratification of the Fourteenth Amendment.

A second Reconstruction Act authorized the military government of each state to use soldiers and officers to aid in the registration of voters and to supervise the election of delegates to the state constitutional conventions. Even after constitutions were duly drafted, a majority of white Southerners decided to defeat them by registering to vote but refraining from voting. Congress responded by changing the requirement for ratification of the constitutions from a majority of *registered* voters to a majority of those who cast ballots.

In June 1868, Arkansas was readmitted to the Union, and its military government stepped down. In July 1870, Georgia became the last state to be readmitted. But the feelings of bitterness, the acts of injustice, and the attitudes of inequality could not be erased by a handful of votes and a few strokes of the pen.

The Least You Need to Know

- John Wilkes Booth assassinated Abraham Lincoln and intended to kill Vice President Johnson and Secretary Seward in an effort to decapitate the government to give the Confederacy time to reorganize.
- Andrew Johnson tried to carry out what he saw as Lincoln's program of Reconstruction, but he was repeatedly blocked by an uncompromising Congress.
- Reconstruction was motivated in Congress by mixed objectives: on the one hand were such noble purposes as achieving full citizenship rights and equality for the freed slaves, and on the other hand was the desire simply to destroy the Democratic Party by keeping Southern Democrats out of office.
- Reconstruction was motivated by a sincere desire to protect African Americans in the South, but the program was often administered so punitively as to have the opposite effect.

War Without End?

In This Chapter

- Impeachment and acquittal of Andrew Johnson
- The effects of Reconstruction on the South
- The Ku Klux Klan is born
- The struggle for civil rights
- Reemergence of Civil War issues

It is difficult to study the Reconstruction period without sadness. Thousands had sacrificed lives, health, and property to achieve a victory that won—what? The slaves were freed, but they were hardly treated as equal citizens of the United States. The white people of the South were impoverished, punished, and humiliated by harsh Reconstruction laws. Intended to protect "freedmen," Reconstruction cast Southern African Americans into the unwilling role of scapegoat, the minority against which the white majority vented an already deep-seated racism.

Still, it all could have been much worse. Many civil wars never end. The formal battles might cease, but one faction or another typically continues to resist, waging chronic and debilitating guerrilla warfare. Although Reconstruction brought much misery, the Civil War, as a *war*, did end—though some issues associated with it continue to resonate.

Articles of Impeachment

The Civil War might have ended, but the war between Andrew Johnson and the U.S. Congress was just getting started. Congress sought to assume executive (presidential) powers, even as the president sought to thwart Congress by purposely interfering with the execution of the Reconstruction laws it had passed.

On March 2, 1867, over President Johnson's veto, Congress passed the Tenure of Office Act, which barred the president from dismissing, without senatorial approval, any civil office holder who had been appointed with senatorial consent. The act was part of the general effort of Congress to usurp as many executive prerogatives as possible, but more specifically it was aimed at preventing Johnson from removing Secretary of War Edwin Stanton, who was strongly allied to the cause of the Radical Republicans. When a defiant Johnson dismissed Stanton in 1868 despite the law, the House of Representatives voted to *impeach* the president.

Under our Constitution, only the House of Representatives may bring impeachment charges against the president, who is then tried before the Senate. The charges against Johnson were weak and transparently motivated by partisan purposes. The Tenure of Office Act was a dubious law and Johnson had defied it, in large part, to bring it to a constitutional challenge before the Supreme Court. That is the arena in which the next stage of the debate should have been held. Instead, there was a trial in the Senate spanning March through May 1868. The key votes, on May 16 and 26, 1868, fell one short of the two thirds required for conviction. Seven Republicans, men of conscience, voted with Johnson's Democratic supporters.

DEFINITION

Impeachment is often misunderstood to mean *removal* from office. In fact, to *impeach* is merely to *charge* a public official with misconduct in office before a legally constituted tribunal. President Johnson, like Bill Clinton 131 years later, was *impeached*, but, also like Clinton, was acquitted of wrongdoing and was not removed from office.

Reconstruction—or Deconstruction?

Johnson's acquittal was a triumph for the system of checks and balances, but the gulf between him and Congress was so deep that he was effectively neutralized as a political leader. With Johnson still in office, but essentially powerless, the Radical Republican Congress tore into the South more aggressively than ever, using Federal troops to enforce a Reconstruction program that was both genuinely reform-minded and frankly punitive.

Although it is true that, in the course of Reconstruction, a series of laws were passed to achieve equal rights for African American citizens, to establish state-supported free public schools, to provide more equitable conditions for labor, and to apportion taxes more equitably, the frenzy of radical Reconstruction also levied many heavy taxes and led to widespread local corruption. In a punitive spirit, those who administered Reconstruction thrust former slaves into high-level positions in state and local government, for which they were entirely unprepared. The result was, more often than not, self-righteous bitterness among whites.

The political agenda of Reconstruction was hardly subtle. It was to take vengeance on the former Confederacy while simultaneously destroying the Democratic Party.

Forrest and the KKK

The South felt besieged—economically and, what was worse, culturally. Northerners were telling Southern people how to live their lives, and the Yankees delighted in putting former slaves in positions of power and authority, as if to make the humiliation of the South complete.

A grassroots resistance movement grew up in response to the abuses of Reconstruction, and Nathan Bedford Forrest, late of the Confederate army, was one of its prime movers. In 1866, in Pulaski, Tennessee, a band of Confederate veterans formed a social club. Like many self-respecting fraternities, it looked to classical Greece for its name, transforming the Greek word for circle, *kyklos*, into *Ku Klux*, and adding, for good measure, the alliterative *Klan* to the end of it.

Within a remarkably short time, the Ku Klux Klan became the principal vehicle for covert resistance to radical Reconstruction. In the summer of 1867, the Klan met in Nashville, where it was styled as the "Invisible Empire of the South." Its first leader, or "Grand Wizard," was Forrest, under whom the Klan became a kind of shadow government, a combination vigilante force (for violent lawlessness was rampant in the postwar South) and terrorist army.

The target of KKK terrorism were the newly freed, newly enfranchised Southern African Americans. At first, terror was achieved primarily by means of the robes, sheets, and other secret society mumbo jumbo—all intended to play on the superstitions of uneducated former slaves—while also providing a disguise against detection by Federal troops and other officials. Soon, the psychological terror turned physical; Klansmen engaged in "night rides," whipping, beating, even murdering freedmen, and any whites who supported them.

Ratification of the Fifteenth Amendment, which explicitly prohibited states from denying the vote to persons on the basis of "race, color, or previous condition of servitude," came in March 1870 and served, in some parts of the South, to increase the influence and power of the KKK. Largely because of the Klan, white rule was restored in North Carolina, Tennessee, and Georgia. However by 1869, Forrest was convinced that KKK violence had gotten out of hand, and he disbanded the organization. In defiance of this order, local branches ("klaverns") continued to flourish, prompting Congress to pass the Force Act in 1870 and the Ku Klux Act in 1871, which authorized the president to suspend the writ of habeas corpus, suppress disturbances by force, and impose other penalties on terrorist organizations.

The Elevation of "His Fraudulency"

Andrew Johnson's troubled term ended in 1869, and Ulysses S. Grant, elected the year before, assumed office. The corruption that had taken root in the South bloomed fiercely nationwide in the Grant administration. Although the former Union general-in-chief was personally honorable, he was inattentive to the fraud, chicanery, and outright larceny that flourished during his two terms in office.

WAR NEWS

A new Ku Klux Klan reappeared in the twentieth century, organized in 1915 by Colonel William J. Simmons. Although African Americans were still a prime target of the Klan, so were "Bolsheviks," immigrants, Catholics, Jews, and organized labor. By the 1920s, the Klan boasted over four million members. Klan membership declined during the Depression, and the KKK even officially disbanded in 1944. It was revived in the South during the early 1960s as the civil rights movement developed. The KKK was involved in numerous bombings, whippings, and shootings in Southern states. Today, the Klan is relatively small and fragmented, occasionally associated with other right-wing extremist and neo-Nazi groups.

As Grant paid little heed to the lawlessness of his political subordinates and associates, so was he lax in exercising the authority Congress had provided for dealing with the KKK. Although he did send Federal troops into the areas of most intense Klan activity, suspended habeas corpus in nine South Carolina counties, and arrested many Southerners, local Klan activity remained widespread and, during the 1870s, achieved most of what the "Invisible Empire" had set out to do: it terrorized blacks into submission. This accomplished, the KKK disappeared during the 1880s.

This illustration, a romantic glorification of the Ku Klux Klan, is from Thomas Dixon, Jr.'s 1905 racist novel The Clansman, *the book on which D. W. Griffith based his epic Civil War film,* The Birth of a Nation *(1915).*

Indeed, during the 1870s, the white supremacy movement was becoming open and public in the South. There was little need for robes and hoods. So-called *redeemers* managed to enact state laws that institutionalized the social, legal, and economic subjugation of Southern African Americans. Such legislation came to be called *Jim Crow laws.*

DEFINITION

Redeemers were Southern political activists who promoted passage of **Jim Crow laws,** state and local ordinances that enforced racial segregation, and other forms of discrimination, aimed at subjugating African Americans. They were named after a racially demeaning song and dance familiar from blackface minstrel shows.

By 1876, the political clout of the redeemers reached the national level. In that year, Democrat Samuel J. Tilden captured the vote of the *Solid South* and outpolled Republican presidential candidate Rutherford B. Hayes by 250,000 votes. But the Republicans used Reconstruction laws to reverse the electoral tally in three Southern states, on the grounds that black citizens had been intimidated to keep them from voting, and thereby challenged the outcome of the election.

The election was thrown into the House of Representatives, which failed to resolve it as inauguration day, March 4, loomed. There was talk of authorizing the current secretary of state to serve as interim chief executive, and many in the South were actually talking about secession and were already setting up rival governments.

Just two days before the inauguration deadline, Congress authorized a bipartisan Electoral Commission while legislators negotiated a behind-the-scenes deal to decide the issue. Republican politicians struck a deal with Southern Democrats: admit Hayes into office, and no Republican administration would ever again disturb the Southern world of segregation and Jim Crow.

DEFINITION

The **Solid South** referred to the unified Democratic voting block that domi- nated the Southern states from the 1870s through the late 1960s, making the South virtually a region of one-party politics.

The deal was made, Reconstruction came to an abrupt end, and even Hayes's friends and supporters took to calling the new president, with cruel humor, "Your Fraudulency."

Separate and Unequal

The election of 1876 made it apparent that radical Reconstruction had backfired. The price of Hayes's presidency was three quarters of a century of legally sanctioned and institutionalized racism and racial segregation in the South, bolstered by custom and enforced by intimidation and terror.

The Cotton States

After the destruction of war, most of the South reverted to an economy based on its antebellum staple crops: tobacco, rice, and, above all, cotton. For labor, the region replaced slavery with *sharecropping*, in which relatively few landowners parceled out their property to freedmen and poor white tenant farmers. In 1880, 36 percent of Southern farmers (black and white) were sharecroppers. By 1930, 55 percent were.

The South settled into a strictly enforced policy of racial segregation, supported by a one-party (Democratic) political system, dominated by locally and regionally powerful political bosses. African Americans, no longer slaves, were now a kind of permanent underclass, the American equivalent of a feudal peasantry.

 DEFINITION

> **Sharecropping** is the practice of tenant farming, in which the tenant gives to the landlord a share of the crops he raises in lieu of cash rent.

The South's new feudalism was a heavy drag on its economic recovery and, not surprisingly, it was among the regions hit hardest by the Great Depression of the 1930s, which essentially bankrupted the cotton economy.

Lynch Law

President Franklin D. Roosevelt's Depression-era economic-recovery programs brought some relief and recovery to the South, but failure to diversify economically and, even more importantly, failure to reform socially kept many of its citizens in poverty. Because of its institutionalized bigotry, the South was shunned by the North, and many Americans felt that the United States really was two nations almost as separate as the Union and the Confederacy had been.

Under a barrage of criticism, Southerners frequently pointed to the hypocrisy of the North, in whose cities African Americans were segregated and discriminated against—not by law, but by custom and common consent. This was true. But the South *was* nevertheless quite different. There racial inequality was a matter of *law*, and when state-constituted law proved insufficient to enforce bigotry and subjugation, some Southerners turned to *lynch law*.

 DEFINITION

> **Lynch law** applies to the activity of vigilantes who abduct and execute, without trial, those they consider wrongdoers.

If discriminatory Jim Crow laws were the everyday means of enforcing the social status quo in the South, lynching was the ultimate weapon of terrorism. Blacks who spoke out against local whites or against discrimination and injustice or who attempted to organize others for social change were often marked for death by the KKK and other white mobs. Between 1882 (the first year for which we have reliable figures) and 1968 (when lynchings became rare), 4,743 persons were murdered by lynching, of whom 3,446 were African Americans. And these figures represent only *recorded* lynchings; certainly, many more must have occurred. Well into the twentieth century, the Civil War had ended, but racially motivated killing had not.

From the Back of the Bus

The manufacturing and agricultural demands of World War II brought a measure of prosperity to the South, as it did to the rest of the nation. The war also brought the beginnings of social change. Although World War II–era armed forces were racially segregated, blacks and whites did serve and work together, and—in many cases for the first time—white and black Southerners got to know one another more or less as equals. After the war, on July 26, 1948, President Harry S. Truman signed Executive Order 9981, which mandated "equality of treatment and opportunity" in the armed forces regardless of race. The integration of the armed forces was a modest degree of social change that gradually spread to civilian society.

On May 17, 1954, the U.S. Supreme Court ruled in the case of *Brown* v. *The Board of Education of Topeka* that public-school segregation was unconstitutional. The following year, in Montgomery, Alabama, an African American seamstress named Rosa Parks (1913–2005) boarded a city bus and, in defiance of city ordinance, refused to yield her seat to a white male passenger. Her arrest triggered a black boycott of Montgomery city buses, which in turn focused national attention on civil rights in the South.

After Rosa Parks's ride and arrest, Martin Luther King, Jr. and others shaped an intensive civil rights movement that dominated the late 1950s and early 1960s and that helped to bring down many racial barriers in the South. In 1959, President Dwight D. Eisenhower federalized the National Guard to enforce integration in the schools of Little Rock, Arkansas, and, in 1964, a new, sweeping Civil Rights Act was passed, followed by the Voting Rights Act in 1965.

Change was resisted, and often violently. But change came, and it is no coincidence that, with social change, the economic position of the entire South, white and black, greatly improved. By the 1970s, many American industries and people eagerly flocked to an area no longer called the Cotton Belt, but, more invitingly now, the Sun Belt.

Regional Politics in the Twenty-First Century

With the administration of Franklin D. Roosevelt (1933–1945), the Democratic Party became increasingly associated with civil rights and racial justice. By the era of Republican President Ronald Reagan (1981–1989), the Solid South was no longer solidly *Democratic*, but increasingly conservative *Republican*.

When the nation elected its first African American president, Democrat Barack Obama in 2008, much of the South voted as a block for his white Republican opponent, John McCain. To many Americans it appeared as if the Republican Party had become the regional party of the South.

As of 2011, the sesquicentennial of the Civil War's beginning, it is still far too soon to judge whether this perception is valid. Nor can we fairly assess what role (if any) race played in the election of 2008. But there can be no question that the election year, and the first year and a half of the Obama presidency, have seen the emergence in the nation of a defiant "hard right" political movement opposed not only to the Democratic Party, but also to the moderate wing of the Republican Party. Discontent with the mainstream of both major parties, so-called "Tea Party" activists speak loudly of "taking back our government" and "taking back our country," and some conservative Southern politicians have begun freely using terms such as "states' rights" and "nullification," the very vocabulary that preceded the Civil War. Indeed, no less a figure than the governor of Texas, Rick Perry, addressing an anti-tax "Tea Party" in Austin, Texas, on April 15, 2009, declared, "We've got a great union. There's absolutely no reason to dissolve it. But if Washington continues to thumb their nose at the American people, you know, who knows what might come out of that. But Texas is a very unique place, and we're a pretty independent lot to boot." His remarks were greeted with a few shouts of "Secede!"

While few Americans believe the Union is in danger of actually dissolving, 150 years after the surrender of Fort Sumter, the Civil War has yet to recede into history's shadow.

The Least You Need to Know

- The impeachment of Andrew Johnson threatened the principles of American government almost as profoundly as secession did.

- The Radical Republican program of Reconstruction brought some benefits to Southern African Americans, but, ultimately exacerbated the racist bitterness that doomed the majority of Southern blacks to decades of inequality, injustice, and even terror.

- The civil rights movement that began in the 1950s, while bitterly resisted in the South, ultimately helped to return much of the region to prosperity.

- A century and a half after the Civil War, important political, cultural, and economic divisions remain in the United States.

Memory

In This Chapter

- Civil War legacy
- Historical approaches
- Civil War genealogy, reenactments, and other passions
- The war in popular literature and film

"We are not enemies, but friends. We must not be enemies." The words near the end of Abraham Lincoln's First Inaugural Address echo with a heartbreaking poignancy. For of course, war did come, and it came with a violence and bitterness far greater than anyone—save, perhaps, William Tecumseh Sherman—ever imagined possible.

And yet the rest of the close of the inaugural address proved, in the long run, prophetic: "Though passion may have strained it must not break our bonds of affection. The mystic chords of memory, stretching from every battlefield and patriot grave to every living heart and hearthstone all over this broad land, will yet swell the chorus of the Union, when again touched, as surely they will be, by the better angels of our nature."

For despite the often ill-tempered pitch and volume of recent divisive political rhetoric, it remains a fact that the unity of the United States as one nation, indivisible, was reaffirmed by the outcome of the Civil War. No wonder that the epic struggle has figured as a subject of continual fascination to millions of Americans.

From Killing Fields to Subdivisions

If we still taste something of the bitterness that once tore a nation in two, the physical scars of the old wounds have long since healed. Many major battlefields have become national parks, and Manassas, for example, site of the first and second battles of Bull Run, is now a pleasant Washington suburb, whereas the area of Atlanta that saw the most intense combat of the Atlanta campaign, the vicinity of Peachtree Creek, is now an elegant urban neighborhood called Peachtree Battle.

No matter how the landscape might change, the Civil War is unlikely ever to fade from our collective memory. Since 1865, more than 65,000 books have been published on the subject. To that add countless movies, television shows, and more than a dozen popular interactive Civil War battle and strategy computer games. Thousands of enthusiasts regularly meet at "Civil War Roundtables" to discuss arcane aspects of the conflict, and an estimated 50,000 more periodically don impeccable reproduction period uniforms and tote reproduction period weapons into reenactments of key Civil War engagements.

Confederate Civil War reenactors at the 1997 Civil War Encampment, Atlanta History Center: one Johnny Reb prepares lunch (left), while another explains the intricacies of his musket to visitors.

The Birth of a Nation and *Gone with the Wind*

The film that marked the transition from the infancy of motion pictures to its early maturity as a vivid storytelling art form, *The Birth of a Nation*, debuted on February 8, 1915 in Los Angeles. The work of D. W. Griffith, son of a former Confederate colonel, it tells the epic story of two families during the Civil War and Reconstruction. Controversial (and even censored in some areas because of its sympathetic portrayal of the Ku Klux Klan), the film cost $110,000 to produce—a staggering budget in 1915—but brought untold millions in profits. Film historians believe it still holds the record as the most profitable film of all time.

There is no need to guess about the financial success of the most famous of all Civil War movies. *Gone with the Wind*, based on Atlanta author Margaret Mitchell's best-selling novel, used 3 directors, 15 screenwriters, and extravagantly recreated the burning of Atlanta, but returned $24 million in revenues during its first release in a day when most movie tickets were under a dollar each. Some 25 million people saw the movie. It has been rereleased several times since 1939, always to great profit.

WAR NEWS

President Woodrow Wilson, who saw *The Birth of a Nation* at a private White House screening, remarked that it was "like writing history with lightning. And my only regret is that it is all terribly true."

Defending the Flag

At times, the Civil War resurfaces as a subject of more than mere fascination. In 1962, the all-white South Carolina state legislature voted to fly the Confederate battle flag from the top of the statehouse. Over the years, other Southern states removed similar flags from their statehouses, but South Carolina held on and held out until April 12, 2000, when the South Carolina state senate voted 36 to 7 to remove the flag and to substitute a "more traditional version" of the battle flag (square, not rectangular) to be flown in front of the Capitol, next to a monument honoring fallen Confederate soldiers. The House passed the bill on May 18, 66 to 43, and on July 1, the flag was removed from the South Carolina statehouse.

As of 2011, Mississippi is the only Southern state whose flag prominently retains the Southern Cross of the Confederate battle flag.

The Historians

Although many Civil War books are fiction, and others are memoirs by politicians and generals, most are the work of historians. The most distinguished popular general works on the war are those by Bruce Catton (*This Hallowed Ground, Mr. Lincoln's Army, Glory Road, A Stillness at Appomattox, The Coming Fury, Terrible Swift Sword,* and *Never Call Retreat*) and Shelby Foote (*The Civil War: A Narrative,* published in three volumes). Catton's *A Stillness at Appomattox* was awarded both a Pulitzer Prize and a National Book Award, and Foote's trilogy was the basis of a detailed and moving film documentary series by Ken Burns, which first aired on public television in 1990 and brought the Civil War home to yet another generation.

WAR NEWS

The great American humorist Mark Twain owned a controlling interest in a publishing company and solicited from Ulysses Simpson Grant a book of memoirs. Bankrupt, in political disrepute, and dying of throat cancer, Grant accepted the offer and began writing in the summer of 1884. He finished proofreading galleys on July 14, 1885, then died on the 23rd. *Personal Memoirs of U. S. Grant* is the greatest firsthand account of the Civil War and, as Twain himself opined, "the best of any general's [memoirs] since Caesar." A literary masterpiece, the book was also a financial triumph, netting Grant's widow more than a half-million dollars in royalties.

The Presence of the Past

Most historians say that we're fascinated by the Civil War because, even more than the American Revolution, it shaped our nation and national character. Of course, the war also presents a gripping, exciting, moving, tragic, epic story, displaying, all at once, the meanness, brutality, compassion, and greatness of which human beings are capable.

As the preceding chapter suggests, the Civil War is an unfinished story. The divisions, disputes, and injustices that spawned the war have yet to be eradicated.

Civil War Archaeology

The process of fighting the Civil War produced untold quantities of debris, the physical evidence of historical events.

Among the many archaeological projects devoted to Civil War study was the work of the Southeast Archaeological Center of the National Park Service at the site of

Georgia's notorious Andersonville POW camp during 1987 to 1990. Artifacts recovered ranged from buttons, buckles, and tools to animal bones, which revealed much about what prisoners and slaves (who worked as laborers in the camp) ate.

A number of battlefields, ranging from major sites such as Gettysburg to more minor ones, such as Monroe's Cross in Hoke County, North Carolina (scene of one of the war's few all-cavalry clashes), have been investigated archaeologically in an effort to augment, with physical evidence, eyewitness accounts of battles and accounts gathered from official records. As discussed in Chapter 20, the discovery, recovery, and ongoing restoration of the Confederate submarine *H. L. Hunley* is one of the most important and exciting projects in the history of marine archaeology.

The Enthusiasts

In contrast to many other specialized fields, Civil War study is not the exclusive province of historians and archaeologists. A lot of ordinary people, without advanced training but with plenty of passion and curiosity, take an extraordinary interest in the war.

Do-It-Yourself Scholarship: The Sources

In addition to the many thousands of books devoted to the Civil War, anyone interested in learning more can find a great many scholarly resources readily available—no special credentials required.

Those interested in a particular battle or other event should begin by finding out if the battlefield or other site can be visited. Many of the important sites have been, in varying degrees, preserved and interpreted, and they usually welcome visitors. See the National Park Service website at www.nps.gov or cwar.nps.gov/civilwar/.

The Library of Congress (www.loc.gov) in Washington, D.C., maintains an unparalleled collection of Civil War research materials, including documents, images, maps, and sheet music. Also based in the nation's capital are the National Archives and Records Administration (www.nara.gov), which holds detailed records relating to the war and the soldiers and sailors who fought it, both Union and Confederate.

Important sources of records, artifacts, and other materials are located in various states. Some of the most important include the following:

- Alderman Memorial Library at the University of Virginia, Charlottesville (www2.lib.virginia.edu/alderman/)

- Atlanta History Center, in Atlanta, Georgia (www.atlhist.org)

- Bowling Green State University Center for Archival Collections, Bowling Green, Ohio (www.bgsu.edu/colleges/library/cac/cwar/cwbio.html)

- Center for American History, at the University of Texas, Austin (www.cah.utexas.edu)

- Charleston Museum, Charleston, South Carolina (www.charlestonmuseum.com)

- Chicago Historical Society (www.chicagohs.org)

- Civil War Center at Louisiana State University, Baton Rouge (www.cwc.lsu.edu/cwc)

- Colonel Eli Lilly Civil War Museum, Indianapolis, Indiana (www.in.gov/iwm/2335.htm)

- Confederate Museum (Memorial Hall), in New Orleans (www.confederatemuseum.com)

- Filson Club Historical Society, in Louisville, Kentucky (www.filsonhistorical.org)

- Maine State Archives, in Augusta (www.state.me.us/sos/arc/archives/military/civilwar/civilwar.htm)

- Mariner's Museum, Newport News, Virginia (www.marinersmuseum.org)

- Museum of the Confederacy, Richmond, Virginia (www.moc.org)

- National Civil War Museum, Harrisburg, Pennsylvania (www.nationalcivilwarmuseum.org)

- National Museum of Civil War Medicine, in Frederick, Maryland (www.civilwarmed.org)

- New York Public Library, New York City (www.nypl.org)

- U.S. Army Military History Institute, at the Army War College, Carlisle, Pennsylvania (www.carlisle.army.mil/ahec/index.cfm)

- Virginia Historical Society, Richmond (www.vahistory.org)

- VMI Archives at the Virginia Military Institute, Lexington (www.vmi.edu/archives)

- West Point Museum at the United States Military Academy, West Point, New York (www.usma.edu/Museum)

- William L. Clements Library at the University of Michigan, Ann Arbor (www.clements.umich.edu)

- Wilson Library at the University of North Carolina, Chapel Hill (www.lib. unc.edu/wilson)

A Confederate (or Yankee) in the Attic

Perhaps you have a connection with the Civil War that goes well beyond intellectual interest and imaginative affinity. If you know or believe that you are a relative of someone who fought in the Civil War, you can investigate—or discover—your ancestor or ancestors through genealogical research.

A good way to begin is to consult "A Brief Introduction to Genealogy and the American Civil War," a webpage at www.illinoiscivilwar.org/cwgeneal.html, and Bertram H. Groene's helpful book, *Tracing Your Civil War Ancestor* (John F. Blair, 1987). Those Civil War descendants who are interested in meeting with others might want to contact and perhaps join an organization of descendants. The largest of these are the following:

- Daughters of Union Veterans of the Civil War, 1861–1865 (www.duvcw.org)

- Sons of Confederate Veterans (scv.org)

- Sons of Union Veterans of the Civil War (suvcw.org)

- United Daughters of the Confederacy (www.hqudc.org)

Reenactors and Reenactments

"Learn by doing" is a time-honored maxim among educators, and some 50,000 enthusiasts have taken this to heart to enhance their knowledge and understanding of the Civil War. These individuals participate in various reenactment projects, ranging from Civil War blacksmithing, Civil War cooking, Civil War sewing, to Civil War "encampments" (living-history recreations of life in soldiers' camps) and full-scale, historically faithful reenactments of battles.

Perhaps the best way to find out more about—or get started in—Civil War reenactments is by consulting the "Civil War Reenactment Organizations and Related Links" page of the website maintained by the Sons of Union Veterans of the Civil War: suvcw.org/reenact.htm.

Civil War Literature

The Civil War gave rise to a large number of novels. *Uncle Tom's Cabin* (1852) was discussed in Chapter 3, and many other novels came out during and shortly after the war. While most of these are of interest mainly to literary historians, there are exceptions of enduring general appeal. John W. De Forest's *Miss Ravenel's Conversion* (1867), a story of a New Orleans physician who moves to Boston because he abhors slavery, is fascinating literature with some thrilling battle scenes. Ambrose Bierce's wry, bitter, and extraordinary short stories collected in his *Tales of Soldiers and Civilians* (1891) are not to be missed. Most important of all nineteenth-century Civil War novels is *The Red Badge of Courage*, published in 1895 by Stephen Crane. This literary classic presents a soldier's-eye view of battle so stunningly real that many assumed its author was a veteran. Crane, however, was born in 1871.

More recent "must-read" Civil War fiction includes the following:

- *Andersonville* (1955), by MacKinlay Kantor, a novel of life and death in the notorious POW camp

- *Cold Mountain* (1997), by Charles Frazier, about the struggle of a wounded soldier to return home

- *Gods and Generals* (1996), by Jeff Shaara, the "prequel" to the great novel of Gettysburg

- *The Killer Angels* (1974), by Shaara's father, Michael

- *Gone with the Wind* (1936), by Margaret Mitchell, the most famous of all Civil War novels and not to be missed if all you know is the 1939 film

- *Jubilee* (1966), by Margaret Walker, the story of a slave family during the war period

- *The Oldest Living Confederate Widow Tells All* (1989), by Allan Gurganus, a yarn spun by a 100-year-old woman

- *The Unvanquished* (1938), by William Faulkner, a tale of Mississippians who refuse to surrender after the fall of the Confederacy

Not surprisingly, notable Civil War nonfiction abounds. Some of the best includes the following:

- *Apostles of Disunion: Southern Secession Commissioners and the Causes of the Civil War* by Charles B. Dew (University Press of Virginia, 2001)

- *Battle Cry of Freedom* by James M. McPherson (Oxford University Press, 1988)

- *Blood on the Moon: The Assassination of Abraham Lincoln* by Edward W. Steers (University Press of Kentucky, 2001)

- *Confederate Reckoning* by Stephanie McCurry (Harvard University Press, 2010)

- *The Confederate War* by Gary W. Gallagher (Harvard University Press, 1999)

- *Gettysburg* by Stephen S. Sears (Houghton Mifflin, 2003)

- *The Grand Design: Strategy and the U.S. Civil War* by Donald Stoker (Oxford University Press, 2010)

- *Grant Moves South* and *Grant Takes Command* by Bruce Catton (Little, Brown, and Company, 1961, 1968)

- *Race and Reunion: The Civil War in American Memory* by David Blight (Harvard University Press, 2001)

- *Reconstruction: America's Unfinished Revolution, 1863–1877* by Eric Foner (Harper & Row, 1988)

- *A Savage Conflict: The Decisive Role of Guerrillas in the American Civil War* by Daniel Sutherland (University of North Carolina Press, 2009)

- *This Hallowed Ground* by Bruce Catton (Simon & Schuster, 1955)

And to stay current with Civil War scholarship, consult *North & South: The Official Magazine of the Civil War Society* (www.northandsouthmagazine.com).

Hollywood Battlefield

The Civil War, and the years on either side of it, were the subject of what most film historians regard as the greatest movie of the silent era, D. W. Griffith's *The Birth of a Nation* (1915), discussed earlier in this chapter. Another Civil War classic of film's silent era is, unlikely enough, a classic comedy: Buster Keaton's *The General* (1927), based on the exploits of Union raiders who stole a Confederate locomotive.

SITES AND SIGHTS

In April 1862, 22 Union raiders, including leader James J. Andrews, a civilian, hijacked *The General*, a locomotive owned by the Western and Atlantic Railroad, in an effort to disrupt Confederate supply lines. This precipitated the "Great Locomotive Chase" on April 12, which began a spree of sabotage against Confederate railroad track and bridges. *The General* and other artifacts can be seen at the Southern Museum of Civil War and Locomotive History in Kennesaw, Georgia. Contact the Kennesaw Civil War Museum, 2829 Cherokee Street, Kennesaw, GA 30144; 770-427-2117 (www.southernmuseum.org).

Other notable Civil War movies include the following:

- *Friendly Persuasion* (1956), adopted from the novel by Jessamyn West, the story of a Quaker family struggling to remain at peace while the nation is at war.

- *Gettysburg* (1993), a meticulous, if sometimes stilted, adaptation of Michael Shaara's novel, *The Killer Angels*.

- *Glory* (1989), the inspiring story of 54th Massachusetts, the war's most famous African American regiment.

- *Gods and Generals* (2003), the film version of Jeff Shaara's "prequel" to his father's *The Killer Angels*.

- *Gone with the Wind* (1939), which, long as it is, omits a good deal of Margaret Mitchell's famed novel, but is a must-see nevertheless.

- *The Red Badge of Courage* (1951), an extraordinary, starkly straightforward adaptation of Stephen Crane's classic novel.

"Our" War

The Civil War is "our" war: an event enacted by men and women with whom we cannot help but feel a profound kinship and sympathy.

They were not, for the most part, professional soldiers, and they were certainly not hirelings of a warlike state. America, North and South, has never been a military or militaristic society.

The people of the Civil War were doctors, lawyers, clerks, brokers, farmers, brothers, sisters, fathers, mothers, sons, daughters, husbands, wives, lovers. They were people like us, and their lives were like the lives most of us live. Only theirs were fiercely moved by patriotic passions, pierced by bugle calls, shattered by bullets, torn by the cries of the wounded, and, perhaps, buried in the silence of the slain. But for the accident of time, we could have been them and they us.

The Least You Need to Know

- No event or period in American history commands more and more enduring modern interest than the Civil War.
- The Civil War is the focus of historical and archaeological specialists, as well as legions of amateur enthusiasts, including reenactors, nonprofessional scholars, and amateur genealogists.
- The Civil War remains a fertile source of popular culture, including many novels and movies.
- The Civil War continues to fascinate us because we identify strongly with its issues and its people.

Words of War

abolitionists   Those who advocated abolishing slavery immediately.

Anaconda   The nickname of the Union's naval blockade of the South.

battalion   An operational unit composed of two or more companies or (in the case of an artillery battalion) batteries. *See also* battery, company, and regiment.

battery   In a Civil War artillery regiment, the operational unit comprising four to six cannon, equivalent to a company in an infantry or cavalry regiment. *See also* company.

bivouac   A temporary encampment.

blockade runner   A vessel—or its captain—specializing in evasion of the Union naval blockade of the South.

border ruffians   Proslavery Missourians who periodically raided eastern Kansas, intimidating and sometimes murdering antislavery settlers.

border states   Slave states that did not secede. They included Delaware, Maryland, Kentucky, and Missouri. The counties forming present-day West Virginia declared themselves loyal to the Union and seceded from the rest of Virginia when that state left the Union. On June 20, 1863, West Virginia was admitted to the Union as a new slave state; it is usually counted among the border states.

breastworks   Temporary, improvised defensive barriers, made of earth, stone, wood—whatever materials are available—usually affording protection that is breast high.

brevet   An honorific military promotion for conspicuous bravery or meritorious service.

brigade   In the Civil War, an operational unit consisting of two or more regiments. Two or more brigades were organized into a division. *See also* battalion, battery, company, and division.

bummers   Soldier foragers in General Sherman's columns during the March to the Sea, partaking in the looting and destruction visited by the Union army.

bushwhacker   The generic term for pro-Confederate guerrillas especially active in the Kansas–Missouri border region.

canister shot (or **canister**)   A type of artillery shell designed to explode upon firing, spraying out the lead or iron shot that was packed within the canister.

carpetbaggers   Northerners who descended on the South after the war, usually to exploit the freedmen in order to control local governments and profit from corruption. *See also* scalawags.

commerce raider   A naval or civilian vessel authorized by the Confederate government to intercept U.S. merchant ships and seize their cargo.

commissary   In the military jargon of the period, the store from which rations were drawn, as well as the officer in charge of provisions.

company   The basic operational unit in the Civil War–era army. In the Union army, it officially consisted of 100 men, including one captain, one first lieutenant, one second lieutenant, one first sergeant, four sergeants, eight corporals, two musicians, and one wagoner; the remaining personnel were privates. Actual numbers were often smaller. *See also* battalion, battery, and regiment.

Copperhead   The disparaging term applied to Peace Democrats.

corps   In the Civil War, an operational unit consisting of two or more divisions and typically commanded by a major general in the Union army and a lieutenant general in the Confederate army. *See also* division.

cotton gin   A device, invented by Eli Whitney (1765–1825) in 1793, for separating the seeds from cotton fiber so that the fiber could be woven into cloth.

counterreconnaissance   An effort to foil the attempt of the enemy to carry out his reconnaissance mission. *See also* reconnaissance.

cracker barrels   Crates or barrels used to store crackers or hardtack—and often used as impromptu camp furniture.

crackers   Hardtack biscuits made with flour and water.

defeat in detail   The time-honored tactic of attacking the spread-out elements of an enemy force one by one, before they have time to concentrate into a single, more powerful unit.

derringer   A pocket-size handgun with a short barrel and large bore. It is named for gunsmith Henry Deringer (whose name is spelled with one *r*).

division   In the Civil War, an operational unit consisting of two or more brigades. Two or more divisions made up an army corps. *See also* battalion, battery, brigade, and company.

double envelopment   A tactic in which the enemy army is completely surrounded by two separate attacking forces.

earthworks   Entrenchments or mounded earth parapets used as defensive positions.

emancipate   To free from bondage or involuntary servitude.

embargo   A government-imposed ban on the exportation or importation of certain goods, or on trade with certain other countries.

endemic disease   A disease chronically characteristic of a certain place or population. *See also* epidemic disease.

epidemic disease   An acute, severe, and widespread outbreak of a disease among a certain population. *See also* endemic disease.

fatigue duty   Military jargon for manual labor.

Federal army   A commonly used term, on both sides, for the Union army.

fire-eater   A Southerner who enthusiastically and unconditionally advocated secession.

flag officer   During the Civil War, a naval rank intermediate between captain and rear admiral.

flank   As a noun, the right or left elements of a body of troops; as a verb, to attack against the side of an enemy force.

foreign secretary   The British government equivalent of the secretary of state in the government of the United States.

Freedmen's Bureau   The popular name for the United States Bureau of Refugees, Freedmen, and Abandoned Lands, which was established by Congress to provide practical aid to newly freed African Americans in their transition from slavery to freedom.

frigate   In the middle nineteenth century, any high-speed, medium-size warship.

gentlemen's agreement   As used in diplomacy, an understanding between two nations, usually drawn up in the form of a diplomatic letter rather than a fully binding treaty.

grape or **grapeshot**   A type of ammunition, usually used on warships, consisting of a cluster of small iron balls used as a cannon charge.

graving dock   A dry dock where major work is done on ships.

Greek fire   An improvised incendiary weapon consisting of highly flammable fluid that bursts into flame when suddenly exposed to air.

gunboat   In the Civil War era, a squat, shallow-draft vessel, often clad in iron plates to deflect cannonballs, and designed mainly for use on rivers as a floating artillery platform.

high ground   Any elevated ground, such as a hill, on which troops can be placed so as to command clear fields of vision and fire over the ground below.

impeachment   Often misunderstood to mean *removal* from office, to impeach is merely to *charge* a public official with misconduct in office before a legally constituted tribunal.

indentured servitude   A colonial-era form of voluntary servitude, in which a person bound himself to laboring service for a fixed period (usually seven years) in return for passage to the New World.

independent command   The label applied to the highest level of operational command and usually applied to commanders of armies.

Jayhawkers   Self-appointed abolitionist guerrillas active in the Kansas–Missouri border region. The most aggressive of them were called "Red Legs," after the red leggings they wore as their only uniform.

Jim Crow laws   Named after a racially demeaning song and dance from blackface minstrel shows, Jim Crow laws were state and local ordinances that enforced racial segregation and other forms of discrimination aimed at subjugating African Americans.

line officers   Military field commanders who directly command troops, as distinguished from staff officers, who do not directly command troops.

Louisiana Purchase   In 1803, the United States acquired from France territory extending from the Mississippi River to the Rocky Mountains between the Gulf of Mexico and the Canadian border for the bargain price of $15 million.

minister   In the eighteenth and nineteenth centuries, U.S. ambassadors were generally called ministers.

monitor   Borrowed from the name of the first Union steel-hulled warship, the term was applied generically to all steel-built or ironclad vessels with gun turrets, especially those designed for coastal bombardment.

mortar   A short, thick-walled artillery piece designed to lob a heavy projectile in a steep, high trajectory.

nullification   The principle that a state may nullify and refuse to obey or enforce any federal law it considers unconstitutional. The concept rested on the related principle of states' rights.

parole   From the French word for *word* or *promise*, during the Civil War it meant the act of releasing a POW to his own lines on condition that he give his word of honor not to fight until he was officially exchanged for a prisoner held by the enemy.

Peace Democrat   Any Northerner who advocated a negotiated settlement of the war, with concessions to the South. *See also* Copperhead.

peculiar institution   The euphemism Southerners (and some others) adopted when referring to slavery.

picket   During the Civil War, a synonym for a guard or sentry.

picket line   The outer perimeter, usually around a camp, which was manned by sentries ("pickets").

pincer movement   A tactic of attacking an enemy army from opposite directions, effectively squeezing it between the jaws of a pincer.

plug uglies   Pro-Confederate thugs who attacked Union troops when they marched through Baltimore to Washington at the beginning of the war.

pocket veto   When a bill is presented for presidential signature within 10 days of congressional adjournment, the president may indirectly veto it by holding ("pocketing") it, unsigned, until after Congress adjourns.

political generals   Inexperienced commanders taken from civilian life and given high military rank, usually in order to secure the support of some political or ethnic group.

pontoon bridge   A transportable temporary bridge resting on floating pontoons or pontoon boats rather than permanent piers or pilings.

popular sovereignty   The doctrine and policy introduced in the Compromise of 1850 that provided for the people of a territory to vote on whether the territory would apply for admission to the Union as a free state or a slave state.

privateer   A privately owned armed vessel commissioned by a warring state to attack enemy vessels of commerce. The word can also be applied to the captain of the privateer vessel.

prize   In naval jargon, a captured vessel and any cargo it carries.

protective tariff   A tax imposed on imported goods with the purpose of discouraging importation and, therefore, promoting the manufacture and sale of domestic goods.

Pyrrhic victory   Victory at a self-defeating cost. The word derives from Pyrrhus (319–272 B.C.E.), king of Epirus, who defeated a Roman army at the Battle of Heraclea (280 B.C.E.), but lost so many men in the triumph that he remarked, "One more such victory and I shall be lost."

Radical Republicans   Northern Republicans who advocated continuation of the war to absolute, total victory, and who further proposed severe punishment for the South following its defeat.

ram   A vessel built with a specially reinforced prow (or "beak") for the purpose of deliberate collision with other ships.

rebels, rebel army   Terms often used (especially by Union forces and the Union government) to refer to the Confederates and Confederate army.

reconnaissance   An exploration to ascertain military information.

Reconstruction   The general term for the transition of the former Confederate states from federal control to restoration of statehood. The period of Reconstruction spanned 1865 to 1877.

redeemers   Late nineteenth-century Southern political activists who promoted passage of Jim Crow laws aimed at curtailing the civil rights of African Americans.

regiment   In the Civil War, regiments were units consisting of 12 companies. Two or more regiments were organized into a brigade. *See also* battalion, battery, brigade, and company.

retreat   The orderly withdrawal of troops from battle. *See also* rout.

rifle pit   A hastily dug emplacement that afforded riflemen a degree of protection.

rout   Withdrawal in panic and disorder. *See also* retreat.

rump   In political terms, a legislature having only a fraction of its original membership; it has no legal authority, but acts as if it did.

salient   Any strong or strongly fortified position, or concentration of troops, projecting from the main line.

sambo   One of the many offensive and demeaning names whites applied to African Americans during the nineteenth century.

sappers   In eighteenth- and nineteenth-century armies, soldiers who were sent in advance of a column or in preparation for an attack. Armed with axes, the sappers' mission was to clear debris, undergrowth, obstructions, and other obstacles to marching or attacking. Also called *pioneers*.

scalawags   Disparaging term for white Southerners who supported the Reconstruction policies of the federal government. *See also* carpetbaggers.

schooner   A fore-and-aft-rigged sailing vessel.

scow   A large flat-bottomed boat with square ends fore and aft, used for transporting freight.

screw sloop   A small armed vessel powered by a steam-driven propeller ("screw").

secede   To withdraw from membership in an organization, association, alliance, or, in the case of what became the 11 Confederate states, from the union that was the United States.

servile insurrection   A period synonym for slave rebellion.

sharecropping   The practice of tenant farming, in which the tenant gives to the landlord a share of the crops he raises in lieu of cash rent.

Sherman necktie   General Sherman's troops destroyed hundreds of miles of Southern railroad by ripping up rails, heating them over open fires, and twisting them into pretzel-like shapes that made them impossible to repair. Such a piece of ruined rail was called a Sherman necktie.

shoddy   Today an adjective meaning cheap, poorly made, and generally faulty, the word is derived from a Civil War–era noun meaning a kind of cloth made from scraps of material felted together—compounded and glued—rather than woven and, therefore, subject to disintegration.

soldier's battle   A battle in which the outcome is determined more by the action of the enlisted soldiers and the junior officers than by the leadership of principal commanders.

Solid South   The unified Democratic voting block that dominated the Southern states from the 1870s through the late 1960s.

staff officers   Assistants to a commander in performing planning and administrative functions. Staff officers do not directly command troops. *See also* line officers.

states' rights   The doctrine that the individual states command all powers and authority not *explicitly* assigned to the federal government by the Constitution. It was the basis of nullification.

straggler   Slang for a soldier who lags behind or wanders away from his unit.

subordinate command   The label applied to command positions responsible for executing the orders and achieving the objectives issued by those in independent command positions.

Three-Fifths Compromise   Article I, Section 2.3 of the U.S. Constitution stipulated that slaves (although that word is not used) may be counted as three-fifths of a person for purposes of levying taxes and apportioning representation in Congress. This provision was a compromise made by the framers of the Constitution between Northern interests (which did not want slaves counted at all) and Southern interests (which wanted slaves counted as persons).

torpedo   At the time of the Civil War, a stationary mine, often no more elaborate than a beer barrel made watertight and tightly packed with explosive black powder. It would explode when struck by a vessel.

total war   Combat waged against civilian as well as military targets with the object not only of destroying the enemy's capacity to fight, but also his will to fight.

Underground Railroad   A secret network that helped fugitive slaves escape from the South to the free states of the North and, sometimes, into Canada.

works   Fortifications. *See also* breastworks and earthworks.

Who Was Who in the Civil War

For military figures, entries include the subject's affiliation (**CSA**, Confederate States Army; **CSN**, Confederate States Navy; **USA**, U.S. Army; **USN**, U.S. Navy) and the highest rank the subject attained by the end of the war. If the subject held command of a major military unit, the unit is listed, followed by the nature of the command (in parentheses, sometimes with time served) and the major engagement(s) in which the subject fought. For example:

> **Bragg, Braxton (1817–1876), General CSA** Army of Mississippi (corps commander): Shiloh; Army of Mississippi (commander): Perryville; Army of Tennessee (commander): Murfreesboro, Chickamauga, Chattanooga; adviser to Jefferson Davis, February 1864 to January 1865.

This means that Bragg was a general in the Confederate States Army, a corps commander in the Army of Mississippi at the battle of Shiloh, commander of that army at Perryville; then commander of the Army of Tennessee at Murfreesboro, Chickamauga, and Chattanooga; after this, he was an adviser to Davis.

If the subject held no overall command of a major unit, but participated in a major battle, only the battle is noted. For example, George A. Custer first distinguished himself at the First Battle of Bull Run, but did not hold any overall command in that engagement.

Finally, early in the war, commanders were not always assigned to specific military units; thus, for example, you will note that the entry for P. G. T. Beauregard begins "Received surrender of Fort Sumter; had field command at First Bull Run"; only after this was he assigned command of the Army of Mississippi.

Adams, Charles Francis (1807–1886) U.S. minister (ambassador) to Great Britain (1861–1868).

Anderson, Robert (1805–1871), Major General USA   Surrendered Fort Sumter.

Baker, Lafayette C. (1826–1868)   Union spy and spymaster.

Banks, Nathaniel P. (1816–1894), Major General USA   Massachusetts governor 1858 to 1861; Army of the Potomac (corps commander): Shenandoah Valley, 1862; Army of Virginia (corps commander): Cedar Mountain; Department of the Gulf (commander): Port Hudson, Red River Campaign.

Barton, Clara (1821–1912)   "Angel of the Battlefield"; solicited and distributed medical supplies for the wounded; founder and first president of the American Red Cross, 1881.

Beauregard, P. G. T. (1818–1893), General CSA   Received surrender of Fort Sumter; had field command at First Bull Run; Army of Mississippi (commander): Shiloh; Departments of South Carolina, Georgia, and Florida (commander), August 1862 to April 1864; Departments of North Carolina and Southern Virginia (commander, April 1864 to March 1865): Petersburg, Carolinas.

Benjamin, Judah P. (1811–1884)   Confederate secretary of war, September 1861 to February 1862; secretary of state, March 1862 to April 1865.

Booth, John Wilkes (1838–1865)   Assassin of Lincoln, April 14, 1865.

Bragg, Braxton (1817–1876), General CSA   Army of Mississippi (corps commander): Shiloh; Army of Mississippi (commander): Perryville; Army of Tennessee (commander): Murfreesboro, Chickamauga, Chattanooga; adviser to Jefferson Davis, February 1864 to January 1865.

Breckinridge, John C. (1821–1875), Major General CSA   U.S. vice president, 1857 to 1861; Army of Mississippi (corps commander): Shiloh; Army of Tennessee (division commander): Murfreesboro, Chickamauga; Army of Tennessee (corps commander): Chattanooga; Army of Northern Virginia (division commander): Cold Harbor; Confederate secretary of war, February 1864 to April 1865.

Buchanan, Franklin (1800–1874), Admiral CSN   First superintendent of U.S. Naval Academy (Annapolis), 1845 to 1847; became a Confederate and commanded ironclads CSS *Virginia* (ex-USS *Merrimack*) at Hampton Roads, March 8, 1862, and CSS *Tennessee* at Mobile Bay, August 5, 1864.

Buchanan, James (1791–1868)   Fifteenth U.S. president, 1857 to 1861; blamed for doing nothing to prevent the Civil War.

Buckner, Simon Bolivar (1823–1914), Lieutenant General CSA   Surrendered Fort Donelson; Army of Mississippi (division commander): Perryville; Army of Tennessee (corps commander): Chickamauga.

Buell, Don Carlos (1818–1898), Major General USA   Department of the Ohio (commander, November 1861–March 1862); Army of the Ohio (commander): Shiloh, Perryville; relieved of command, October 1862; resigned, June 1864.

Buford, John (1826–1863), Major General USA   Army of Virginia (cavalry brigade commander): Second Bull Run; Army of the Potomac (chief of cavalry): Antietam, Fredericksburg; Army of the Potomac (cavalry division commander): Gettysburg.

Burnside, Ambrose E. (1824–1881), Major General USA   Brigade commander: First Bull Run, Roanoke Island; Army of the Potomac (corps commander): Antietam; Army of the Potomac (commander): Fredericksburg; Army of the Ohio (commander): Knoxville; Army of the Potomac (corps commander): the Wilderness, Spotsylvania, Cold Harbor, Petersburg; effectively relieved, August 1864.

Butler, Benjamin F. (1818–1893), Major General USA   Occupation of Baltimore; occupation of New Orleans; Army of the James (commander): Bermuda Hundred, Fort Fisher; relieved, January 1865.

Cameron, Simon (1799–1889)   Corrupt U.S. secretary of war, March 1861 to January 1862; minister to Russia, 1862.

Canby, Edward R. S. (1817–1873), Major General USA   Military Division of West Mississippi (commander): capture of Mobile; received surrender of the last Confederate armies.

Chase, Salmon P. (1808–1873)   Ohio governor, 1855 to 1859; U.S. secretary of the treasury, March 1861 to June 1864; chief justice of the United States, 1864 to 1873.

Crittenden, George B. (1812–1880), Major General CSA   Son of John J. Crittenden; defeated at Mill Springs; resigned, October 1862.

Crittenden, John J. (1787–1863)   U.S. senator from Kentucky, 1854 to 1861; proposed Crittenden Compromise to avert war, December 1860; U.S. congressman, 1861 to 1863; his Crittenden Resolution declared the preservation of the Union as the sole war aim, July 25, 1861; father of both a Confederate and a Union general.

Crittenden, Thomas L. (1819–1893), Major General USA   Son of John J. Crittenden; Army of the Ohio (division commander): Shiloh; Army of the Cumberland (left wing commander): Murfreesboro; Army of the Cumberland (corps commander): Chickamauga; resigned, December 1864.

Custer, George A. (1839–1876), Major General USA   First Bull Run; Army of the Potomac (cavalry brigade commander): Peninsula to Petersburg; Army of the Shenandoah (cavalry division commander): Shenandoah Valley; Appomattox; slain at the Battle of Little Big Horn, Montana, 1876.

Dahlgren, John A. (1809–1870), Rear Admiral USN   Inventor of Dahlgren naval gun; South Atlantic Blockading Squadron commander, July 1863 to July 1865.

Davis, Jefferson (1808–1889)   U.S. senator (Mississippi), 1847 to 1851 and 1857 to 1861; U.S. secretary of war, 1853 to 1857; Confederate president (1861–1865).

Du Pont, Samuel F. (1803–1865), Rear Admiral USN   Port Royal; directed attacks on Charleston, April to July 1863; relieved, July 1863.

Early, Jubal A. (1816–1894), Lieutenant General CSA   Brigade commander: First Bull Run; Army of Northern Virginia (brigade commander): Peninsula, Second Bull Run; Army of Northern Virginia (division commander): Antietam, Fredericksburg, Chancellorsville, Gettysburg, the Wilderness, Spotsylvania; Army of Northern Virginia (corps commander): Cold Harbor, Shenandoah Valley.

Ericsson, John (1803–1889)   Designer and builder of the Union ironclad USS *Monitor*.

Ewell, Richard S. (1817–1872), Lieutenant General CSA   Army of Northern Virginia (division commander): Shenandoah Valley, Peninsula, Second Bull Run; Army of Northern Virginia (corps commander): Gettysburg, the Wilderness, Spotsylvania, Richmond defenses; captured at Sayler's Creek, April 6, 1865.

Farragut, David G. (1801–1870), Vice Admiral USN   West Gulf Blockading Squadron (commander): capture of New Orleans, bombardment of Vicksburg, Port Hudson, Mobile Bay.

Foote, Andrew (1806–1863), Rear Admiral USN   Upper Mississippi River fleet (commander), August 1861 to May 1862; capture of Fort Henry, Fort Donelson, Island Number 10.

Frémont, John C. (1813–1890), Major General USA   Western Department (commander, July–November 1861); relieved, November 1861; Mountain Department (commander, March–June 1862): Shenandoah Valley (1862); relieved, June 1862; Republican nominee for president, May 31, 1864; withdrew, September 22, 1864.

Gibbon, John (1827–1896), Major General USA   Army of Virginia (brigade commander): Second Bull Run; Army of the Potomac (brigade commander): Antietam; Army of the Potomac (division commander): Fredericksburg; Army of the Potomac (corps commander): Gettysburg; Army of the Potomac (division commander): the Wilderness, Spotsylvania, Petersburg, Cold Harbor; Army of the James (corps commander): Appomattox.

Gordon, John B. (1832–1904), Major General CSA   Army of Northern Virginia: Peninsula, Antietam; Army of Northern Virginia (brigade commander): Chancellorsville, Gettysburg, the Wilderness, Spotsylvania; Army of Northern Virginia (division commander): Shenandoah Valley, 1864; Army of Northern Virginia (corps commander): Petersburg, Appomattox.

Grant, Ulysses S. (1822–1885), Lieutenant General USA   Commander: Belmont, Fort Henry, and Fort Donelson; Army of the Tennessee (commander): Shiloh, Vicksburg; Military Division of the Mississippi (commander): Chattanooga; general-in-chief of Union armies, March 12, 1864; directed campaigns of Army of the Potomac, 1864 to 1865; received Lee's surrender at Appomattox, April 9, 1865; 18th U.S. president (1869–1877).

Greeley, Horace (1811–1872)   Abolitionist editor of the *New York Tribune*, 1841 to 1872; condemned Lincoln's lukewarm abolition policies in "The Prayer of Twenty Million" editorial, August 20, 1862.

Halleck, Henry Wager ("Old Brains") (1815–1872), Major General USA   Department of the Missouri (commander, November 1861–March 1862); Department of the Mississippi (commander, March–July 1862); general-in-chief of Union armies, July 1862–March 1864; chief of staff, March 1864 to April 1865.

Hamlin, Hannibal (1809–1891)   U.S. vice president during Lincoln's first term, 1861 to 1865.

Hancock, Winfield Scott (1824–1886), Major General USA   Army of the Potomac (brigade commander): Peninsula; Army of the Potomac (division commander): Antietam, Fredericksburg, Chancellorsville; Army of the Potomac (corps commander): Gettysburg, the Wilderness, Spotsylvania, Cold Harbor, Petersburg.

Hardee, William J. (1815–1873), Lieutenant General CSA   Army of Mississippi (corps commander): Shiloh; (left wing commander): Perryville; Army of Tennessee (corps commander): Murfreesboro, Chattanooga, Atlanta, Carolinas; Department of South Carolina, Georgia, and Florida (commander, September 1864–April 1865).

Heth, Henry (1825–1899), Major General CSA   Army of Mississippi (division commander): Perryville; Army of Northern Virginia (division commander): Chancellorsville, Gettysburg, the Wilderness, Spotsylvania, Petersburg, Appomattox.

Hill, Ambrose Powell (1825–1865), Lieutenant General CSA   Army of Northern Virginia (division commander): Peninsula, First and Second Bull Run, Antietam, Fredericksburg, Chancellorsville; Army of Northern Virginia (corps commander): Gettysburg, the Wilderness, Cold Harbor, Petersburg; killed at Petersburg, April 2, 1865.

Hill, Daniel Harvey (1821–1889), Lieutenant General CSA   Big Bethel; Army of Northern Virginia (division commander): Peninsula, Antietam; Army of Tennessee (corps commander): Chickamauga; relieved October 1863; Army of Tennessee (division commander): Carolinas.

Hood, John Bell (1831–1879), General CSA   Army of Northern Virginia (brigade commander): Peninsula; Army of Northern Virginia (division commander): Second Bull Run, Antietam, Fredericksburg, Gettysburg; Longstreet's corps (commander): Chickamauga; Army of Tennessee (corps commander): Atlanta; Army of Tennessee (commander): Atlanta, Franklin, and Nashville; voluntarily relieved, January 1865.

Hooker, Joseph (1814–1879), Major General USA   Army of the Potomac (division commander): Peninsula, Second Bull Run; Army of the Potomac (corps commander): Antietam; Army of the Potomac (Center Grand Division commander): Fredericksburg; Army of the Potomac (commander): Chancellorsville; Army of the Cumberland (corps commander): Chattanooga, Atlanta; voluntarily relieved, July 1864.

Howard, Oliver O. (1830–1909), Major General USA   Brigade commander: First Bull Run; Army of the Potomac (brigade commander): Peninsula; Army of the Potomac (division commander): Antietam, Fredericksburg; Army of the Potomac (corps commander): Chancellorsville, Gettysburg; Army of the Cumberland (corps commander): Chattanooga, Atlanta; Army of the Tennessee (commander): Atlanta, March to the Sea, Carolinas.

Jackson, Thomas J. "Stonewall" (1824–1863), Lieutenant General CSA   Brigade commander: First Bull Run; commander: Shenandoah Valley (1862); Army of Northern Virginia (division commander): Peninsula; Army of Northern Virginia (left wing commander): Second Bull Run; Army of Northern Virginia, "Jackson's Command": Antietam; Army of Northern Virginia (corps commander): Fredericksburg, Chancellorsville; victim of friendly fire at Chancellorsville, May 2, 1863; died, May 10, 1863.

Johnson, Andrew (1808–1875)   Governor of Tennessee, 1853 to 1857; U.S. senator, 1857 to 1862; military governor of Tennessee, 1862 to 1865; U.S. vice president, November 8, 1864; succeeded to the presidency, April 15, 1865.

Johnston, Albert Sidney (1803–1862), General CSA   Western Department (commander, September 1861–April 1862); Army of Mississippi (commander): Shiloh; killed at Shiloh, April 6, 1862.

Johnston, Joseph E. (1807–1891), General CSA   Commander: First Bull Run, Fair Oaks; Division of the West (commander, November 1862–December 1863); Army of Tennessee (commander, December 1863–July 1864): Atlanta; Army of Tennessee (commander, February–April 1865): Carolinas.

Lee, Fitzhugh (1835–1905), Major General CSA   Army of Northern Virginia (cavalry commander): Peninsula; Army of Northern Virginia (cavalry brigade commander): Antietam, Chancellorsville, Gettysburg; Army of Northern Virginia (cavalry division commander): Spotsylvania, Shenandoah Valley (1864); Army of Northern Virginia (cavalry corps commander): Appomattox.

Lee, Robert E. (1807–1870), General CSA   Commander of Virginia troops, April to November 1861; Department of South Carolina, Georgia, and Florida (commander, November 1861–March 1862); adviser to Jefferson Davis, March to June 1862; Army of Northern Virginia (commander, June 1, 1862–April 9, 1865): Peninsula to Appomattox; named Confederate general-in-chief, February 6, 1865; surrendered to Grant, April 9, 1865.

Lincoln, Abraham (1809–1865)   Sixteenth president of the United States, 1861 to 1865; assassinated April 14, 1865.

Longstreet, James (1821–1904), Lieutenant General CSA   Brigade commander: First Bull Run; Army of Northern Virginia (division commander): Peninsula; Army of Northern Virginia (right wing commander): Second Bull Run; Army of Northern Virginia, "Longstreet's Command": Antietam; Army of Northern Virginia (corps commander): Fredericksburg, Gettysburg; Army of Tennessee (left wing commander): Chickamauga; Confederate commander: Knoxville; Army of Northern Virginia (corps commander): the Wilderness, Petersburg, Appomattox.

Lyon, Nathaniel (1818–1861), Brigadier General USA   Department of the West (commander, May–July 1861); killed at Wilson's Creek, August 10, 1861.

Magruder, John B. (1810–1871), Major General CSA   Commander: Big Bethel; Army of Northern Virginia, "Magruder's Command": Peninsula; district commander, Texas and Arkansas, October 1862 to May 1865.

Mallory, Stephen R. (1813–1873)   Confederate secretary of the Navy, 1861 to 1865.

Mason, James M. (1798–1871)   Confederate commissioner to Great Britain, August 1861; captured in *Trent* Affair, November 8, 1861.

McClellan, George B. (1826–1885), Major General USA   Department of the Ohio (commander, May–July 1861): Philippi, Rich Mountain; District of the Potomac (commander, July–August 1861); Army of the Potomac (commander, August 1861– November 1862): Peninsula, Antietam; Union army general-in-chief, November 1861–July 1862; relieved, November 1862; Democratic candidate for president, 1864.

McDowell, Irvin (1818–1885), Major General USA   Army of the Potomac (division and corps commander): First Bull Run; October 1861–April 1862; Army of the Rappahannock (commander, April–June 1862); Army of Virginia (corps commander): Second Bull Run; relieved, September 1862.

McPherson, James B. (1828–1864), Major General USA   Chief engineer: Fort Henry and Fort Donelson, Shiloh; Army of the Tennessee (brigade commander): Iuka; Army of the Tennessee (division commander, October 1862–January 1863); Army of the Tennessee (corps commander): Vicksburg; Army of the Tennessee (commander): Atlanta; killed at Atlanta (Battle of Peachtree Creek), July 22, 1864.

Meade, George Gordon (1815–1872), Major General USA   Army of the Potomac (brigade commander): Peninsula, Second Bull Run; Army of the Potomac (division commander): Antietam, Fredericksburg; Army of the Potomac (corps commander): Chancellorsville; Army of the Potomac (commander, June 1863–April 1865): Gettysburg to Appomattox.

Morgan, John Hunt (1825–1864), Brigadier General CSA   Shiloh; led Kentucky raids, July, October, December 1862; led Ohio Raid, July 1863; captured and escaped July 26–November 26, 1863; killed at Greeneville, Tennessee, September 4, 1864.

Mosby, John S. (1833–1916), Colonel CSA   First Bull Run; Shenandoah (1862); commander of Partisan Rangers, January 1863 to April 1865; "Gray Ghost" of the Confederacy.

Ord, Edward O. C. (1818–1883), Major General USA   Commanded Washington defenses, October 1861 to March 1862; Army of the Tennessee (division and district commander, June–October 1862); Army of the Tennessee (corps commander): Vicksburg; Department of the Gulf (corps commander, September 1863–February 1864); Army of the James (corps commander): Petersburg; Army of the James (commander): Appomattox.

Paine, Lewis (1845–1865)   Booth co-conspirator; attempted assassination of Secretary of State Seward, April 14, 1865; hanged, July 7, 1865.

Pickett, George E. (1825–1875), Major General CSA   Army of Northern Virginia (brigade commander): Peninsula; Army of Northern Virginia (division commander): Fredericksburg, Gettysburg ("Pickett's Charge"); Department of Virginia and North Carolina (commander, September 1863–May 1864): Drewry's Bluff; Army of Northern Virginia (division commander): Cold Harbor, Petersburg, Appomattox.

Pinkerton, Allan (1819–1884)   Union detective, spy, counterespionage agent; Army of the Potomac (chief detective, August 1861–November 1862).

Pleasonton, Alfred (1824–1897), Major General USA   Peninsula; Army of the Potomac (cavalry division commander): Antietam, Fredericksburg, Chancellorsville; Army of the Potomac (cavalry corps commander): Gettysburg.

Polk, Leonidas (1806–1864), Lieutenant General CSA   Western Department (commander, July–September 1861): Belmont; Army of Mississippi (corps commander): Shiloh; Army of Mississippi (commander): Perryville; Army of Tennessee (corps commander): Murfreesboro; Army of Tennessee (right wing commander): Chickamauga; Army of Tennessee (corps commander): Atlanta; killed at Pine Mountain, Georgia, June 14, 1864.

Pope, John (1822–1892), Major General USA   Army of the Mississippi (commander, February–June 1862): New Madrid, Island Number 10; Army of Virginia (commander): Second Bull Run; Department of the Northwest (commander, September–November 1862 and February 1863–February 1865).

Porter, David Dixon (1813–1891), Rear Admiral USN   Capture of New Orleans; Mississippi Squadron (commander, October 1862–July 1863): Fort Hindman, Vicksburg; Lower Mississippi River fleet (commander, August 1863–October 1864): Red River; North Atlantic Blockading Squadron (commander, October 1864–April 1865): Fort Fisher.

Porter, Fitz-John (1822–1901), Major General USA   Army of the Potomac (division commander): Yorktown siege; Army of the Potomac (corps commander): Peninsula, Second Bull Run, Antietam; relieved, November 1862; removed, January 1863, for conduct at Second Bull Run; exonerated, May 1882.

Price, Sterling (1809–1867), Major General CSA   Missouri State Guard (commander): Wilson's Creek, Lexington, Pea Ridge; Army of the West (commander): Iuka; Army of West Tennessee (corps commander): Corinth; led Price's Missouri Raid.

Quantrill, William C. (1837–1865), Colonel CSA   Wilson's Creek; led guerrilla raids: Independence, Missouri, Lawrence, Kansas, and Baxter Springs, Kansas; killed in Kentucky, May 10, 1865.

Reynolds, John F. (1820–1863), Major General USA   Army of the Potomac (brigade commander): Peninsula; Army of the Potomac (division commander): Second Bull Run; Army of the Potomac (corps commander): Fredericksburg, Chancellorsville, Gettysburg; killed at Gettysburg, July 1, 1863.

Rosecrans, William S. (1819–1898), Major General USA   Rich Mountain; Army of Occupation and Department of West Virginia, July 1861 to March 1862; Army of the Mississippi (commander): Iuka, Corinth; Army of the Cumberland (commander): Murfreesboro, Chickamauga; relieved October 1863.

Ruffin, Edmund (1794–1865)   Rabid Virginia secessionist; long (mistakenly) credited with firing first shot at Fort Sumter; committed suicide, June 18, 1865.

Schofield, John McAllister (1831–1906), Major General USA   Wilson's Creek; Missouri district and department commander, November 1861 to January 1864; Army of the Ohio (commander): Atlanta, Franklin, Nashville, Carolinas.

Schurz, Carl (1829–1906), Brigadier General USA   U.S. minister to Spain, 1861 to 1862; Army of Virginia (division commander): Second Bull Run; Army of the Potomac (division commander): Chancellorsville; Army of the Cumberland (division commander): Chattanooga; voluntarily relieved, 1864.

Scott, Winfield (1786–1866), Lieutenant General USA   General-in-chief, USA, 1841 to 1861; crafted Anaconda Plan; retired, 1861.

Seddon, James A. (1815–1880)   Confederate secretary of war, November 1862 to February 1865.

Semmes, Raphael (1809–1877), Rear Admiral CSN   Commander of Confederate commerce raiders *Sumter*, June 1861 to January 1862, and *Alabama*, August 1862 to June 1864; lost naval battle with USS *Kearsarge* off French coast, June 19, 1864; returned to Confederacy to assume command of James River squadron until April 1865.

Seward, William H. (1801–1872)   U.S. secretary of state, 1861–1869; wounded in assassination attempt, April 14, 1865.

Sheridan, Philip H. (1831–1888), Major General USA   Army of the Ohio (division commander): Perryville; Army of the Cumberland (division commander): Murfreesboro, Chickamauga, Chattanooga; Army of the Potomac (cavalry corps commander): the Wilderness, Spotsylvania, Richmond Raid, Cold Harbor, Appomattox; Army of the Shenandoah (commander, August 1864–March 1865).

Sherman, William Tecumseh (1820–1891), Major General USA   Brigade commander: First Bull Run; Department of the Cumberland (commander, October–November 1861); Army of the Tennessee (division commander): Shiloh; Army of the Tennessee (corps commander): Chickasaw Bluffs, Fort Hindman, Vicksburg; Army of the Tennessee (commander, October 1863–March 1864): Chattanooga, Meridian; Military Division of the Mississippi (commander, March 1864–April 1865): Atlanta, March to the Sea, Carolinas.

Sickles, Daniel E. (1825–1914), Major General USA   Army of the Potomac (brigade commander): Peninsula; Army of the Potomac (division commander): Fredericksburg; Army of the Potomac (corps commander): Chancellorsville, Gettysburg.

Sigel, Franz (1824–1902), Major General USA   Organizer of German-American troops and war support; Wilson's Creek; division commander: Pea Ridge; Army of Virginia (corps commander): Second Bull Run; Army of the Potomac (corps commander, September 1862–February 1863); Department of West Virginia (commander, March–May 1864): New Market; relieved, July 1864.

Slidell, John (1793–1871)   Confederate commissioner to France, August 1861; captured in *Trent* Affair, November 8, 1861.

Smith, Edmund Kirby (1824–1893), General CSA   Brigade commander: First Bull Run; Department of East Tennessee (commander): invasion of Kentucky; Trans-Mississippi Department (commander, March 1863–May 1865): Red River; commander of last Confederate operational unit to surrender, May 26, 1865.

Stanton, Edwin McMasters (1814–1869)   U.S. attorney general, December 1860 to March 1861; U.S. secretary of war, January 1862 to May 1868.

Stephens, Alexander H. (1812–1883)   Confederate vice president.

Stevens, Thaddeus (1792–1868)   U.S. congressman from Pennsylvania and Radical Republican leader.

Stoneman, George (1822–1894), Major General USA   Army of the Potomac (cavalry division commander): Peninsula; Army of the Potomac (corps commander): Fredericksburg; Army of the Potomac (cavalry corps commander): Chancellorsville; Cavalry Bureau chief, July 1863 to January 1864; Army of the Ohio (cavalry division commander): Atlanta; captured near Macon, Georgia, July 30, 1864, and exchanged; Department of the Ohio (commander, November 1864–January 1865); District of East Tennessee (commander, March–April 1865).

Stuart, J. E. B. (1833–1864), Major General CSA   First Bull Run; Army of Northern Virginia (cavalry commander): Peninsula, first ride around McClellan, Second Bull Run, Antietam, second ride around McClellan, Fredericksburg, Chancellorsville; temporary command of Jackson's corps: Brandy Station, Gettysburg Raid, the Wilderness, Spotsylvania; mortally wounded at Yellow Tavern, May 11, 1864; died May 12, 1864.

Sumner, Charles (1811–1874)   U.S. senator from Massachusetts, 1851 to 1874; leading abolitionist and Radical Republican; caned in Senate by Representative Preston S. Brooks of South Carolina, 1856.

Sumner, Edwin V. (1797–1863), Major General USA   Army of the Potomac (corps commander): Peninsula, Antietam; Army of the Potomac (Right Grand Division commander): Fredericksburg; voluntarily relieved, January 1863.

Thomas, George H. (1816–1870), Major General USA   Army of the Ohio (division commander): Mill Springs; Army of the Ohio (second in command): Perryville; Army of the Cumberland (commander of the center): Murfreesboro; Army of the Cumberland (corps commander): Chickamauga ("Rock of Chickamauga"); Army of the Cumberland (commander): Chattanooga, Atlanta, Franklin, and Nashville.

Toombs, Robert (1810–1885), Brigadier General CSA   Confederate secretary of state, March to July 1861; Army of Northern Virginia (brigade commander): Peninsula, Second Bull Run, Antietam; resigned March 1863.

Vallandigham, Clement L. (1820–1871)   U.S. congressman from Ohio, 1858 to 1863; leader of Copperhead Democrats; banished to the South, May 1863; ran in absentia for Ohio governorship, October 1863; defeated, returned to the North to write peace platform at Democratic convention, August 1864.

Van Dorn, Earl (1820–1863), Major General CSA   Army of the West (commander): Pea Ridge; Army of West Tennessee (commander): Corinth, Holly Springs; murdered by a civilian, May 8, 1863.

Wallace, Lew (1827–1905), Major General USA   Division commander: Fort Donelson; Army of the Tennessee (division commander): Shiloh, Monocacy; served on court-martial of Lincoln's assassins and was president of court-martial that convicted Andersonville Commandant Henry Wirz.

Welles, Gideon (1802–1878)   U.S. secretary of the navy, March 1861 to March 1869.

Wheeler, Joseph (1836–1906), Lieutenant General CSA   Shiloh; Army of Mississippi (cavalry brigade commander): Perryville; Army of Tennessee (cavalry brigade commander): Murfreesboro; Army of Tennessee (cavalry corps commander): Chickamauga, Knoxville, Atlanta, March to the Sea, Carolinas.

Wilkes, Charles (1798–1877), Commodore USN   Captain of USS *San Jacinto* who removed Confederate commissioners James M. Mason and John Slidell from British vessel *Trent*, November 8, 1861.

Wirz, Henry (1822–1865), Major CSA   Andersonville Prison commandant, January 1864 to April 1865; convicted of responsibility for inhumane prison conditions and executed, November 10, 1865.

Index